The Apocalypse of Saint John

Emil Bock

The Apocalypse of Saint John

Floris Books

Translated by Alfred Heidenreich

Originally published in German under the title *Apokalypse.*
Betrachtungen über die Offenbarung des Johannes
by Verlag Urachhaus in 1951.
First published in English by the Christian Community Press,
London in 1957. Third reprint 1996.

British Library Cataloguing in Publication Data

Bock, Emil
The apocalypse of St John.
1. Bible. New Testament. Revelation
I. Title
228'.06   BS2825.5

ISBN 0-86315-045-4

Printed in Great Britain
by Biddles Ltd, Guildford

CONTENTS

TRANSLATOR'S NOTE

The Book of Revelation has always exercised a powerful fascination over the mind of English speaking people. Allusions to Revelation by English writers throughout the centuries are plentiful.

I do not know whether in any literature such discerning lines can be a found as these: "I think of it as an awful and spontaneous energy of spiritual life going on, of which the prophet was enabled to catch a glimpse. Those 'voices crying day and night', 'the new song that was sung before the throne', the cry of 'come and see'—these are but part of a vast and urgent business, which the prophet was allowed to over-hear. It is not a silent place, that highest heaven, of indolence and placid peace, but a scene of fierce activity and the clamour of mighty voices." (A.C. Benson in *Joyous Gard*.) And quite recently J.B. Phillips in his foreword to *A New Translation of the Apocalypse* (1956), coming from a fresh and intimate meeting with the book, admirably testifies to its power and quality. "Once we are gripped by the mysterious compulsion of these visions we find the 'silence in Heaven for what seemed to be about half an hour' almost intolerable. The 'solitary eagle flying in mid-air', crying out in pity for the inhabitants of the earth is, out of its context, bizarre to the point of absurdity, but, set as it is, it is almost unbearably poignant."

Emil Bock's studies present a key to a conscious understanding of the Apocalypse. They do not offer a running commentary, but they attempt an introduction to the sphere out of which the Apocalypse was written and where alone an adequate understanding can be sought.

Michaelmas 1957   ALFRED HEIDENREICH

FOREWORD

THIS book is an attempt to point to sources of inward security and strength amidst the perplexities of our time. It witnesses to the conviction that the destinies of the present age are charged with a deeper and more far-reaching significance than calmer and more settled periods of the past.

The human mind comes up against a special barrier when it endeavours to comprehend the events of the immediate present. We require some distance from the events in order to understand them. We are unable fully to grasp the historic significance of present facts, and the historic facts which we do seem to grasp belong to the past and are no longer accessible to our immediate experience. Thus our understanding always lags behind the actual event.

This is inevitable because—to quote Rudolf Steiner—real history is made in the sphere of the supersensible. High above our heads, above the plane of external events, above the tumult of battles history is made in the realm of the spirit. Earthly history is but a shadow of this meta-history. If we were able to watch the events on the meta-historical plane, we could read the significance at every single moment of the events in which we are involved on earth.

The Revelation of St. John is a magic mirror which, held up against events of the time, makes visible not only the external but also the inward and hidden countenance of a historic period.

For our present age constant reference to the supersensible events is particularly indispensable. As though by invisible hands humanity is moved towards the threshold of the unseen, we might almost say thrown against it. Only the spell of materialism, as yet still unbroken, obscures the view. In reality, human actions themselves, even in the sphere of political tensions, are today a constant opening of sluicegates through which the floods of the supersensible world pour into the world of men. What poets and writers of earlier ages expressed in prophetic terms is becoming factual reality.

Our present time is not lacking in revelation. The angels are active. They are descending from heaven, they produce dramatic pictures, they blow their trumpets, they draw away the veil which hides the Spirits behind the scene. Not revelation itself, but our sense for revelation is wanting.

9   A*

The Revelation of St. John can help us to wake up; and we may begin to read in the book which discloses the meaning of what so often appears utterly meaningless.

The present studies are based on lectures held in the winter of 1940–1941 at Stuttgart, Berlin and Munich under the auspices of The Christian Community. The dramatic events of that time made their own immediate contribution. The latter half of the lectures was often given while the air-raid sirens sounded. The series was barely concluded when in June 1941 The Christian Community was suppressed by the Hitler Government. Its literature was confiscated and destroyed; its ministers put in prison and concentration camps.

The manuscript of this book, in part already prepared for publication, was also lost. In re-writing these studies after the war (in 1951) I asked myself whether they were still relevant to the events which have moved with such inexorable momentum since then. But it may seem that a study of the Apocalypse is today more relevant than ever.

In 1908 Rudolf Steiner, who was the principal "helper and adviser" of The Christian Community at its foundation, gave at Nuremberg a cycle of basic lectures on the Book of Revelation, published in the Series "Esoteric Studies" by the Anthroposophic Publication Company at Dornach, Switzerland. This publication is referred to here as representative for the whole of the epoch-making work of Rudolf Steiner who placed his Anthroposophy as a comprehensive Apocalypse into the present time. The studies of this book owe their inception to this great inspirational impulse. Individual works by Rudolf Steiner are quoted in footnotes.

EMIL BOCK

INTRODUCTORY OBSERVATIONS ON THE CHARACTER AND STRUCTURE OF THE APOCALYPSE

THE Revelation of St. John has a strange reputation. For many people it has a strong sectarian flavour. Many imagine that it contains nothing but the superstitions of days long past. But rightly understood it is the guide-book of advanced Christianity.

It is not without reason that the Revelation of St. John stands at the end of the Bible, its compass reaching far beyond the Gospels. One must already have gone through everything else—the Gospels, the Acts of the Apostles and St. Paul's Epistles—before one can approach it. It stands at the peak, the highest level of the New Testament. Had Christianity already attained to the level of the Apocalypse, one might more confidently face the facts of our Age, which is becoming more and more apocalyptic.

Christianity rightly understood is the religion of the open heavens; the religion of men before whom the curtain has been drawn aside which divides the earthly world of the senses from the sphere of the supersensible. The worship of the Old Covenant was the religion of the closed heavens. The veil before the Holy of Holies in Solomon's Temple was the central symbol of Old Testament religion. But in the hour of Golgotha the religious principle of the veiled mystery lost its validity and power. The rending of the veil in the Temple was a significant gesture of God, a telling spiritual act.

The Revelation of St. John teaches men to read in the world from which the curtain has been drawn aside. Great patterns and spheres of evolution emerge out of one another. At the beginning the seer encounters Christ at a moment which might well be called his Damascus. This encounter awakens in him a new consciousness. The Johannine Eagle now begins to soar aloft and to rise in spiral movements, as it were, into the world behind the curtain.

The first cycle remains still close to the Earth. It is reflected in the Seven Messages (Chapters 1 and 2). Seven perhaps insignificant early Christian congregations in Asia Minor appear as a quintessence of mankind, arranged in a circle, like a cyclical collection of phases of history. This preparatory round is followed by the Seven Seals (Chapters 5–8), the Seven Trumpet Blasts (Chapters 8–14), and the outpouring of the Seven Vials of Wrath (Chapters 15–18). The Seven Seals contain spiritual *pictures*, indicating that an inner faculty of seeing has been developed. The Trumpet Blasts are a higher form of *speech*, presupposing an inner faculty of hearing. In the last and holiest cycle, *reality* follows picture and word. Real contact with super-earthly forces and beings opens up inner organs which are a spiritual octave of the sense of touch.

Each of the three higher stages contains a main theme: the Seals are connected with the *Book*, the Trumpets with the *Altar*, and the Vials of Wrath with the *Temple* in Heaven. The description found in Rudolf Steiner's writings of the three stages of supersensible know-ledge, which he calls Imagination, Inspiration and Intuition, supplies an important key to the architecture of St. John's Apocalypse. In Steiner's teaching dogmatic talk of inspiration and the supernaturally inspired origin of the New Testament Scriptures is replaced by a concrete description of three spheres of higher perception, to which the human mind, raised by the grace of God, can ascend. The structure of the Apocalypse is a veritable map of these provinces and spheres of an increasing supersensible knowledge. The Seals of the Book, the Trumpet Blasts at the Altar, the outpoured Vessels from within the Temple—these are the apocalyptic forms of expression for the three stages of supersensible perception.

The three higher planes of knowledge are today reflected in all walks of life. People today have a tremendous *hunger for pictures*. This has brought into existence the immense number of illustrated papers with which we are inundated. This hunger is a symptom of the fact that Man, through the destiny of our time, is being urged towards the sphere of *imaginative* perception. Unfortunately, as this is not properly understood, substitutes like the cinema and television endanger and perhaps kill the true picture-sense in the soul. Similarly we observe a growing *hunger for music* in men of today. Many are feverishly hungry for music, not only for the sake of entertainment and amusement. From the surging world of the supersensible, the powers of *Inspiration* are exercising a magnetic influence on souls. The spiritual sphere of Harps and Trumpets is dimly sought after. But in spite of the hunger for music, under the influence of modern civiliza-tion people have forgotten how to listen. Their souls have grown deaf to the real sound-world behind the music. Here too a substitute is palmed off on men as they dimly yearn for new spiritual experiences.

However useful the radio may be for many purposes in everyday life, it has nevertheless not improved or deepened the faculty of hearing in souls.

The most irresistible desire in our age is a chaotic influence from the plane of *Intuition*. It is not necessary to specify in detail the forms assumed by the *hunger for love*. A veritable ocean of wishes and urges has engulfed men and women. Errors and perplexities abound. The chaos is made complete by the false fulfilments which the hunger for love finds. The foaming waves of this ocean can only be smoothed when mankind perceives that its longing points beyond the earthly domain.

Here, incidentally, the comprehensive task is set for a Renewal of Religion. The hunger for pictures is satisfied when Man is taught a new wisdom which is capable of Imagination. Hunger for music longs for an artistic life pervaded by real Inspiration. Hunger for love ultimately aims at the sphere of a religious practice which touches the sphere of Intuition, and so orders and sanctifies the turbulent depths of the human will.

The Apocalypse stands at the end of the New Testament, and hence of the whole Bible. It is the completion both of the New Testament and Old Testament Scriptures. Its structure comprising all levels of higher knowledge throws into relief retrospectively the order and sequence of the whole of the New and Old Testament. The grouping of the Biblical Scriptures is by no means accidental. It follows the stages of ascent revealed in the Apocalypse. The canon both of the New and the Old Testament arranges the Biblical Scriptures in three groups, of which each one represents one of the three stages of supersensible perception. The Old Testament trinity of the historical, poetic and prophetic books, and the corresponding New Testament trinity of the Gospels, the Epistles and the Revelation of St. John, lead through the spheres of Imagination, Inspiration and Intuition, as do the three circles of Seals, Trumpets and Vials of Wrath in the Apocalypse. The books of Moses, Judges, Kings, together with the other "historical" Scriptures in the Old Testament, represent with their graphic stories the *Picture stage*. The same is true of the four Gospels and the Acts of the Apostles in the New Testament (although the source of St. John's Gospel lies beyond the sphere of Imagination). These are holy picture-books, drawn from spiritual vision. Just as the historic Scriptures of the Old Covenant look back into the very beginning of Creation and the story of the Chosen People, so these books picture the life of Christ as the very beginning of a new Creation, which begins to unfold in the story of the apostolic age.

The stage of Inspiration is represented in the Old Testament by the Psalter, the Proverbs of Solomon, the book of Job and the other so-called poetic books; and in the New Testament, by the Epistles of St. Paul and the other Apostles. Here the *Word element* prevails, drawn from the fount of the Spirit. In the human word, be it the poetic word of prayer or the word of instruction spoken by the Apostles out of their deep spiritual maturity, the message of a higher world flows too.

On the plane of Intuition a real *Contact with the Spirit* and permeation with power take the place of picture and word. To this third stage belong, in the Old Testament, the prophetic books, and in the New Testament only the Apocalypse of St. John. This last book of the Bible is the authoritative work on intuitive spiritual experience; every word in it is saturated with divine presence.

The Revelation of St. John has flowed complete out of the well-spring of higher knowledge described in the last of the sevenfold cycles. Out of the Temple in Heaven, the ministering priestly angels bring forth the golden Vials. Will men experience the sense of Intuition when they drink the Love of God out of these Vials, or must what flows from the Temple-vessels be changed into the opposite of Love to the hurt of men? The Apocalypse is the intuitive warning of God. It is intended to show men the way to the true fulfilment of their being.

I

THE GATE OF PERFECTION:
THE SON OF MAN

THE FIRST CHAPTER

THE Book of Revelation is framed by a Prologue (i, 1 to i, 8) and an
Epilogue (xxii, 6 to xxii, 21). In these chapters many passages correspond, yet in such a way that the themes of the Introduction, after
passing through the cycles of the book, appear at the end transformed
and completed. The principal theme of the Apocalypse, the Second
Coming of Christ, is expressed both in the Prologue and the Epilogue.
At the beginning we read: "Behold He cometh" (i, 7). At the end the
sentence is spoken significantly three times, now no longer in the third
person, but by Christ Himself in direct speech: "Behold I come
quickly" (xxii, 7, 12, 20). In the Prologue, the sentence in its entirety
which indicates the Coming of Christ is a short comprehensive
epitome of the whole Apocalypse, especially with regard to the
storms and trials described throughout the book: "Behold He cometh
with clouds and every eye shall see Him, and they also which pierced
Him; and all kindreds of the Earth shall wail because of Him" (i, 7).
The full force of this passage, however, is not grasped if the returning
Christ is pictured in the usual manner as a Judge appearing at a definite
point of time, passing judgment and sentence as in a court of law.
The Second Coming of Christ is the coming of a whole sphere. The
supersensible world approaches as a whole. The clouds which have
hitherto veiled the returning Christ will be rent asunder. And that
part of the human race which has grown earthbound and loveless,
without realizing that in doing so it has inflicted continual injury on
the Godhead—"has pierced Him"—will be inescapably exposed to
perceiving the cosmic storm. But it is not that the part of mankind
hostile to Christ will see Him and be terrified because it must now fear
Him as Judge, but rather that mankind, convulsed by a thousand fears
and shocks, will be forced to perceive the effects of the onrushing
Spirit-sphere without seeing the Being from Whom these effects proceed, and Whose renewed presence alone gives meaning to all these
alarms and renders them bearable. A sense of terror will surge through

humanity, and men will not know whence it comes. The cry of anguish at the approach of the sphere of Christ will take the most varied forms. Among other things men will take refuge in material strength and in striving after power, the more the approach of the supersensible demonstrates how little mankind is prepared to face the reality of the Spirit. It cannot be simply an unmixed blessing when the Christ reveals Himself anew. In so far as men have not yet developed the power to penetrate the clouds and the veil, as long as they only dimly notice that something is approaching which they are not able to comprehend, they are helplessly exposed to all the storms and afflictions which appear in the Apocalypse (the Seven Seals, the Seven Trumpets, and the Seven Vials of Wrath) and which in reality signify the great break-through of Heaven into the Earth.

In order to understand the precise wording in which the theme of Christ's Coming—"I come quickly"—is three times expressed in the last chapter of the book, we must appreciate the special language of the Revelation of St. John. Another sentence in the Prologue and in the Epilogue may help us: "For the time is at hand" (i, 3 and xii, 10). Unfortunately, modern languages are rather inadequate to reproduce the Greek of the Apocalypse. The concise, condensed language in the original text of the Apocalypse has been attributed by many theologians to a special relationship with Hebrew, thus supporting their opinion that St. John's Revelation is in fact a Jewish book written in Hebrew, translated into Greek, and elaborated by Christianity. In reality, however, the Apocalypse is saturated with Intuition even in its language. The Greek of the Gospels is much more human; in the Apocalypse we are dealing with a Greek such as Archangels would speak if they made use of human speech. If we translate the sentence ὁ καιρὸς ἐγγύς (ho kairos engys) "the time is at hand", we are likely to misunderstand it seriously. It would be more correct to say: "the time is limited—time presses." The sentence is indeed a description of how the inner tempo, the spiritual vigour of the age will be different when mankind enters the apocalyptic era. When Christ comes, the time is laden with force, charged with vast destinies. In addition, the Greek text does not employ the ordinary word for "time", but speaks of the *kairos*. This means time which has matured, which is "fulfilled". In the same way the sentence thrice repeated at the end of the book: "Behold I come quickly", should not be understood as meaning that early Christendom expected to be separated only by a short span from this event. The sentence does not promise an early approach; it is rather a characterization of the dynamic quality of time. The meaning is, "I come in the pressing, the urgent time; the time which bears within it an immense spiritual hastening, breaking in with power upon a humanity which is for ever too slow." There is a challenge in these words. That Christ comes quickly can very well mean that He comes "too quickly" for an unprepared and sleeping humanity. That the time is "near" may mean that it is "short"; that it is actually too short considering the slowness and laziness of human souls.

Unlike the Prologue, however, the Epilogue of the Apocalypse no longer surrounds the motif of the Coming with the terrors of a cosmic storm. The air has been cleared and purified. And so, between the second and third repetition of the sentence concerning the Coming of Christ, the motif of the Coming can be heard in a wonderful dialogue between Heaven and Earth: "The Spirit and the Bride say 'come', and let him that heareth say 'come', and let him that is athirst come. And whosoever will, let him take the water of life freely" (xxii, 17). To the Coming of Christ must correspond a Coming of Humanity. If the Christ-sphere is to come down to the level of men, the souls of men must endeavour to come nearer to the Spirit. That is the meaning of the cry which rings out from the Spirit-world, "The Spirit and the Bride say 'come'." Those who are able to hear this cry and to respond to it, may themselves, through the power of prayer, call upon the Christ-sphere and say "Come". And then again it is Heaven which invites mankind to come. The Coming of Christ is no longer to be feared; on the contrary, it gives a share of the Water of Life to those whose hearts are open to it. Thus, at the very end of the apocalyptic book, when Christ's cry sounds for the third time, once more a wonderful dialogue takes place, born out of the reciprocal approach between Christ and Mankind. To Christ's cry, "Surely I come quickly", the human heart which is open to Christ replies, "Even so, come Lord Jesus" (xxii, 20).

In the opening sentence, which may very easily be read as a mere formality, the Revelation of St. John expresses its theme: "The Revelation of Jesus Christ". Not only the *book* is to be understood by the word Revelation, but the whole *process* of the Apocalypse. The Christ-Being having passed through Death, Resurrection and Ascension is revealed in the glory of His future-bearing Presence. The book that begins with these words is the manifested revelation of the nature of Christ, Who, however, does not remain static, but as the world-creative Principle can be seen in continual combative activity and metamorphosis. "This is the revelation (un-

17

veiling) of Jesus Christ which the Father God gave unto Him to show unto His servants." Christ has received His "glory", His radiant light-body from the Father. Through the Resurrection the words of Jesus were fulfilled: "Father, the hour is come; glorify thy Son" (John xvii, 1). But the light-body of the Risen One appeared to a humanity whose spiritual eyes were blinded. It is the Father's will that Christ should show "His servants" the glory, that the glory which He has given Him should be visible to them. Thus a complete change of consciousness, a healing of human blindness must come to pass. In order that the light-nature of Christ already revealed in the Spirit may some day be also revealed to the consciousness of men, the book of the Apocalypse is given to the "servants of Christ". It is the Being of Christ displayed in words and pictures, and indeed in such a manner that these words and pictures become seeds of a future direct seeing, hearing, and touching. The Spirit-figure of Christ becomes a book; and this book is intended to lead mankind to a vision of the Spirit-figure of Christ. This is the meaning of the sentence: "He signi-fied it and sent it by His Angel to His servant John." The nature of Christ Himself is, as it were, converted into written symbols and ciphers so that men may possess a book through the decoding and correct reading of which they may be educated and initiated to the realization of the nature of Christ.

In the opening sentences a hierarchical sequence is observed. "The Revelation of Jesus Christ, which God gave unto Him to show unto His servants briefly things which must come to pass: and He sent and signified it by His Angel unto His servant John. . . . Blessed is he that readeth, and they that hear the words of this prophecy and keep in their heart those things which are written therein: for the time is at hand (or presses)" (i, 1–3). The Father God, the all-embracing Ground of the World, gives to the Son the revelation of light. The Son gives it converted into words and signs to His Angel who, as in-spiring genius, radiates it into the soul of John. In the seer of Patmos, that which proceeded from the Father reaches mankind after passing through Christ and the realm of the Angels. Divine self-surrender flows from the heights, through all spheres of Heaven to Earth. What the Father gives is His own being; all the kingdoms of Heaven are members of the body of God. Christ becomes the sum of all, the heart and pulse-beat of the whole. The Being of the Father is converted into the Son, and the Son, having passed through His Incarnation, imparts Himself to mankind as the substance of the revelation, hence also, as the seed of a new consciousness. We see the hierarchical origin,

18

the heavenly pedigree of the Revelation of St. John. That which was given from the heights is passed on from one realm of Heaven to another until it reaches the Earth. And then the aged John—by tradition almost a hundred years old—stands there on Patmos as the man who continues the descending series of hierarchies. But the continuation of the gift in the hierarchical succession of stages is not yet ended. "Blessed is he that readeth, and they that hear." It should be noticed that first the singular, and then the plural is used: he who reads, they who hear. Obviously the reference is not to abstract reading; that has only started since books like the Apocalypse have been printed on paper and can be carried in the pocket. "Reading" is here the reading of the Gospels like a heraldic proclamation, as it was carried out by the priestly *anagnosts* in the early Christian congregations.

Today, reading is a taking and receiving. It should also be a giving, an active hearing. He who wishes to receive Revelation, must hear with the ear of the soul, with the acquired faculty of recognizing the voice of God through the words of men. Thus the heavenly ladder on which the Revelation descends to Earth continues further into the human sphere: Father, Son, Angels, John, the priestly reader, the congregation of devout listeners. Out of the fullness of Heaven comes the word of the Apocalypse working as a community-building force among men. The self-characterization with which the Book of Revelation begins, shows how fundamentally the spell of the Old Testament is broken. The chasm between God and Man is bridged over. God's great confidence in Man, founded on Christ; *belief in Man*, as a cosmic principle of the new creation: this is the basis of the Apocalypse. It is a proof of the confidence of God in Man.

He who has united himself with Christ is joined to the hierarchies of Heaven; he is received into them as their lowest member. Hence at the very beginning of the Apocalypse the lofty words may be spoken: "He hath made us Kings and Priests" (i, 6). Through Christ Man is invested with new dignity. The spiritual *freedom* attained in a Christ-filled ego-consciousness is the divine crowning of human personality; it is the secret of the inner kingdom. And if the free personality, after the pattern of Christ Himself, *serves* instead of ruling, if in brotherliness he helps his fellow men, the secret of the spiritual priesthood is revealed: it is *Love*.

The first chapter is a little Apocalypse complete in itself. It might be called a "prefatory Apocalypse" just as the first two chapters of

St. Luke's Gospel containing the history of the childhood of Jesus might be called a "prefatory Gospel". We take part in the biographical moment of the birth or dawn of St. John's Revelation.

During the Domitian persecution of the Christians in one of the last years of the first century, the aged presbyter of Ephesus was subjected to cruel torture, and then taken as a prisoner and exile to the rocky island of Patmos. There, as the outward drama into which the Messianic and the anti-Messianic tensions of the age had drawn him was nearing its end, an inward drama began for him. His mind was stirred by the Apocalypse which was brought to him by the Angel of Christ, and which was in effect the very revelation of Christ Himself.

"It was on the Lord's day" (i, 10). This is not merely an outward indication of time whereby we learn that St. John's illumination on Patmos began on a Sunday. The first Christians had made Sunday their weekly festival because it was the day of the Resurrection. But they combined with it more than the regular devotional commemoration of a great event in the past. The cosmic background, the planetary colouring of the several weekdays was still an accepted reality. Nor did the Resurrection of Christ fall accidentally on the day of the Sun. It revealed the Sun-character of Christianity, the essential connection of Christ with the Sun. Henceforth the Sabbath, the day of aged Saturn, was replaced by the day of the bright Sun which, because Christ was the Lord of the Sun, was called at the same time the "day of the Lord". The solemnities on the Lord's day were developments of the Sun-mysteries which had received a new content on Earth through Christ. The festival experience of Sunday was also charged—and this is important—with a strong feeling for the future. From Easter Sunday, now lying in the past, the early Christians looked towards the new Coming of Christ, which would be a mighty sunrise and daybreak in the realm of soul and spirit. This promise of the Day of the Sun was fulfilled for St. John on Patmos. The new Christ-day dawned; a new world rose for him; he was one of the first witnesses of the break-through of the Sun which was to form the content of advancing Christianity.

The first manifestation which penetrated to the soul of John "in the Spirit" was a sound, a manifestation to the spiritual hearing: "I heard behind me a great voice as of a trumpet" (i, 10). He turned round wishing to see the Being who was speaking to him, and a mighty vision rose before his soul. Trembling, he sank to the ground as dead before the Figure which met his eyes. Then he felt that a hand was laid upon him; and the touch, like a living current thrilling through him, restored life to him again. The apocalyptic spark on Patmos flashed across in three stages: the hearing of the voice, the seeing of the Figure, and the life-awakening touch. St. John first *hears* the Sunrise of the Coming of Christ, the Day of the Lord. And only when the sound of the Trumpet which penetrated his whole being is hushed do the eyes of his soul open to the great Vision.

The human figure of great and dignified stature proved to be the speaker whose voice rang out like a Trumpet. Is it Christ? The words "I am He that liveth and was dead" assure us of this. The Apocalypse characterizes the great Vision as the "likeness of the Son of Man". The "Son of Man" is the Spirit-Man born as a higher being in the Man of Earth. "Son of Man" is not necessarily always a description of Christ; but Christ can be so designated because He is "The Man".

During the primal, "paradisal" age the true image of Man, the figure of the "Spirit-Man", overshadowed earthly man. Through the "Fall" Man fell away from his divine likeness. In and through Christ the Spirit-Man rose again. Christ Jesus was the first bearer of the true, restored human form. On Patmos St. John saw Christ and at the same time the true human ideal, the higher Man, restored to mankind in and through Christ. And by placing this picture in its solemn grandeur at the beginning of the Apocalypse, he discloses the goal to which all stages of the path must lead. The door that leads into the Temple of the Apocalypse reveals at the same time the fulfil-ment of apocalyptic development. The vision of the Spirit-Man is an epitome of the whole Apocalypse. What is imparted to mankind first as a picture, through John, must be finally attained through all the circles of apocalyptic ascent. The Apocalypse starts from Man as he was conceived in the mind of God, and as restored after the Death and Resurrection of Christ. The new foundation is laid: God's faith in Man. Should not then Man himself also learn once more to believe in men?

The Revelation of St. John renews and lifts to a Christian level the Greek proverb: "Man is the measure of all things." If the vision of the Heavenly City at the end corresponds to the vision of the Son of Man at the beginning, this means that Man becomes a World. Man can build up through the epochs of history a world corresponding to the thought of God if he copies its measurements and laws from Man; not from the natural man with his selfish materialism, but from the true nature of Man, the Spirit-Man.

The picture of the Son of Man (i, 13–20) is described as having nine attributes. All the nine Angel-hierarchies have shared in its fashioning and have given of their best for their christening-gifts, so that the Spirit-Man might be accepted as the tenth member of their choir. The nine characteristics fall into three groups of three.

Solemn brightness, maturity and calm proceed from the first trinity; the Son of Man is clad in a long white vesture flowing down to His feet. About His breast He wears a golden girdle. His head and His hair are gleaming white, like white wool or snow.

The second group of characteristics is, in contrast, charged with dynamic force. There is something elemental about it; the elements of fire, water and earth unite their voices and fill everything with evolutionary suspense. The Son of Man has eyes like flames of fire. He has feet like glowing brass fresh from the furnace. And He has a voice like the rushing of mighty waters.

The nature of the last three hierarchical characteristics shows the Son of Man far and high above the earthly elemental sphere. The sun and the stars are no longer above Him, but in Him. He has authority to effect grave world-decisions. In His right hand He holds seven stars. Out of His mouth goes forth a sharp two-edged sword. And His countenance shines as the Sun, radiant in full strength.

The solemnity of the first trinity reveals the spiritual dignity of the Son of Man. The long white garment shows the purity of willing and being. The golden gleam of the girdle round the breast is the light and warmth of feeling, and at the same time the form-giving solidity to which all chaotic and disharmonious confusion must submit. The snow-white head and hair show mature thinking illumined by wisdom. The central trinity is the radiation of a basic strength of soul. The human being must not be faint-hearted while growing upward to the Spirit-Man; the earthly soul must be so purified in the fire of the Spirit that it becomes itself a burning fire. The flames which give the eyes their immense vitality are the enthusiasm and the longing for knowledge. They transform the perception that sees only from out-side into a vision that penetrates within. Feet like glowing brass signify a firm grip on the Earth. By mining metals out of the earth Man takes hold of the hardest earthly substance. But Man should not leave the earth as it is; he should not stride over it unconcernedly. Creative and constructive, he should not confine his sphere of action to the plane of the merely useful. A real creative change of earthly conditions is possible through the fire of the Spirit. The voice which is like the rushing of great waters is acquired by the Son of Man when He learns how to cause the creative force of the cosmic word, God's word, to flow into the human word. Much of the future of mankind depends upon whether the "lost word" is found again, and whether Man attains to that power of speech in which the overtones of a higher world can be heard.

Finally, Spirit-Man is in control of cosmic life-forces. The seven stars in the right hand of the Son of Man show that Man is not a tool with no volition of his own, but can be master of his destiny. The sharp two-edged sword proceeding from the mouth of the Son of Man suggests the cosmic authority with which he, as master, confronts the discord between good and evil. The countenance which shines as the Sun shows that Man himself can be a Sun. If he bears within him the Lord of the spiritual Sun, he will become the source of a light which enlightens the world and conquers all darkness. The centre of the world is within him, signifying an inner mainstay, a force dispensing life and order for mankind. Thus the first chapter of St. John's Revelation reveals the vision of Christ and at the same time of the ideal human being. It reads like an illustrated breviary of Christian idealism.

As John turns round to see the One who spoke to him like a trumpet, he sees the Son of Man in the midst of seven golden candlesticks. An altar is not mentioned yet; the symbol of the altar belongs to a later stage. Nevertheless the sight of the seven candles prepares us for the idea of an altar. That on which the seven candlesticks stand can be imagined as an altar, and the figure of the Son of Man as looking down upon us from above the seven lights of this altar. In the renewed sacramental life as it is observed in The Christian Community, the picture of the altar on which the seven lights burn, and over which the countenance of Christ shines forth, has become once more familiar and homely to many. The experience of worship before these new altars may make it easier in reading the first chapter of the Apocalypse to become a St. John, as it were, and to see with the eyes of his soul the Son of Man in the midst of the seven golden candlesticks. Conversely, a study of the first vision of the Apocalypse may inspire us to see—either before a physically present, or before a spiritual altar—in the picture of Christ a mirror of our higher self, a picture of what we ought to be.

The first chapter closes with the sentence, "The mystery of the seven stars, which thou sawest in my right hand, and the seven golden candlesticks. The seven stars are the angels of the seven churches: and the seven candlesticks which thou sawest are the seven churches" (i, 20). Presently, in the seven messages directed to the Seven Churches the beginning of a new order of mankind is made.

Around Christ, communities arise which represent a stage in the evolution of a new world lying, as it were, between the first vision of the Son of Man and the final picture of the heavenly Jerusalem. A new heaven of stars springs from the Earth. And each Church has its genius, its Angel, hovering over it. Men on earth make it possible for Heavenly Beings to dwell upon earth and to work together in earthly events according to the will of Christ.

II

THE MESSAGES:
STAGES IN THE EVOLUTION OF MANKIND

THE SECOND AND THIRD CHAPTERS

WHEN Parsifal, in Wagner's opera, sets foot for the first time upon the territory of the Grail, he becomes aware that his pace alters. A strange new, unsuspected relationship to Time and Space occurs to him. Astonished, he says, "I have hardly taken a step, yet I feel I have gone far." And his aged guide Gurnemanz explains, "You see, my son, here Time becomes Space."

In its whole construction, the Apocalypse is Grail country where for those who traverse it and who pass all the tests Time becomes Space. This appears in the different laws of number by which it is governed at the beginning and at the end; it advances *from the Seven to the Twelve.* For us today numbers normally express only quantities. But books like the Revelation of St. John still reckon throughout with the qualitative character of numbers.

Seven is the number of Time; it expresses the rhythm of evolution. Its simplest manifestation is the week with its seven days. Twelve is the number of Space. Its best illustration is the twelve signs of the Zodiac. There we experience what Space is.

The first part of the Apocalypse advances entirely in rhythms of seven. In the very first chapter the number seven occurs in the significant context of the Seven Stars and the Seven Golden Candlesticks. Then the great circles of Seven unfold, their progress measured as it were by cosmic dials. Seven Messages, Seven Seals, Seven Trumpets, and Seven Vials of Wrath follow each other.

Where the mounting circles leave the earthly plane, between the Messages and the Seals, the quiet note of the number Twelve, the number of Space, begins to be heard for the first time. The promise of lasting existence, eternity, is foreshadowed in variations and multiples of Twelve: in the four cherubic Creatures, in the ring of four and twenty Elders around the throne of God. Time is about to turn into Space. At the end, everything is taken up into the twelve-fold rhythm of the cosmic firmament. When the 144,000 throng round the

Lamb on the holy mountain; when the heavenly city appears, with the twelve gates and the twelve foundations, with the twelve precious stones and the twelve pearls, then Time is fulfilled and has become Space altogether.

In the first cycle equality is the rule. The Seven Messages are wonderfully balanced against one another; each occupies about the same space. In the next cycle equality is continued through the first stage. The first four Seals balance one another in their condensed style. Then, however, events gather momentum. The fifth Seal bursts its bounds, expanding beyond the space which each of the preceding ones occupied. The sixth Seal goes further still. Whereas the first five Seals together occupied only half a chapter, the sixth takes one and a half for itself alone. Finally, the seventh dissolves altogether into the next sevenhood; its content is the Seventh Trumpets, the whole of the subsequent greater cycle.

The first four of the Trumpet-blasts pass in uniform, condensed brevity. The content of the fifth stage extends and stretches. An immense growth begins. The first four Trumpets together form the content of one chapter; the fifth occupies rather more than half a chapter; the sixth more than two whole chapters; finally the seventh Trumpet resounds through nearly four and a half chapters. So we advance into a structure of ever-widening dimensions.

What is expressed in this progress? Since the Seven Cycles are dealing with a succession of great epochs of time and stages in Man's evolution, we might think that if one Seal or one Trumpet occupies more space than the ones before it, a longer lapse of time must be indicated. In reality, it is not a quantitative but a dynamic principle which is involved. Not the duration of time, but the contents of the events and of the destiny of a section of time grow and multiply continually in the successive cycles. Time becomes swifter, more condensed. Its momentum increases. Time becomes apocalyptic. The nearer the seventh day approaches, in one of the great cosmic weeks, the more it seems as if time can hardly contain its inner fullness, and comes near to bursting asunder. Something works increasingly into earthly evolution out of higher worlds to resolve Time into Space. At such times men can only keep pace with their destiny if they do not resist the drive and pull of events, and are prepared to live with death at their elbow. These are the very times of which we read also in the Gospel, "Except that the Lord had shortened those days, no flesh should be saved" (Mark xiii, 20).

At first sight, the uniformity with which the Apocalypse begins in the circle of the Seven Messages seems to recur at the end in the Seven Vials of Wrath. But as we shall see later, in this last Cycle of Seven a new aeon begins. The "Last Trump" points to the end of the planetary life of the Earth, and ushers in the concluding drama which leads to the duality of the "Bride, Jerusalem" descending from Heaven, and the "Harlot, Babylon" plunging into the abyss.

There is symmetry between the beginning and the end of the book. *Before* the Seven Messages the great *One* appears, the vision of the Son of Man, the spiritual prototype of Man, which is the origin and fulfilment, the Alpha and Omega of everything. Out of Him proceeds the sevenfoldness of the Churches to which the Messages are addressed. Out of Spirit-Man humanity proceeds, "informed" by the sevenfold order of the succeeding stages of evolution. *After* the Seven Vials of Wrath which again follow one another uniformly, comes the great *Two*, the cleaving of Earth and Mankind into two worlds which appear in the picture of the two cities. The apocalyptic tragedy lies in the fact that it is a divided world which will pass into the next aeon.

(We shall eventually see that it is a *Three* which in the end confronts the initial *One*. Between the two great pictures of the final conditions of our Earthly cycle of time there stands the transformed picture of the Son of Man, the *White Horseman* who in the decisive battle leads the advancing part of mankind into the future.)

The Seven Messages are addressed to seven early Christian Churches which actually existed in Asia Minor: Ephesus, Smyrna, Pergamos, Thyatira, Sardis, Philadelphia and Laodicea. They formed the circuit of the aged presbyter John. It may have been in the middle of the first century when the disciple whom Jesus loved began from Ephesus his quiet activity, holy and beneficent, which he was able to carry on until the end of the century to a ripe old age. There is no reason to doubt the traditions which report him as working in Ephesus, together with Mary the Mother of Jesus. The Churches to which the Messages are addressed may have been the focusing points of the pastoral activities to which St. John was devoted. The three Epistles of St. John in the New Testament are moving testimonies of this labour of love and wisdom harmoniously fused.

If we try to visualize the path which the old man had to travel from Ephesus, whenever he wished to visit the seven Churches, the symbolic pattern of this group becomes apparent. Ephesus was the city by the sea. A wide bay opened out to far horizons. Today the place has become quiet and insignificant, since the harbour is silted up and the town lies inland. Nevertheless, the great natural arena of ancient Ephesus, lying in a circle round the Castle Hill, is still clearly discernible. In early Christian times the sun of Homer still shone over Ephesus as over no other city of the Johannine Churches. In the very landscape in which St. John's Gospel was written, the writings of Homer came into being a thousand years earlier. And the soul of the great and populous city was still infused with the Mysteries of the oft-destroyed, oft-rebuilt, age-old temple of Artemis-Diana.

To reach Smyrna one must travel northwards by sea round the promontories. Smyrna lies also on the sea-coast, but it does not share the sunny character of Ephesus. A solemn gloom lies over the city. Black forbidding mountains tower up immediately behind the city, very unlike the bright green plains of Ephesus. Time and again, the city has been razed to the ground. Thus there are no remains whatever of the Smyrna of the early Christian age. The Smyrna of today, a great commercial town, can only maintain itself—as it has always done —by the hard work and almost militant industry of its people.

To reach the site of the third Church, Pergamos, we must turn north-east, and proceed more inland. On majestic heights with sweep-ing views, the city lay crowded closely round the castle and temple hill. Its temple buildings gave it a character of concentrated greatness. The little Christian community had to lead their quiet life in an environment of powerful heathen cults.

Towards Thyatira the road goes further inland and we arrive at the plateau of Asia Minor. The landscape is more monotonous than at the coastal strip. Life is simpler, and less full of history. No shadow of a gigantic past falls upon it. Now having described a semi-circle in a north-easterly direction, we draw, in order to reach the other Churches, Sardis, Philadelphia and Laodicea, another semi-circle south-westwards, so that the Johannine journey through the seven Churches approxi-mates a full circle. The last stages take us into a mysterious land-scape. Laodicea lay quite close to Colossae to which St. Paul's Epistle was directed. In the Epistle to the Colossians St. Paul urges the two Churches to exchange the letters addressed to them. Not far away from these two towns Hierapolis was situated which has played a very important part in religious history. Hierapolis was the home of the Plutonion, one of the most famous oracles of the ancient world. Here a cave penetrated deep into the interior. A sinister atmosphere, a sense of terror, issued from this sub-earthly rocky cave. It was known that it was filled continually with poisonous gases from the interior of the Earth and that whoever entered it would be asphyxiated. Despite or even for that very reason, this inferno concealed a sanctuary. It was thought to be the dwelling-place of Pluto, the God of the Underworld. A mysterious rite was performed there by the priests of Cybele. These priests must have made use of an early chemical knowledge whereby they protected themselves from the deadly effects of subterranean gases. Thus, by means of these forces flowing from the interior of the Earth, they succeeded in transporting themselves, like the Pythia at Delphi, into a somnambulistic condition which enabled them to give oracular answers from the gods to the questions of men. The exterior landscape surrounding this subterranean Delphi corresponded to the sinister nature of these chasms. In the country near the cities of Hierapolis, Laodicea and Colossae, the surface of the Earth is like an inverted stalactite cave. In the past, hot mineral springs issued here from the interior of the Earth, and trickled over the soil so that through stalactite activity a kind of porcelain or glassy crust was formed. Fantastic, needle-like points of rock deposited and crystallized by the mineral waters rise up from the glassy formation of the ground like the surface of an alien, dead planet. All verdant life is scorched by the death-dealing subterranean breath. Here is a complete contrast to the country of Ephesus. There, by the sea, everything was still illumined by the dreams of the gods and echoes of the original paradisal harmony with heaven. Here in the interior of Asia Minor the powers of hell tread openly in the daylight bringing death to all living things.

The road leading up in a wide curve from the sea to the mountain heights, from the first to the seventh apocalyptic Church, repeats the path of humanity. It starts in cities which still live in an age-old heritage of culture and wisdom, and leads into surroundings which, though indeed far removed from the centres of life in these days, yet anticipated the future. In our day something of the Plutonion principle has spread over the whole of modern civilization. We have had to learn on a large scale how to work with subterranean forces such as gases, electricity, or latterly, atomic energy. A kind of glazed crust covers every landscape in which Nature has been thrust back by industry. In Laodicea, a prophetic anticipation of modern conditions may have been at work.

The Seven Churches represent in miniature the great human epochs in the course of history. Echoes of a past still near to Heaven and God, as in the ancient Indian culture, create the magic of Ephesus. Smyrna has something of the old Persian epoch, wherein Man awoke to the struggle between light and darkness, and gained from it the urge to active work and practical labour. Pergamos, on the soil of the former Trojan lands, echoed the Mycenic-Trojan wisdom, sister of the Egyptian-Chaldaic temple culture. The presbyter of Ephesus met his own epoch in Thyatira, the central city of the Seven. At the middle point of history, Christ descended to His Incarnation on Earth, and the current of Christian life could begin to flow into the historic evolution of mankind. Thus the central city of the Seven depicts the time of the Apostles, that is, the "present time" of the Johannine epoch. Travelling deeper into the interior of the country, from the cities of the preservers to those of the precursors, we come last to Sardis, Philadelphia and Laodicea. Although linked together by contemporary existence, the Seven Cities and Churches conceal within their proximity in space a great succession of stages in time, which anyone who together with the aged John visited the Seven Churches one after another, would have experienced in their symbolic significance.

In the Seven Messages to the Churches the Apocalypse itself lifts our gaze from the facts about the actual congregations of those times to a higher level of archetypes: what John was to write to the Churches was not addressed to the Churches themselves, but to the "Angels of the Churches". It has been remarked by theological writers that in the early Christian Churches the priestly leaders were called Angels, and so the Messages are to be considered as addressed to the priests. But the Revelation of St. John speaks quite concretely and precisely of supersensible conditions. A Church is something more than the mere sum of the men who meet together in it. An organized community of interests, a co-operative association, an audience listening to a lecture consists in most cases simply of the sum of the individuals present. From a cosmic point of view, however, a group of people is only valuable when it forms a fellowship, and thereby becomes a "Church". Where true fellowship is achieved, Heaven co-operates. An Angel Being becomes the genius of this fellowship and is incorporated in it, just as a human ego is incorporated in the organs of the physical body. The sum-total of the men becomes the sum-total of the organs of the Angel who is embodied in the Church. Only the spiritual Being who hovers, as it were, over the heads of human beings, can maintain a real and lasting cohesion in a community. Then perhaps a feeling penetrates into the consciousness of the people involved: "We are not alone; we are privileged to be the Body of a higher Being who is working through us." It is an enhancement of this mystery that a Christian community becomes at the same time the body of Christ, of which (as St. Paul describes it in 1 Corinthians, xii) individual

30

men are the members, which should work together in harmonious concord. Every true Church receives its position in the colour-scale of humanity, the type of its soul, the pitch of its key, from the particular apocalyptic quality of the Son of Man which prevails and is realized in it. When the Son of Man tells John what he is to say in the Messages to the Churches, He speaks out of the various aspects of His nature one after the other. This gives to the Angel of the Church, and through him the community inspired by him, its special human and archetypal character. Only the sum total of the Churches can mirror the complete Christ Being. Goethe's words, "Only the whole of humanity is the true Man," touch upon this secret. When we are told that He "that holdeth the Seven Stars in his right hand, who walketh in the midst of the Seven Golden Candlesticks" speaks to the Church of Ephesus, we realize that the magic of this Church lay in the harmonious integrity of the spiritual light still at its command. It possessed the seven-branched candlestick spiritually. The seven-hued rainbow of potential developments in human history was still present there in its archetypal origin. It had not yet developed any one-sidedness. And if the Seven Candles burn again on the new altars of the Christian Community, the secret of an omnipresent Ephesus begins to radiate from them. Where true progress is achieved, all forms of one-sidedness are gathered before the altar into one new complete humanity. With the quality of Ephesus, the long-lost ages when the Gods were at hand will be renewed in the midst of the storms of the present day.

To the Church of Smyrna He speaks Who is "The First and the Last, which was dead and is alive". Therewith the second of the Seven Churches is marked out by the divine will as a community which, through "dying and becoming", must continually struggle forward to new beginnings and resurrections. To the third Church, in which the wisdom of the temples of Egypt survives, speaks "He which hath the sharp sword with two edges." This picture points to the power of the magic Word which gave the special character to the temple-rites performed in the civilizations between the Euphrates and Tigris and on the Nile—a spiritual character which through Christ was bestowed on mankind anew and in freedom. An interesting detail can illustrate this point. In the third Message the sentence occurs, "I have a few things against thee, because thou hast there them that hold the doctrine of Balaam." A figure of the Old Testament emerges, one of the great opponents of Moses, who met the Chosen People when after forty years in the wilderness they came to the borders of the

Promised Land. The kings of the Palestinian territory wished to drive back the intruders with the help of magic, and called Balaam to their defence; he was to curse the Israelites by the power of the magic word which he possessed. They were convinced that Balaam's curse was able to break the power of Israel. Astonishingly, however, his curse became a prophetic blessing against his will. The sword of the magical priestly Word revealed its two-edgedness. It could both curse and bless. It proved that Balaam was in reality no longer master of the word-magic employed by him.

What can the third Message mean when it says there are men in Pergamos who hold the doctrine of Balaam? It is not easy to imagine that magical adversaries of the type of Balaam should belong to a Church under the guidance of the aged presbyter John. Yet the phrase has a concrete purpose. In the churches of early Christendom, "speaking with tongues", a relic of the magical use of the "Word", was practised in many places. There were individuals who, in a state of trance, could speak a language which was not like any earthly speech. It needed those who had other capacities at their command to interpret and explain "the unknown tongue". St. Paul's Epistles show that he held no brief for speaking with tongues. He says that for him a single word proceeding from clear knowledge is of more value than a thousand words spoken in an unknown tongue. He did not care for such echoes of old spiritual faculties. John turns even more sharply than Paul against speaking with tongues when he calls those who speak in an unknown tongue "followers of Balaam". He knows the danger that might ensue to the Churches from these remnants of an effete spiritual life, and urges a spiritual soberness, a Christ-filled, wide-awake consciousness. Christ Himself must be the bearer of the Word in the Church. Not the babble of Balaam, but the Word of Christ can illumine and inspire the world with light and warmth.

To the Church in Thyatira, the middle one of the Seven Churches, speaks "the Son of God, who hath his eyes like unto a flame and his feet like fine brass". At the turning point of time a highest Divine Being enters into earthly life. The human figure which it assumes stands firmly with both feet on the Earth, but carries at the same time the fiery power of the Spirit into the sphere of Earth. But the fourth Message contains also a passage corresponding to the reference to Balaam in the third letter. "I have a few things against thee, because thou sufferest that woman Jezebel, which calleth herself a prophetess, to teach and to seduce my servants to commit fornication, and to eat things sacrificed unto idols." Again a figure emerges from the Old

32

Testament. This time it is the great opponent of Elijah, Queen Jezebel who, as daughter of a Phoenician king and high priestess of Baal, brought the priests of Baal into the land. Again it is difficult to imagine how in a Church where John had been at work the influence of Jezebel should have taken such root. But here, too, something concrete is referred to. The spiritual life of those days was still extensively influenced by "Sibyls". These were women of a type easily excited to ecstasy, who became mediums and were able to speak as oracles. Important Sibylline localities were scattered over the whole world. Thus Nero could seek counsel from the Cumaean Sibyl. There were, however, also Christian Sibyls, and the Sibylline Books, collections of Sibylline maxims on a Christian basis, formed a large part of the apocryphal literature of Early Christendom. The significant part played by the Sibyls in Early Christian times is evident from the paintings of Raphael and Michelangelo. Raphael's picture of the Sibyls in the church of Santa Maria della Pace in Rome, and the monumental paintings of Michelangelo on the ceiling of the Sistine Chapel, which show Prophets and Sibyls alternately, belong to the marvels of Renaissance Art. Just as he turned against "speaking with tongues" so did St. Paul turn against the Sibylline influence, in so far as it reared its head in the Christian Churches. He rejected everything vague; anything that would dull sober, clear-thinking consciousness. That is the meaning of his often quoted saying, "*mulier taceat in ecclesia*" (let your women keep silence in the churches). Again John rejects the Sibyls more sharply than Paul, by calling the Sibyls "children of Jezebel". He desires that in the Churches which are to embody the spirituality of the present, Christ and not the Sibyls is to be sought as the only one Whose eyes flash flames of fire. He is to be seen as the Lord of a new type of spirituality. Normal consciousness is not to be suppressed; on the contrary, it is to be enhanced. Everywhere the spirit of the Apocalypse urges a conversion of the remnants from bygone phases of humanity into a balanced, dignified Christ-filled ego-consciousness appropriate to the present and the future.

To the Church of Sardis, Christ speaks as "He that hath the seven Spirits of God and the Seven Stars". He seems to have the same characteristics as when he spoke to the Church of Ephesus. At the fifth stage, mankind has passed the middle point, and must endeavour to recover on a new level those forces which it once possessed and lost in the course of its earthly pilgrimage. The Church in Philadelphia is addressed as follows: "These things saith he that is holy, he that is true, he that hath the key of David, he that openeth and no man shutteth;

and shutteth and no man openeth." When mankind enters those cycles of evolution which are under the sign of the number six, that is, those which lead towards an ending in time, Christianity is standing before open doors. The gates of the supersensible world burst open; the doors of human hearts must open also. Out of the open gates of Heaven, Angels and Messengers of God desire to come to men; but out of the doors of Hell, simultaneously opening, demonic powers mingle among men. Then the way is prepared for a dividing of souls among mankind. On the one hand there will be those who, although perhaps going on their way quite unobtrusively, yet possess the inner power of opening their hearts to the good Spirits and to Christ. Others, out of a fear which delights to pose as strength, will close their hearts, and for that reason fall the more readily under the influence of the dark forces. The seventh Church in Laodicea was addressed by Him who is called "the Amen, the faithful and true witness, the beginning of the creation of God". Here a new cosmic beginning is announced, a beginning born out of the Amen, the solemn final Word of the preceding phase of evolution. This last Message also speaks of Him who stands at the door and knocks, to whom we must open the door if we are to be united in communion with Him.

The name of the sixth Church is Philadelphia, which means "brotherly love". From that name the words, "I have set before thee an open door," have generally been understood as referring to open-heartedness in human companionship which produces brotherly affection and mutual confidence. But the themes of the "key of David" and the "open doors" refer in reality to the new relationship between the sense-world and the supersensible world. An open Heaven implies that the gates of Hell are also opened. The power of the keys in the hands of the Son of Man ushers in apocalyptic ages with great tensions. At such times mankind is, to start with, farther from the secret of brotherly love than at any other. Wars rage through the world, and no one seems able to bring the avalanche of catastrophe to a standstill. We know this clearly enough from the story of our own age. At such times one becomes painfully aware, if one did not know it before, that true brotherly love is a high and distant goal. Love, the highest purpose of earthly life, can only be learnt in slow stages. The history of humanity is the school of love, and in this school we have taken only the very first steps at most.

The mysterious subject of love is introduced explicitly into the first and last message. The Church of Ephesus is told "I have this against thee, that thou hast forsaken thy first love". What is the "first love"?

34

We cannot attain to the last love, to the earthly goal, so long as we belong to those who have even forsaken the first love. Such apocalyptic formulae as that of the "first love" should not be taken too humanly. The first love is the love which animates children. The spirit and soul of a human being would not descend to Earth at birth if they were not led to do so by love of the Earth. Only afterwards we forget why we come down into incarnation. But the joyous surrender of a child to all that is earthly is the echo of pre-natal love for the Earth. "*Love for the Earth*" is the meaning of the apocalyptic expression "the first love". It lies hidden in the depths of our own being. In the course of life we fall all too easily into the temptation to look back longingly to Heaven, and hence to be disloyal to the Earth. The cultivation of this first love forms the first step on the path to Philadelphia. Nor must our religious life cause us to forget the first love in egoistic yearning for the world beyond. This is the error with which the Church of Ephesus is reproached. The "last love" is spoken of in the conclusion of the Seven Messages. He who has opened the door when Christ knocks, and is in communion with Him Who enters, may be enthroned with Him; and as Christ "sits at the right hand of the Father" to carry out the deeds of the Father, so may he sit at the right hand of Christ, and share in the fullness of His creative and transforming power. The last love is the guiding love of God to men. By it Man can participate in the goal of evolution.

The drama of Christ's passion, as He passed through the stages of death and resurrection, marks out the same path. The Washing of the Feet is the most wonderful realization of the "first love". In the picture of the Ascension, Christ appears in the mystery of the "last love", as it is expressed at the conclusion of the Messages. Before this goal lies Philadelphia. From a true harmony between reverence for that which is below us and reverence for that which is above us, we learn step by step reverence for that which is beside us, the secret of brotherly love, of loving one's neighbour. The path of human history leads to Philadelphia if it is at the same time the path with Christ from the Washing of the Feet, through Death and Resurrection to Ascension.

To each of the Seven Churches a particular promise is given which corresponds to the facet in the Being of Christ which is directed to that particular Church. Each time it is said, "To him that overcometh shall be given." It refers each time to those who have stood the tests of one stage, and are able to pass on to the next. The promise to those who overcome in Ephesus runs, "I will give them to eat of the Tree of

Life, which is in the midst of the Paradise of God," i.e., I will give them nourishment through higher strength, feeding even the bodily nature of a man.

To those who stand the tests in Smyrna is promised "the crown of life", and that they "shall not be hurt of the second death". Those to whom this promise refers will not escape physical death but will be spared the fate of those who, after death, forfeit immortality and sink into darkness because during their lifetime they have absorbed so much death into themselves. Suffering, duly borne and mastered, gives the soul the shining crown of such powers of individual consciousness as are not extinguished in the darkness of the kingdom of death. The promise to Pergamos is "te hidden manna" and "the white stone" on which is written "a new name which no man knoweth save he that receiveth it". Just as Ephesus has received the spiritual gift of the physical body, and Smyrna that of the life-forces, so to those in Pergamos is assigned the spiritual gift of the enlightened soul. The illumined soul is fed by the hidden manna; hence there shines in her the secret of the white stone, the bright jewel on which stands the name "I" which none can understand or utter except the bearer of this "I".

The promised gift of the fourth Church is the "rod of iron which shall break the potter's vessels to shivers, and the bright morning star". At the fourth stage, he who has come through all the tests will attain to the power of true egohood. The ego-impulse expresses itself at first negatively. It breaks the primitive tribal basis of fellowship. All the old bonds of fellowship are lost. But the true Self bears within it the principle of spiritual individuality, shining like the morning star which precedes the rising of the Sun. In it lives the power to bring forth a new, free fellowship in the Spirit.

To those who overcome the Sardis stage it is promised that they "shall be clothed with white raiment and that their names shall not be blotted out of the book of life". The Sun of higher humanity rises on them. And they themselves begin to shine from within. They have outgrown the purely earth-bound intellect and have filled their hearts and minds with radiating spiritual thoughts. In the sixth Church the victors become "pillars of the temple". The temple is built in which Man himself may be both building stone and pillar.

The promise made to the seventh Church is participation in the Ascension of Christ, in His divine creative power—"I will grant him to sit with me in my throne." Man becomes part creator of the new world. All the seven promises to those that overcome together build again the seven-membered Spirit-Man, after the Son of Man seen in the great opening vision as the Archetype of Man has poured Himself out into the seven basic groups of humanity.

The Seven Messages can become a golden book of rules for the training of our inner life. We learn how to prepare our souls for the Coming of Christ. True, this Coming of Christ is itself spoken of only in negative sentences which add a solemn warning to the positive instruction: if you do not do this or that, disaster will befall you. The "two-edged sword" of the new experiences is impressed upon us.

Both the negative sentence and the motif of the Coming are, however, absent in the second Message. The Church of Smyrna has to pass through the school of suffering. "Fear none of those things which thou shalt suffer." Therefore the special sentence which expresses apocalyptic severity is not needed. In the seventh Message, the sentence with the motif of the Coming of Christ has ceased to be a threat and has become a comforting promise. If we pass the sentences in review one by one as they are found in the Authorized Version, we read in the first Message, "Remember from whence thou art fallen, and repent . . . or else I will *come* unto thee quickly and will remove thy candlestick" (ii, 5). In the third Message, "Repent, or else I will *come* unto thee quickly and will fight against them with the sword of my mouth" (ii, 16). In the fourth Message, "That which ye have already, hold fast till I *come*" (ii, 25). In the fifth Message, "Be watchful and strengthen the things which remain that are ready to die . . . remember what thou hast received and heard, and hold fast, and repent. If therefore thou shalt not watch, I will *come* on thee as a thief, and thou shalt not know what hour I will *come* upon thee" (iii, 2–3). In the sixth Message, "Behold I *come* quickly, hold fast that which thou hast, that no man take thy crown" (iii, 2). In the seventh Message, "Be zealous and repent. Behold I stand at the door and knock. If any man hear my voice and open the door, I will *come* in to him and will sup with him and he with me" (iii, 19–20).

The stern formula with which the Coming of Christ recurs everywhere implies that the Second Coming cannot pass by simply unnoticed. Even that section of humanity which sleeps through this spiritual event cannot remain unchanged. Either blessing or curse flows from it. He who succeeds in having a real share in this experience will receive great spiritual riches. He who at the times of the Coming of Christ shuts himself away from the spiritual world will lose even that measure of spiritual grace which he has hitherto possessed.

37

He will fulfil on a grand scale the saying, "Unto everyone which hath shall be given; and from him that hath not, even that he hath shall be taken away from him." The turn of phrase employed in the fifth Message, which also appears frequently in the Gospels, that Christ will come like a thief, is popularly understood to be only an indication of the unexpected and surprising nature of the Second Coming. The apocalyptic picture should, however, be understood quite literally. When thieves have broken into a house during the night, the inhabitants are poorer next morning than they were the day before. Just so, those who shut themselves away from the advent of Christ will of necessity become spiritually impoverished by doing so. It is not the demonic powers which rob these souls; Christ Himself passes over the Earth as the cosmic thief for this section of humanity. Among the tempests released by His presence in the arena of human destiny, souls are losing their merely inherited forces far more rapidly than they would in non-apocalyptic times. However paradoxical it may sound, it is a sign of the new nearness of Christ that so many people feel today as if they had become inwardly poor overnight.

The third Message presents the picture of the coming Christ fighting with the sword of His mouth against that section of mankind that has shut itself away from Him. Thrusts and blows of fate, dealt as it were by invisible hands, attack these people. Events become more incalculable and well-laid plans are frustrated. People think that all the spirits and demons of opposition are in league against them. In fact it is the approaching spiritual world, and the Christ-Being Himself, which disturb their purely human plans and calculations.

In the first, third, fifth and seventh Messages, the same warning is given which John the Baptist uttered before the first Coming of Christ, "Change your outlook, re-think all things." (It is inadequate to translate "Repent ye".) Before the Second Coming of Christ the necessity for change of heart is even greater, since the Christ is now only revealed in the realm of Spirit and is not perceived unless the earthly heart is changed and opened, and the soul awakened to the supersensible world. It is as though something of the sound of the Trumpets rings out in this four times repeated challenge: "Change your outlook, re-think all things (*meta noëson*)." The exhortation in the fourth and sixth Messages, "Hold fast what you have", "Hold fast that thou hast," appears at first sight as if it were easy to follow. But this is an illusion. Did we not all as children have a paradisal feeling about life and a happy carefree outlook on the world which later on in life we were unable to hold fast? Nature endows us

38

with many forces and powers of divination which we can only keep alive, or even preserve in some form or other, by unceasing endeavour. How difficult it is to obey Christ's words, "Become as little children"— as adults to achieve on a higher level a new inner, childlike simplicity. The burden of the Messages, which sounds so easy, is that the Second Coming of Christ will particularly require an account of whether we have made our natural gift our own inalienable possession.

When the fifth Message exhorts us to strengthen those things which are ready to die, a similar point is made. In the evolution of humanity as a whole, as well as in the course of an individual life, a gradual decline of the natural forces is inevitable. A revival and transformation of these forces by spiritual exercise and inward discipline may not only strengthen those things which are ready to die, but the eye of the soul for the spiritual world will be opened.

In the first and fifth Messages we read, "Remember from whence thou art fallen . . . remember what thou hast received and heard." These sentences speak of the active cultivation of memory. Memory is a remnant of the ancient powers of supersensible vision. Calm, patient exercises in remembering, such as looking back in the evening and reviewing the events of the day, raise the soul slowly back to those heights from which it has fallen. And as the soul learns to realize in the act of remembrance its heavenly origin, it brings to flower the new vision wherein the sphere of the Coming of Christ can be seen.

The last Message concentrates on the need for zeal and perseverance in the new consciousness. Behind the noise of the world is heard the knocking on the door of Him who comes to sup with us.

Thus the Seven Messages form a book by itself, a catechism of exercises for the soul—a breviary of selfless prayer whereby we can open ourselves to Him Whose in-dwelling is the great communion of our souls.

III

THE CREATION OF THE WORLD AND
THE SACRIFICE OF THE LAMB

THE FOURTH AND FIFTH CHAPTERS

THE Revelation of St. John leads us through several forecourts and antechambers before we are shown into the Temple of great trials and decisions. After we passed the Gate of the initial vision of the Son of Man, the Seven Messages made us survey the whole circle of humanity.

Even now the trials do not begin at once. The patience of God with men is reflected in the structure of the apocalyptic book. Not without preparation can we face the storms and tempests which are to come. We must receive strength from the primal well of being. Before our souls are raised to the successive planes of vision, spiritual hearing, and immediate contact with the Spirit, they are first invited to share in the calm solemnity of a cosmic sabbath. Never again, even to the very end, does the Apocalypse lead us through such wonderful, profound stillness, as in the two chapters between the Seven Messages and the Seven Seals. In quick succession through the three stages of Picture, Word, and Being (which later unfold in the three cycles of Seven) we witness with the writer a sublime act. First a *picture* appears: "After this I looked, and behold a door was opened in Heaven." What panorama will appear at this first glance? The dramatic experience awaiting him who enters remains hidden at first. The door stands high above mankind; only he who is able to rise to the heavenly level can see through it, perhaps even pass through it. To the picture is added a *sound*: the voice which is like a trumpet says, "Come up hither and I will show thee things which must be hereafter." A foretaste of the trumpet blasts had opened the soul of the apocalyptic writer to the vision of the Son of Man, and raises him now, too, to the higher level of the open door. Presently the door becomes a window. We gaze with the apocalyptic writer into the interior of the world. The sphere of first principles is revealed. The perception which now begins penetrates to the very *substance* of the Spirit: "Immediately I was in the Spirit."

The solemn picture which now appears before the soul of the Seer consists of several symmetrical figures, arranged in concentric circles. The centre is formed by a throne, and one that sits on it. But while we are tempted to picture the one who sits on the throne in human form, the Seer deters us from doing so: "He that sat was to look upon like a jasper and a sardine stone." He is a starry centre of light, from which two diversely coloured rays proceed. Jasper is a greenish shimmering jewel; but in the past the type of jasper which was almost white was considered the most valuable; it shone like a diamond, its pure white light gleaming green only from a distance. The sardine stone is, like the carnelian, a blood-red gem. From the throne, which forms the central point of the heavenly sphere, red and white beams of light issue in harmonious accord; these are the revelation of the very Godhead. Here, in the realm of prototypes, we meet the polarity of white and red, familiar everywhere in fairy tales, legends and the symbols of historical life. Whether it is the charming story of Snow White and Rose Red, or the legend of Flos and Blanchefleur, the Red Rose and the White Lily, or the polarity of the Red and White Roses in English history, the duality of white and red always expresses the consonance between spirit and soul. The spiritual element shines in the clear white light; the soul-element glows in the colour of red blood. He who sits on the throne is the radiant source of the original light differentiated according to spirit and soul, as in light and heat, revealing the eternal consonance of soul and spirit.

The first of the concentric figures round the throne is the coloured circle of the rainbow. It is described as "in sight like an emerald". Green, the colour of life and centre of the sevenfold colour-harmony, gives its character to the whole.

Round the central point of light another circle is seen, not erect like the rainbow, but horizontal, "Round about the throne were four and twenty seats, and upon the seats I saw four and twenty elders, clothed in white raiment; and they had on their heads crowns of gold." For the first time beings emerge from the darkness of the cosmic background. Twenty-four representatives of the world become visible. Their white garments show their complete permeation by the Spirit, and by their golden crowns they are recognizable as stewards and bearers of the thoughts of God; they are the true cosmic thinkers. Perhaps the twenty-four Elders may be pictured—unlike the Throned One—in human form. Yet they belong to exalted superhuman realms of existence.

The ring-encircled centre is not standing motionless; it is a central point of scintillating force. Rays and currents proceed from it, only comparable to what on Earth is thunder and lightning. The lightning issues in flames: in seven creator-beings, light-bearing like flaming torches and thronging closely round the throne. These are the seven Elohim, which in the beginning created Heaven and Earth.*

"Out of the throne proceeded lightnings and thunderings and voices, and there were seven Lamps of fire burning before the throne, which are the Seven Spirits of God." In the twenty-four Elders and the seven Lamps of fire the powers and principles of Space and Time are revealed; the former, majestic and calm; the latter charged with fiery power, yet holding back their creative work. Around all this, in an enigmatic picture, appears a sphere. To the circles and symmetrical polygons, an all-embracing globular form is added: "Before the throne there was a sea of glass like unto crystal." A spherical sea in the process of crystallizing surrounds the throne and its circles.

Finally, the fullness of the heavenly figures is completed by the Four Living Creatures: "Four beasts full of eyes before and behind. The first beast was like a lion, the second beast like a calf, the third beast had a face as a man, and the fourth beast was like a flying eagle. And the four beasts had each of them six wings about him, and they were full of eyes within and without; and they rest not day and night saying, Holy, holy, holy, Lord God Almighty, which was and is, and is to come." The Four Beasts are clearly described. They now begin really to look like earthly creatures. They are the beholders of the divine cosmic principles, grouped around the radiant central point of heaven. They are utterly absorbed in contemplation of the Throne and its surroundings; and their tranquil contemplation releases from within them the eternal hymn of praise, the eternal *Sanctus*.

The symmetrical groupings seem to be divided into two strata: a giving and taking of cosmic creation seem to confront each other.

* Where the usual translations of the Old Testament say, "In the beginning God created heaven and earth", the Hebrew text uses a plural and really speaks of a number of creative Beings: "In the very beginning the Elohim created heaven and earth". Here, indeed, the Elohim are only named in general; but the fact that seven Creator-Beings (in the New Testament called *exusiai* or Powers, in modern Spiritual Science "Spirits of Form") belong to the Logos and to Christ, that is to say, that they serve progressive creation, has been known to all ages in a tradition of which even Goethe makes use. He points out in his *Theory of Colour* (towards the end of the essay on *The Physical and Moral Effects of Colours*) that the sphere of the Elohim is revealed in the seven colours of the rainbow. "If only the divergence of the yellow and blue is properly grasped, and if especially the deepening into red, whereby the opposite colours lean together and unite in a third, is adequately studied, then assuredly a particularly mysterious manifestation will appear—a spiritual significance will be found underlying these two separated and opposed beings; and, if one sees them producing downwards the green and upwards the red, one can hardly refrain from thinking of the creative activity there on earth and here in heaven, of the Elohim."

Can it really be that in the picture of the Four Beasts the world of creatures is contrasted with the Creators?

The book of the Revelation began with the picture of Man in the great initial vision of the first chapter. Now animal forms appear for the first time. Among these, one indeed has the form of a man. But the figures of the Four Living Creatures no more represent earthly animals than does the vision of the Son of Man stand for Man as an earthly creation. Isaiah describes the majestic winged Beings who sing the sublime *Sanctus* round the throne of God not as animals but as Seraphim. Indeed it is in exalted hierarchical realms that we must seek the Beings who appear to us in the picture of the Four Beasts. We touch a sphere to which the ancient Egyptian works of art also point, a sphere which represents the gods with the head of bulls, eagles or lions. A lofty realm of gods, containing animal prototypes, is revealed to us. The animals on Earth are but copies and reflections fallen from Heaven.

One might be inclined to interpret the circles and figures at the beginning of Chapter IV astronomically. Could not the ring of twenty-four Elders round the Throne reflect the twelve Signs of the Zodiac? Do not the seven spiritual Lamps point to the seven planets? Cannot the empyrean, the crystal heaven, as the ancient world called the sphere above the fixed stars, be recognized in the sea of glass? Even the figures of the Four Living Creatures may be found again in the sky: they are the constellations of the Lion, the Bull, the Water-carrier, and the Scorpion (the Scorpion appears as the counterpart of the Eagle), which form the great cross in the Zodiac. In the heaven of the fixed stars, earlier civilizations saw the "higher animals", of which the animal kingdom on the Earth is a distant shadow. This is why they called the ring of stars, through which the Sun and the planets move, the Zodiac (from the Greek ζῷον = animal).

However, a reference to the constellations of the starry sky is not a sufficient explanation of the apocalyptic symbols. The starlit heaven itself is just another Apocalypse, which in its picture alphabet corresponds in a sense to the Apocalypse of St. John. The one book can illumine the other, but it cannot explain it. We are dealing with two different translations of the same original text. What is the original text?

At this point we must reflect once more on the nature of apocalyptic vision. At the beginning and the end of the Bible, we have two books which deal with facts above the level of rational perception. In Genesis, the Bible begins with a supersensible vision. Genesis springs from a *spiritual retrospect*; for it is not possible by outward methods to look into the ages long past—the first stages of evolution—because creation began before the material phase came into existence. To the retrospect of Genesis is now added the prophetic *prevision* of the Apocalypse which reveals the secrets of the future. The retrospect from which Genesis springs is nothing else than an inverted prophecy. But before the prophetic vision of the Seer John comes to the point of revealing the laws and secrets of the future, in the Seven Seals, Trumpets and Vials of Wrath, it first plunges once again retrospectively into the very beginning of evolution. It is only from this retrospect that the prophetic prevision is brought forth. We might regard the fourth and fifth chapters of the Apocalypse as a New Testament story of the Creation, a New Testament Genesis. Here the picture of the sea of glass may serve as a key. We witness a definite moment in the evolution of the world. Aeons of evolution have already run their course in the spiritual sphere. Now comes the first germination of physical, corporeal existence. Out of the all-enveloping spiritual sphere of the heavenly ocean the material world, the *prima materia*, still pure and virginal, begins to crystallize. The world of matter is born in the form of shining crystals. In the picture of the sea of glass the Seer beholds the moment of birth, the *status nascendi* of the physical world. He is a witness of the beginning of cosmic incarnation. Why does the sight of a rock crystal or an amethyst give us such unusual delight? These star-like forms fascinate us, as if they were not of this world at all. Every crystal is, so to speak, a reminiscence of the original condition of our earthly world. Earthly, bodily existence had its origin in just such transparent crystal purity. But in the course of its evolution it has not been able to preserve its original crystal clarity. Much turbidity and loss of form has overpowered the world of earthly matter. Today crystals are reminders of the world as it was originally planned; and every snow-crystal which we admire in its star-like structure before it melts is like a greeting from the sphere from which earthly things once rose as radiant, strong, paradisal *prima materia*.

The moment of cosmic evolution recognizable in the sea of glass signifies at the same time a stage of development of the human being. Man already existed in the pre-physical aeons, but he was as yet like a drop of water in the sea, completely contained within the divine womb of higher beings. There was as yet no individuality. At the moment when the crystal heavens formed themselves from the ocean of the Spirit as the first spherical seed of physical existence, a first

44

inkling of individual corporeality, and hence of future consciousness of self and spiritual identity, may have passed through the soul of mankind. The sea of glass rose as a mirror. The transparent cosmos formed something corresponding to the foil behind the glass; something which turned the glass into a mirror. The very first reflection of himself, a first consciousness of his individuality, confronted Man in the picture of the crystal. Hence a crystal speaks to us not only of the primal beginnings of the material world, but also of the first tentative sense of ego-consciousness. And it suggests that we become true bearers of an immortal Ego when the crystal clearness of spiritual thought can dwell within us, and radiate out from us like a star. Crystal clear thoughts in the human mind correspond to the crystals in Nature.*

Like the sea of glass the rainbow which the Seer perceives around the heavenly throne is a sign of the spiritual origin of Creation. When a rainbow is formed in the sky today it is as though the world remembers its creation out of light.

Into these pictures of the first beginnings the vision of the Four Beasts is placed. At first sight it seems a step downward when the great opening vision of *Man* in the first chapter is followed in the fourth chapter by the picture of the *Beasts*. But what is it that distinguishes Man from the animals? Man, as he has become in the course of world evolution, has an individual soul, whereas animals have a communal group-soul according to their species. They remain in a condition through which the human being has passed. Man did not appear on the scene as an individual being immediately. But where were men at the beginning, when the Earth was crystallizing as a sea of glass out of the spiritual cosmos? They were already there, but still retained in the womb of higher Beings who, representing them, lent their divine consciousness to take the place of the human consciousness which would come into existence in the future. The Four Living Creatures are seraphic Beings who, like great group-souls, held at first the souls of men concealed within them. Each of the four prepares one aspect of future humanity. One of them dreams the seed of human thinking. He appears as heavenly Eagle. In the second

* This vision of creation seen by John appeared to the poetic gaze of Novalis, the German poet and contemporary of Goethe, as the city Arcturus which he describes in the ninth chapter of his novel *Heinrich von Ofterdingen*. It is a wonderful poetic parallel to the Revelation of St. John. The city, with its houses and palaces and figures consisting purely of ice-crystals, lies in a milky-blue haze. "All this was mirrored in the glassy sea surrounding the mountain on which the city stood." Distant sounds were heard in the city of Arcturus, like the murmur of creation from the cosmic smithy in which the Gods were putting the world together: "Nothing could be clearly distinguished; yet strange noises could be heard over here, as if from some huge workshop in the distance."

45

seraph, the beginnings of human feeling are formed in embryo, the forces of the human heart. This seraph appears in the form of a Lion. The figure of the Bull is assumed by the seraph which prepares the human will. Together with the Eagle, the Lion and the Bull, there is the fourth sphere whose seraph portrays the whole Man, in the consonance of Thinking, Feeling and Willing. In him the human figure itself rises on the horizon of evolution. *

*Note.—The picture of the four heavenly Living Creatures is one of the apocalyptic motifs which from the time of the early Christians has played a specially important part in the life of Christian imagination. The Four Beasts were seen as sublime inspiring genii, standing behind the four Evangelists. The Eagle was regarded as the sign of St. John, the Bull as that of St. Luke; the Lion belonged to the Gospel of St. Mark, and the Man among the Four Beasts to St. Matthew. When the understanding of the spiritual origin of the Gospels was lost, and came to be taught only as a dogma, the connection between the Evangelists and the Four Living Creatures survived in the end only as an ornamental design in ecclesiastical art. There is, however, no more classic expression of the fact that the Evangelists were only able to write their books with the co-operation of higher hierarchical Beings, than the assigning to each of them one of the Four Living Creatures. The same seraphic guardians round the throne of God whom St. John beholds, and from whose divine womb earthly humanity issues, are also the guardians of those spheres whence the four Gospels spring. The four exalted group-genii of humanity have worked together in producing for humanity the angelic message of the Incarnation, Death and Resurrection of Christ.

The Seer on Patmos was not the first to see and describe the four Living Creatures. The repetition of this picture shows, as nothing else does, the spiritual kinship and connection between the Apocalypse of the New Testament and the prophetic books of the Old Testament. In the writings of Isaiah, Ezekiel, and Daniel, there are parallels to the Johannine vision of the Four Beasts. And a theology which knew nothing of inspiration, seeking to trace from literary interdependence the sources from which the New Testament Scriptures had been written, made use in particular of the fact that the Four Beasts already appear in the Old Testament to make the Revelation of St. John appear as a barely Christianized sample of the fantastic apocalyptic books which appeared in the wake of the Old Testament. But in fact the same supersensible realities can be witnessed at different times and places by different seers, just as on the physical plane different men travel independently of one another in a foreign country, and can afterwards give similar reports.

A comparison between the Old Testament descriptions and the Johannine vision of the Four Beasts is very instructive. It may be seen at a glance that in the books of the Prophets the vision only struggles into visibility, whereas in St. John's Apocalypse it stands out clearly. Isaiah and Ezekiel see the sphere of the Four Beasts as the source of their prophetic vision. Isaiah describes the exalted Beings revealed to him above the throne in the Temple not as animals; he calls them by their hierarchical name: Seraphim. Like John, he sees that each of these Beings has six wings; like him he hears them singing the eternal Sanctus. Ezekiel's vision is less calm and clear. Storm rages through his soul. Each of the Four Living Creatures is, through his four faces, a four-fold creature. The flames of burning lamps which John sees surrounding the Four in sevenfold majesty, blaze through everything as Ezekiel sees it in dramatic movement. The turning wheels of fire, the eyes of the divine hierarchical Beings flash through everything. A higher sphere of heavenly tranquillity rules, however, above the Four Living Creatures, where the sea of glass appears as a heavenly crystal and the rainbow forms a circle of colour. On this level the vision of the prophet is in the same sublime atmosphere as the vision of the Apocalyptic Seer. Lastly, Daniel does not immediately perceive the four Living Creatures when the sphere of inspiration is opened to him. Only later, when he is shown the future birth-pangs of a new era, he sees the Four Living Creatures rise out of the sea. But the harmony of Lion, Eagle, Bull and Man is destroyed by the conflict between Heaven and Hell. Only the first Living Creature is of a seraphic order; it is a Lion with Eagle's wings, but it is formed like a human being and has a human heart. Of the three other Beasts, each one in turn is more horrible and satanic than the one before. In the vision of Daniel the Four

46

The apocalyptic vision of the fourth chapter presents Creator and Creatures standing as it were face to face. Soon movement and development will begin. But as yet everything is filled with divine calm and solemnity. Creation still rests in the sphere of perpetuity; the wheel of time is not yet revolving. The hierarchical realm which contains the creatures is full of wonder and worship, absorbed in contemplation of the creative cosmic centre. If we ever wished to ask the paradoxical question how created beings were occupied before the Creation, here we have the answer. Absorption in contemplation of the Creator aroused in the sphere of the created the primal hymn of praise, the great *Sanctus*, which filled the cosmos like an echo of the Creative Word itself.

Proceeding to the fifth chapter, we become aware that movement now enters into the deep calm and solemnity. The divine stillness represented maturing creation. Now in the right hand of Him Who sits on the throne, a book is visible "written within and without". It contains the ground-plans and blueprints of the inner and outer world which is to be created. The building is to begin. But who will loose the seven seals of the book? Not until the book is opened can perpetuity change into the stream of time. A dramatic tension arises. A Being like a herald appears on the scene: "And I saw a strong Angel proclaiming with a loud voice: 'Who is worthy to open the book and to loose the seals thereof?' " Like an incarnation of divine resolve to continue the work of creation, the mighty Angel steps forward. Eternal duration would become cosmic stagnation if nothing further happened. The strong Angel, standing alone, radiates the will to set in motion what was threatening to stagnate. No name is mentioned, but the Being wields something of the authority of the Archangel Michael whom the Apocalypse repeatedly presents as a power intent on overcoming stagnation and on carrying forward new developments. The challenge of the Angel hangs motionless in the cosmos: "No man in heaven nor on earth, neither under the earth, was able to open the book, neither to read therein." Grief-stricken, the Seer John shares in the cosmic tension. He says, "And I wept much because no man was found worthy to open the book." The cosmic anguish engulfs him too.

Heavenly Beasts and the two beasts of the abyss described by St. John in the thirteenth chapter of the Apocalypse are confused.

How clean and pure stands the vision of St. John in contrast to those of Ezekiel and Daniel! Does not the comparison show clearly that between the Old Testament prophets and the New Testament Apocalypse something has happened whereby clarity and harmony and tranquillity have been poured into the world of the Spirit as well as into the soul of the Seer?

At last the tension is relaxed. One of the circle of twenty-four Elders cries, "Weep not: Behold the Lion of the tribe of Judah, the Root of David, hath prevailed to open the book, and to loose the seven seals thereof." We must ourselves enter into the dramatic sequence of the pictured events which now follow. Do not let us suppose that one of the twenty-four Elders had always known what he now proclaims. On him, too, the urgent question had been weighing. He can now announce the solution only because he was the first to recognize the releasing and redeeming power, like a watchman who at last spies on the horizon the sail of an anxiously awaited ship. The perception of this Elder effects the relaxation of tension.

If we maintain the symbolic conception, the words of the Elder indicate the direction from which the rescuing movement will come. It is the heavenly region where, among the Four Living Creatures, the Lion stands: "Weep not, behold the Lion of the tribe of Judah has won the victory." But even from the realm of the seraphic Lion the crucial deed cannot be done unless a change takes place. The liberating cry indicated the region of the Lion; but there, in the place to which all eyes now turn, no longer the *Lion* appears, but the *Lamb*: "And I beheld and lo, in the midst of the throne and of the Four Beasts, and in the midst of the Elders stood a Lamb as it had been slain, having seven horns and seven eyes, which are the seven Spirits of God, sent forth into all the earth." The Lamb approaches the Throne, and takes the sealed book from the hand of Him Who sits on the throne. It is able to loose the seals. But how is it possible that there, where the Lion was standing, suddenly the Lamb appears? Lofty divine Beings have performed a great deed, a divine sacrifice has been offered. Through the sacrificial self-transformation carried out by a most exalted Being creation has overcome the threat of stagnation and begun to flow again.

In his short story of "the Child and the Lion", Goethe has painted a human, poetic picture of the cosmic event to which the Apocalypse here points. In the story, the Child fearlessly approaches the Lion before whom men tremble. He soothes it with his song, and coaxes it to come tamely out of its den, while he lovingly frees it from the thorn which was sticking in its foot. A verse in the child's song runs thus:

> " For the Eternal Rules on earth;
> Over the sea His glance prevails.
> Lions now must lambs become,

And the waves must backward roll.
The bright sword rests and does not strike,
Faith and Hope are both fulfilled,
Wonder-working is the Love
Which reveals itself in Prayer."

Just as in Goethe's story, so in the great cosmic drama of Creation, *Love* is the force which transforms the Lion into the Lamb. From the direction of the seraphic realm wherein the seed of human feeling is sown, a God approaches. He is the bearer of cosmic love. This exalted Divine Being, Who might well rule as a king, assumes the form which makes Him the ministering brother of nascent creation. He offers Himself up and appears in the form of the sacrificial Lamb. Later, the picture of the Lamb was used to represent Him who suffered sacrificial death on Golgotha. But He Who afterwards took upon Himself the sacrifice of incarnation and death on earth had already played a decisive part, through a great primal sacrifice, at the creation of the world itself. Just as He later renewed the world through Death and Resurrection, so at the very beginning of evolution He made the birth of our world possible through His sacrificial intervention. A great sacrifice of Christ, the Lamb of God, was made already at the beginning of the world. Golgotha was, in the human sphere, the decisive renewal and enhancement of the primal sacrifice whereby the world came into being.

This is the deepest principle of the world: from the very beginning a force has been active to overcome the stagnation, to set the wheel of evolution in motion, to give new life to the dying. It is not the superhuman, heroic power of the four seraphic Living Creatures. In the picture of the Lamb we realize the highest magic in all the world: the power of sacrifice and love.

In the apocalyptic images which follow, the Lamb does not supplant the Four Beasts; He is rather a kind of epitome, a further stage of their evolution. In the symbol and sign of the Lamb mankind enters upon the earthly path. Henceforth it remains beholden to the ideal of sacrifice and love.

We are told that the Lamb has seven eyes. He is no longer covered, as the Four Beasts are, with eyes within and without. Once the actual earthly developments have started, progress is not possible without renunciation of the original fullness of heavenly vision. Together with the seven eyes, the Lamb has seven horns. The picture of the horns points to the first earthly organs of the human being which result from densification. The equal number of eyes and horns express the balance between above and below, between the organs of divine vision and the first stage of bodily nature vouchsafed to mankind at the moment of Earth's genesis. The sevenfold eyes through which the Lamb beholds the progress of the creative work initiated by Him counterbalance the sevenfold horns, all the more effectively because in them the sevenfold Creative Spirits are mirrored, the Elohim, described before as Lamps.

When the Lamb appears, the twenty-four Elders fall down in adoration before Him. Each of them carries a golden harp and censer in his hand. Sighs of relief turn into hymns of praise before the throne of God. When the Elders become witnesses of the divine sacrifice which sets Creation in motion, heavenly music and offerings of incense proceed from the realms of hierarchical Beings in gratitude and praise. Seen from the Spirit realm, the Creation of the world appears as a ritual celebration, in which the Angel kingdoms sing and make music. The sound of the harp, however, is not merely an accompaniment; it is like the clangour which in Novalis' tale sounds as from a distant workshop. It belongs to the creative sound which brings forth the world, the "Word in the beginning". And when we read of the Elders, "They sang a new song", we may realize that the song of the Angel kingdom joins in the music of creation which brings to birth a new world.

Later, in the fourteenth and fifteenth chapters of the Apocalypse, pictures arise in the prophetic prevision which correspond to the retrospective pictures of the New Testament Genesis which we are discussing here. For the second time the picture of the Lamb appears; He stands on Mount Sion, surrounded by the 144,000. Now the Lamb Himself forms the centre of future humanity. The universe is filled anew with the sound of harps; "I heard a voice from Heaven as the sound of many waters, and as the voice of a great thunder; and I heard the voice of harpers harping with their harps, and they sang as it were a new song before the throne, and before the Four Beasts and the twenty-four Elders." When the new Creation, the new Heaven and the new Earth, begin to tear themselves away from the ageing cosmos of the old Earth, the music of evolving existence begins to sound again; now, however, it is *men* who throng around the Lamb, *men* who may sing the creative song of progress to the music of the harps.

In the fifteenth chapter the prophetic vision penetrates into the same picture-sphere as in the Seer's first retrospection: "And I saw as it were a sea of glass." But here it is "mingled with fire". When the new planetary incarnation of the Earth is formed, the warmth of soul which advancing humanity will have developed during the Earth age must form the inner fire and the blood-circulation of this new creation. Then by the glassy sea of the future will stand those who, harp-bearers themselves, have followed the Lamb, the ideal of sacrifice and love: "And I saw . . . them that had gotten the victory over the beast and over his image, and over his mark, and over the number of his name, stand on the sea of glass, having the harps of God." Then men will themselves have authority over the Word of Creation which brings forth the new world. The role of the Gods in the story of the first creation passes over to men at the birth of the new Creation. That, however, is only possible if men are strong enough to offer the sacrifice which before was offered by the Gods. Love is a greater magician than force. The line in Goethe's story "Love is wonder-working" expresses the deepest cosmic principle. Sacrifice is the power which calls a new world into being. At the beginning, the middle and the end of earthly existence stands the picture of the Lamb. Christ's great sacrifice made possible the first creation of the Earth; at the turning-point of time, through the sacrifice of the Lamb on Golgotha, the miracle of the Resurrection was brought about; at the end of our Earth-age, through men who have learned to offer themselves together with the sacrifice of the Lamb, the resurrection of the Earth will be added to the resurrection of Man, achieved through Christ.

IV

SEALS:
ARCHETYPES, IMAGES, REFLECTIONS

THE SIXTH AND SEVENTH CHAPTERS

THE Seals are attached to a *Book* which they hold mysteriously closed. Is there in the whole cosmos a power able to open the Seals, and therewith the Book? This fateful question has caused the first tension and motion in the heavenly symmetry around the divine Throne. The Book in the hand of the Throned Figure is the primary symbol of the beginning of evolution in time. It poses a real problem, a problem for God Himself, as it were, demanding a real answer. It contains at the same time the sum-total of all answers, for it is the epitome of those divine thoughts out of which Creation with all its kingdoms is to be produced. It is the aggregate of the yet unuttered Words of Creation. When the Power which can open the Seals of the Book appears, it will at the same time prove to be the mouth through which the unspoken Word of God can be uttered. Not that it can be read with silent thinking as an earthly book; when the contents of the Heavenly Book can be read, a Voice will be raised, and this Voice will be the world-creative speech of the Logos, the Word of God. The Seven Seals are the transitional stage in which the *thinking* of the Godhead turns into creative *speaking*.

The writer of the Apocalypse, and those who follow his words and ways, share in the tenseness of the pause during which the anxious question remains unanswered in Heaven. Then, however, they share also in the release of tension when the Lamb appears. Only through sacrifice and love did the evolution of the world begin. Our world was born out of the serene Cosmos of Heaven by means of great sacrificial deeds in the sphere of the Divine Powers.

But this first stage of creation is not yet a material world. *Pictures* emanate from the opened seals of the Book. The archetypes of divine thought appear first, and pass out of perpetuity into evolution. They move and acquire substance; but there is a long way to go before they crystallize, and materialize into their likenesses in the world of tangible things.

In supersensible Imagination the Seer looks into the evolutionary stream of archetypal existence. He can only do this from the level to which evolution had already advanced in his time. Just as we look up to the stars of Heaven through the layer of air which surrounds the earth, so does he look back through the strata of human history to the primal sources of evolution which begin to well up through the opening of the Seals. In a sense St. John is a Christian Platonist. He assumes a knowledge of the sphere which Plato calls the Realm of Ideas, the realm of archetypes and primal phenomena. Everything earthly which we see with our eyes, has its prototype in the Spirit; but we do not understand the condition of our world fully if we think that it has evolved in an unbroken line from the sphere of the prototypes. A cosmic tragedy has intervened, to which we refer as the Fall of Man. The organic flow was upset by a whirlpool. The heavenly unsealing was followed by an earthly re-sealing. As if bewitched the divine archetypes vanished into external objects. But the eyes of our soul can unseal again the enchanted Book of creation. We can undo the curse and learn to read the heavenly archetypes in their disfigured copies. A new faculty of spiritual sight, to which in our age the path of progress is leading mankind, will effect this unsealing. But this unsealing, like that in Heaven, can only be achieved through the Lamb. It needs the selfless consciousness which comes to life in the human soul through the in-dwelling of Christ. The line at the end of Goethe's *Faust*, "All that is transient is only an image," points to the unsealing of the Book of Nature. What it says may also help us to follow with genuine understanding the unsealing of the Heavenly Book in the Apocalypse.

Out of the first four Seals which the Lamb opens, Four Horses proceed one after the other. Disregarding detail for the moment, we recall once more the pictorial stages through which we have moved. The picture of Man came first. Later, pictures of animals appeared in the form of the Living Creatures surrounding the Throne. Then the picture of one animal was shown, as a kind of epitome of the Four Living Creatures. This was the Lamb, coming forward to open the Book. We have already said that the picture of the Four Beasts indicates the Spiritual realms in which for long ages, before individual human beings started to develop, humanity was grouped under four great group-souls. But it is significant that the picture of Man stands at the beginning of the Apocalypse. Man is the origin and measure of all things. His picture appears in the Spirit-realm before the picture of the animals.

Through the opening of the first four Seals new animals appear. The Four Horses are distinguished from one another by their colour; the White, the Red, the Black, and the Pale Horse. The link between the Four Horses and the Four Beasts is close, for every time the Lamb approaches the sealed Book to open a Seal, one of the Four Beasts, first the Eagle, then the Lion, then the Bull, and lastly the Man, cries with a voice of thunder, "Come". Each time the soul of the Seer is lifted up by this cry to the level at which he is able to witness the unsealing. Each of the Four Beasts round the heavenly Throne has undertaken, as it were, the sponsorship of one of the Four Horses which leap from the Seals. We must keep in mind that we are still far from the plane on which earthly animals exist. What have the Four Horses in the sphere of archetypes to say to us? What divine thought, what primal phenomenon is expressed in them? It is significant that in each case also a human figure appears riding on the animal. The first four Seals really contain the archetype of the horseman. The general idea which emerges at the deciphering of the first Seals is thus that a Creation takes form, in which the archetypes of the human and of the animal kingdoms are shown in the relationship they bear to the divine thought. Man appears as the ruler of the animal. The horse, seen from the point of view of the history of civilization, is the primal example of man's task and achievement in taming animals. A man on horseback has always been the symbol for Man's mastery over the animal kingdom. He must not allow the animal to become its own master, but must control it and hold the bridle firmly in his own hand.

All the same there must be a reason why it is the horse which depicts the relationship between Man and animal corresponding to the divine thought. In pre-Christian mythologies and rituals the horse plays an important part. In Germanic antiquity it was regarded as a sacred animal. People saw in the horse something different from the mere beast of burden, domestic animal, cart-horse or charger. The horse is a symbolic creature and in particular the head of the animal expresses a significant secret. For this reason one can still see even today in many districts of Northern Germany the skulls of horses hanging from the gables of old houses, or the wooden planks lining the angle of the gable may be finished off with a carved horse's head on either side. The Greeks, too, recognized the archetypal and symbolic quality in the horse. The steeds of Helios drew the chariot of the Sun which circles the vault of Heaven. And the helmet of Athene who sprang, as embodied Thought, from the head of the father of the gods and bestows thought upon men, was formed in such a way that it lay like a horse's head with its nostrils slanting over the brow of the goddess. Pericles, too, is represented wearing the helmet of Athene. Thus the symbol of the long forehead of the horse appeared on human as well as on divine heads.

The archetype of the horse must have borne some relation to the archetype of Man. A connection must have existed which, though older than physical Man on Earth, still had significance after Man's entry into physical incarnation and evolution. This significant relationship becomes clearer if we realize that the Apocalypse demands altogether a different conception of the relationship between the human and the animal kingdoms from that which is generally held today. The primitive idea held almost universally today that Man has evolved in straight descent from the animal kingdom is alien to the book of Revelation, and is open to serious doubts generally. It is true that science has been at great pains to reconstruct the animal ancestry of Man, and to describe the individual animal species as the stages through which mankind has passed in its evolution. But "the missing link" has never been found. And from the point of view of the Revelation of St. John the whole idea of Man originating directly from the animal is a disastrous error. Man is descended from the Gods, not from the animals. In his presentation of what he thought to be the true relationship between Man and animal, Rudolf Steiner has often started from Lorenz Oken (a contemporary of Goethe), who took pains to show that Man is the compendium of the animal kingdom, and that the animal kingdom corresponds to the separate parts of the multiple human being. If Man has, physically, also gone through a series of stages which may be characterized as resembling animal forms he has nevertheless *always* been *more* than animal. Throughout a series of evolutionary stages at which he assimilated certain forces and faculties and developed certain functions and organs of his body, the different animal species co-existed as witnesses, so to speak, of the newly acquired organs, as milestones, or even as by-products and "cast-offs". In passing through the stages of his evolutionary career, Man cast the animal element out of himself. Animals are the accompanying phenomena of Man's formation, therefore each animal type is the symbol of a soul-force in Man.

Today we should train ourselves so to energize our Imaginative faculties that remembering "all things transient are but a likeness" we begin to recognize in every animal a part of our own being; but only a *part* of our being, a reflection of *some* of the organs and functions of ourselves.

There is a crucial difference between the Four Beasts around the throne of God in Heaven and the Four Horses proceeding from the Seals of the Book. The Four Beasts still bear the human element *within them*. The Four Horses are found *within Man*. The heathen, mystical valuation of the horse, continued by the pictures of the Apocalypse into the realm of Christendom, was based on the fact that in the ancient symbolic conception of the world men saw in the horse a picture of the stage at which Man assimilated intelligence, the power of thought. In the figure of the horse there is engraved in outward physical symbolism what has become in Man the purely inward capacity for thought. This is why the Greeks seized upon the symbolizing effect of the skull of the horse, which really consists only of an enlarged forehead, and in the statues of Athene and Pericles surmounted the human brow with a horse's forehead shaped like a helmet. At a certain moment in time the power of thought was given to Man from divine heights to help him on his way. This is the moment which we witness when in the Revelation of St. John the Lamb opens the first Seal. Up to that moment the thoughts of God had been latent and silent. They rested unborn in the womb of eternal duration. When the Lamb appears upon the scene and opens one Seal after another, the creative thoughts of God begin to stir and then to ring out as picture-words. But what first arises out of them is by no means the world of *things*. The very beginnings of divine thinking concern *Man*, who is the first-born and the measure of all creatures and all things. Although it may have needed many cycles of time before Man existed in clearly outlined physical incarnation on the solidified Earth, in the sphere of archetypes the full Image of Man was present from the very beginning with all that has since come into being. In the first Seals we see the thoughts of God passing over into the thoughts of men. This is done in four stages of evolution, like four wide-spanned arches through which the faculty of Thought must now pass in its descent from God to Man.

When the first Seal is opened, the White Horse appears. The rider who sits on it is crowned with a gleaming golden crown, holds the bow bent in his hand, and is called a conqueror. This is the apocalyptic picture of the initial stage of human thinking. To suppose that at the beginning mankind was primitive and without intelligence is one of the fundamental errors of the materialistic world-conception. Thinking did not evolve from primitive movements of the brain. At first thinking was a prerogative of the Gods, and then the Gods gave

Man a share in their thoughts. The first stage of human thinking is entirely illumined by divine light. Man himself does not yet really think. On the human brow higher Beings are thinking, Beings who can turn their thoughts into words, and their words into a world. And even when the human being has already entered into physical incarnation on earth he remains steeped in the paradisal light of original revelation. This is the secret of the White Horse. The crown that the rider wears on his head is the light of thought implanted by the Gods on the brow of Man when they gave him a share in their thinking. And the bow in the hand of the rider reveals how through the power of thinking Man acquires the faculty of a sure aim. Without the gift of intelligence, the world and his own being must remain vague to Man for all time. Thought, although not yet his own possession, enables him to see what exists around him and to direct his life to a right goal.

Out of the second Seal the Red Horse proceeds. To him who sits on it power is given to take peace from the earth and to sow strife among men. He holds not a bow but a sword in his hand, with which man fights against man. The transition from the White to the Red colour is very expressive. With it the breaking up of light into the multiplicity of colours begins. Man must begin to make the divine intelligence his own. It must be linked with his blood-stream which, too, has gradually withdrawn from the universal circulation of cosmic forces and grown into a self-contained unit. Thought becomes humanized and compressed into the soul of the individual. In this "ensouled" form thought becomes a source of action in the human being, who thus grows more and more individualized. In the previous chapter the two precious stones, jasper and sardis, were mentioned, symbolizing the harmony of spirit and soul. In the progression from the first to the second Seal, however, discord arises. Man can absorb the power of intelligence into his soul only by forsaking the original divine light. The red colour of his blood tinges his thinking. The secession from the primal light brings in its train the loss of the original harmony and peace. The second apocalyptic rider bears dissension and war to mankind. Egoism arises, and strife flares up.

When the third Seal is opened, another tragic break occurs. After the pure light, colour now fades away also: the Black Horse leaps out. He who sits on it has a pair of scales in his hand; he shouts words like street cries. Wares are offered for money. The transition which first led from spirit to soul, now leads from soul to matter, to the physical plane. There darkness and death rule. The colours of the first three

Horses, White, Red and Black, reveal the primal symbolism of the consonance of spirit, soul and body. This symbolism is frequently used in fairy tales. Thus Snow White in her unearthly beauty is depicted as white as snow, red as blood, and black as ebony. (And has the stork perhaps been made the emblem of human birth because like an archetype made physically visible, he also owns this triple colour?) At the opening of the third Seal, the step from red to black is, therefore, a further tragic descent. It is an inversion of the illuminating and comforting change of colours which accompanies the transition from Good Friday to Easter Day on the altars of the restored sacrament celebrated in The Christian Community. The Black hue of death used during Lent is replaced by the bright Red of Easter, and a breath of resurrection and rejoicing passes through our souls. When in the succession of apocalyptic Riders the Black Horse takes the place of the Red, evolution leads from the sphere of the living to that of the dead.

The Black Horse and its Rider show what happens when Intelligence sinks down to the plane of material opportunities and advantages. Trade and barter begin. There is buying and selling on Earth. The polarity between white and red is still bright. The polarity between red and black conceals dangers. Behind the red, "Luciferic" desires and passions threaten; behind the black, the "Ahrimanic" danger of soulless cleverness is hid.★

But the scale of descent and loss is not yet ended. Out of the fourth Seal leaps the Pale Horse. The word *pale* is *chloros* in Greek. This literally means yellow-greenish in colour, like sulphur. He who rides on this Horse is called Death. He is followed by Hades, the underworld of ghosts. And to him is given the baleful authority to kill a large part of all living beings on Earth.

At the present time it ought not to be difficult to understand this further plunge of human intelligence, a plunge expressed in the transition from the Black to the Pale Horse. Straightforward materialism has still some character; bloodless abstractions are inhuman. With abstractions one can prove and refute anything. Mere intellectualism has no roots left. It ceases to take thinking seriously. It is long since Man first began to absorb into himself what had formerly been the prerogative of God. Now he no longer engages even his own human nature fully in his thought life. He does not even notice how thinking

★ The *double nature of evil* is presented as a fundamental truth in the philosophical and anthroposophical works of Rudolf Steiner. He calls this evil polarity "Lucifer" (Devil) and "Ahriman" (Satan). Cf. also page 104.

slips from him and begins to lead a spectral life. The Black Horse symbolized thinking fettered to the physical body which is subject to death. When the Pale Horse gallops over the Earth, thinking becomes ghostly; it is no longer only within Man, it is beginning to haunt him like an army of spectres. Starting from human thinking, Death permeates the whole surrounding world with processes of decay. The Homeric myths have prophetically foretold in the story of the wooden horse the final apostasy of human intelligence. The Greeks who besieged Troy made use of a stratagem which originated in the brain of Ulysses. They built a wooden horse and carried it to the gate of the beleaguered city. The Trojans took it as a votive offering to the Gods, for they were still living in an older consciousness which knew that Man owes the power of thought to the Gods. However, when they had brought the wooden horse into the city, Greek warriors emerged from it during the night and perpetrated a fearful massacre. Ultimately mankind turns the gift received from Heaven into a source of ruin for itself. With much pomp and circumstance we also introduce death and unfettered hosts of demons into our modern cities.

In the virtual disappearance of the horse from public life, our civilization has undergone a veritable apocalyptic transformation. Only the superficiality of our age obscures the apocalyptic significance of the horse being superseded by machinery. Like the horse the machine which has taken its place can be a reflection of a part of Man's being. The ousting of the horse by "mechanically propelled vehicles" should really make us think. It is only through familiarity that we are no longer terrified at the sight of a vehicle whose source of locomotion we do not perceive. Machines are intelligence set free, become objective; they have placed Man in the position of a magician's apprentice, the slave and whipping-boy of his own inventions. Our intelligence meets us from without as a threatening, spectral force. However paradoxical it may sound, so long as the horse was still at home on the streets of our cities the communal life of man was more human. Since the horse has been superseded by machinery, Man is in danger of being superseded by the beast—the beast or beasts which the writer of the Apocalypse sees rising from the abyss. The Pale Horse has death and the demonic host of Hell in his retinue. The first three Seals depict the descent of divine intelligence to the human level. In the fourth Seal the danger of the human intelligence becoming demonic is revealed.

In the later parts of the Apocalypse, when the fifth and sixth Trumpets sound, the theme of the Pale Horse receives sinister development. In the ninth chapter demonic powers are described spreading over the Earth like swarms of locusts: "And the shapes of the locusts were like unto horses prepared unto battle, and on their heads were, as it were, crowns like gold, and their faces were as the faces of men. . . . And they had breastplates, as it were, breastplates of iron; and the sound of their wings was as the sound of chariots of many horses running to battle. And they had tails like unto scorpions, and there were stings in their tails, and their power was to hurt men . . . (ix, 7). And I saw horses in the vision, and them that sat on them, having breastplates of fire and jacinth and brimstone. And the heads of the horses were as the heads of lions, and out of their mouths issued fire and smoke and brimstone. By these was the third part of men killed" (ix, 17). These are gruesome, machine-like beings which eventually appear on the scene as metamorphoses of the Pale Horse. Of course, it is not the purpose of the Apocalypse to dissuade people from employing technical science. It would be foolish not to make use of the machines which our intelligence has constructed. But when we learn to see our mechanized civilization as a reflected image of our own human condition, we shall be obliged to confess that we can only employ technical science and continue to live at the same time as true human beings, if we add to this external culture such a strengthening and cultivation of our spirit as provides the balance to increasing mechanization; if we can again unite the intelligence which is slipping away from us with the reinforced spiritual core of our being.

It is puzzling and disconcerting that at the very moment when the vision of the Seer soars up from the earthly level to high stages of supersensible perception, and perceives pictures in which the inmost secret of the origin and evolution of the world is revealed, a prophecy of evil running through the pictures should meet him. The first result of Imagination is the vision of the tremendous fall suffered by cosmic intelligence, from divine heights down to the human sphere and then into sub-human, demonic realms. However, if we take the whole of the Apocalypse into account, in the end the redemptive picture of the White Horse appears again. "And I saw Heaven opened, and behold, a white horse, and He that sat upon him was called Faithful and True; and in righteousness he doth judge and make war. His eyes were as a flame of fire and on his head were many crowns" (xix, 2). The one crown worn by the rider of the White Horse in the first Seal has become many crowns. Just as the hosts of Hell follow the Rider of the Pale Horse, so a heavenly army, of which each one is clothed like

Himself in white raiment, follows the White Rider on the White Horse.

The fall of humanity from the divine to the demonic was foreseen in the book of God's purposes. But the downward movement reveals its true purpose only if Man ultimately reconquers the heights by the strength of that freedom which he attains at the bottom of the valley. At first the White Horse is given to him without his own effort or desert. He will be able to win it back in freedom through the strength to which he rises by his own endeavour. One of the names of the White Rider is "The Word of God". When Man finds anew the way to receive the thinking of God into his own thinking, and the Word of God into his own words, the downward movement can turn into an upward movement. If this is achieved, the bud of vision will open in the mind and will grow from the inmost centre of Man, and from the indwelling divine Ego. Man may ally himself with the White Rider on whose brow gleam many golden crowns.

When the Lamb opens the fifth Seal, the image released from the Seal changes. The stirring picture of a Horse with its Rider is not repeated. Instead, the sublime and peaceful vision of an Altar appears. In the sequence of the four apocalyptic Riders which leads to the middle of the Seven Seals, obviously a nadir is reached; after the middle, at the fifth stage, a level is touched from which a return and new ascent is possible. After the heavenly Book, the Altar is the second basic symbol of the Apocalypse. Just as the sevenfold circle of the Seals was released from the Book, so the Altar will later become the place from which the Seven Trumpets originate. The heavenly Book pictures a sphere of cosmic lore and knowledge from which the history of cosmic intelligence proceeded in its metamorphoses throughout human history. Now the symbols indicating thought, teaching and knowledge recede. If intelligence is to be rescued, help must come from another source. The development of the intellect has come to an end. Mechanization, i.e. applied thought divorced from its source and leading an independent existence, reveals the last dangerous stage. Soulless spectres have made their appearance on the human scene. But when the machine turns into an apocalyptic picture in which the threatened fall into the abyss may be seen the Altar must again appear among mankind, and indeed not only as focus of religious tradition, but as apocalyptic fact, as the well-spring of a new spiritual life, a centre from which humanity may ascend to a new, conscious communion with the divine Spirit. The Altar in the fifth Seal is surrounded by those souls who have taken with them across the threshold of death the fruits of an active devotional life. All the souls assembled round the Altar have received a white robe. Beyond the gates of death the first rays of the sunrise are seen in which humanity may regain the pure divine light which it possessed at the beginning of creation.

Why is it the dead who are seen under and behind the Altar? An Altar always has the form of a tomb. The sarcophagus is the prototype of the Altar. Whenever we stand by a coffin we are in fact standing at an altar. At a coffin we are in the presence not only of earthly beings, but also of beings of the spiritual world who overshadow the earthly. The souls of the dead form the lowest rank, the province next to us in the realm of spiritual Beings. Since the empty tomb of Golgotha, however, the Altar has become more than a tomb. It is the place of Resurrection. At Christian altars, therefore, something more can be experienced than the presence of individual departed souls or the universal sphere of the dead. The Risen One is present in the consecration of bread and wine, and the souls of the departed who during their earthly life formed a union with Christ—however humbly—join in the celebration. So do the celestial hierarchies whose charge is to serve the Christ.

The souls shown in the fifth Seal partake in the glory of martyrdom. They are described as victims of the hatred against God among men. In times such as the period of transition from the Pale Horse to the Altar, no genuine Christianity is possible without suffering. These sufferings and persecutions, whether they are intentionally inflicted or are the automatic result of an anti-Christian civilization, are, after death, a very real source of Light. Even in earthly life, union with Christ kindles a light in the soul; but it does not visibly prevail against the darkness which permeates the earthly human being. After death, the white robe is displayed to the eye of the soul in full brilliance, after it has been woven during the life on earth out of the glory of the Risen One at the Altar.

In our day, the erecting of altars and the care of them, in the consciousness that they are a meeting-place between the living and the dead, is a vital necessity. In this spectre-like age of the Pale Horse, the crises of our civilization have caused to enter into the supersensible world within a short space of time such a gigantic army of dead—killed, tortured or starved to death—as never before in the history of humanity. And a monstrous paradox results. Just at this juncture when the number of the dead is so enormous, those who are living on Earth have reached the very nadir of their understanding of and interest in the world of the dead. Never has a generation had so little instinct for, or consciousness of, a life after death and the possibilities of reciprocal help between living and dead, as the present one. Reciprocal influence does, however, take place, both on this side and on the other of the threshold of death, even though people on Earth do not wish to know about it. This reciprocal influence must cause a grievous disappointment to the dead and a disturbance in the health of soul and body in the living, if it is not taken up with conscious devotion and love. The centre for such mutual communion can be the altars which have the form of a tomb, and yet are the place of the Risen Christ.

The sixth Seal is the first to grow beyond the proportion of the other stages. It tends to break through its perimeter. Apocalyptic time is condensed and accelerated. The sound of the Trumpet Blasts is already audible from afar. Instead of one main picture a tense drama in two acts is unfolded. When the Seal is opened, a tremendous earthquake shakes the world. The Sun becomes black "as sackcloth of hair" and the Moon red as blood. The colours of the second and third of the apocalyptic Horses now appear as Sun and Moon. The descent of human intelligence spreads over the cosmos. Man imagines that he can do his work on Earth without influencing the universe, or even the Earth itself. Now he will learn something different. The earthquake in the sixth Seal is not merely a natural catastrophe; it betrays the consequences of the spiritual attitude of Man. The cosmos echoes back the deeds of men. "The stars fall to the earth, and the heaven is rolled together as a scroll." The catastrophic metamorphoses of heaven and earth thus described need not occur in a precisely physical and visible way. If technical science is about to construct projectiles whose speed equals the velocity of the motion of heavenly bodies, is that not an indication that Man has surrounded himself with a field of force whereby the natural influences of the stars upon human beings are eliminated? Although we are not yet fully conscious of it, we are engaged in opposing nature and the cosmos in a most arrogant way. Once Heaven was an open book in which men could read. If we go far enough back into the past this reading was a perception of the supersensible Beings and forces which operate between Heaven and Earth. Later, when the ability to see into the supersensible died away, at least the majesty and beauty of the starry heavens spoke to the souls of men. But now the stars have become chiefly objects of calculation and technical experiment. The real

Heaven is now rolled together like a scroll, and has thus become unreadable. This is a veritable inversion of the Heavenly Book, in which one Seal after another was opened by the Lamb. And likewise the book of Nature and Life, which we imagine we have investigated to the last item, is in reality closed to us.

One effect of the earthquake is described as displacing the mountains and islands. Natural catastrophes of this kind are only the last material result of a process which begins on an inner plane. The spiritual value of the islands and the mountains is lost. What a wonderful secret has been woven, for instance, round the sacred summit of Mount Tabor, where the three intimate disciples experienced the Transfiguration of Christ, and which stands in the countryside even today as the proto-type of all mountains. Once the mountains were the visible revelation of a spiritual secret, an ascent to the heights. Similarly, islands were visible symbols of a withdrawal from the world. "The island of Patmos," where the Apocalypse was born—does it not arouse a sense of sacred significance? One might say, Patmos is not *an* island, but *the* island. Islands are part of God's hieroglyphs, and have their values as letters in the great pictorial script of creation. They are symbols of the sacred solitude in which the soul is laved by the Ocean of the Spirit. In our day a complete unsouling of all earthly landscapes takes place, even of those which have a special symbolism or were once the scene of the most holy events. Men can climb Mount Tabor as often as they like, and spend long hours on the island of Patmos; but hardly anyone will now meet with an echo of the Transfiguration or the Apocalypse there, unless he bears it already in his heart and brings it with him. The secret of the mountain and the island will only be found in the inner place of the soul.

When in the last resort, evoked by Man himself, these great cosmic convulsions overcome mankind, "the kings and the great men and the rich men of the earth hide themselves in the dens and rocks of the mountains." It is irrelevant whether this happens outwardly. The fact is that the more powerfully the supersensible world beats against the shore of physical life, the more do men creep ever deeper into earthly materialism. They have not the inward strength or courage to meet the kingdoms of heaven as they draw near. They become weak and cling more passionately to material existence. It may even be a sign of the approach of spiritual realities that so many people become restless, and drug themselves with narcotics more than ever before.

The first half of the sixth Seal speaks of a cosmic upheaval and the dissolution of the world in terms similar to the twenty-first chapter of St. Luke's Gospel, which is read at the altars of The Christian Community as the Advent Gospel. The same divine purpose of instruction is contained in it. Why are men told, "When these things begin to come to pass, then look up, and lift up your heads, for your redemption draweth nigh"? (St. Luke, xxi, 28). The signs of an Advent, of a Second Coming, may be read from the signs of the apocalyptic disintegration of the world. Happy is he to whom all these catastrophes and convulsions are signs of the approach of Him Who is quick to help.

A turning-point towards salvation is reached in the second act of the drama of the sixth Seal. Once more a check is put upon the rising hurricane of cosmic dissolution. To begin with, four Angels stand at the four corners of the Earth. They are intent on allowing the wheel of destruction, which has just begun to turn, to roll on over all creation. They do not belong to the celestial Hosts who serve the Christ; they are Luciferic Angels rejoicing over the work of destruction which they are allowed to perpetrate. Then, however, another commanding power steps forward: "And I saw another Angel descending from the East, having the Seal of the living God, and he cried with a loud voice to the four Angels to whom it was given to hurt the earth and the sea, saying, 'Hurt not the earth neither the sea, nor the trees, till we have sealed the servants of our God in their foreheads.' "

It is the second time in the Apocalypse that this powerful Being appears upon the scene. We saw him first as the herald of progress who called into the cosmos for the power which could loosen the Seals of the Book. In him the will of God, desiring to lead from permanency to evolution, became vocal. Now in the sixth Seal he commands evolution to stand still. We sense the presence of a power "having the seal of the living God" whose name is, however, revealed only at a much later stage. The great crisis must not begin until those who serve the Spirit are rescued from the destruction to come. With them the seed of a new world is ensured. The light of Christ in their souls is the seed of the new world.

An impressive variation and inversion of the Opening of the Seals is carried out. The Heavenly Book has already been unsealed six times. Now men from all branches of mankind are sealed. The unsealing of the Book signified the emanation of creation from the sphere of archetypal sources. The created kingdoms of earthly life were the ultimate results of this Opening of the Seals. Now it is the heavenly and divine which is starting to grow in man that is sealed. Men are found worthy to become the sealed vessels of a divine seed of life. Those who bear the Seal of God in their foreheads are arrayed in white robes. In the fifth Seal white robes were given to those in the kingdom of the dead who were in union with Christ. Now, since Man has entered amid storms and earthquakes upon a new stage of his evolution, there must also be men on earth who wear the white robe although living still in opaque, earthly bodies. Under pressure of apocalyptic events the inner source of light will become bright enough to irradiate the mortal body from within.

For the first time a *number* is hinted at, which at the end of St. John's Revelation appears as the governing principle of the ordering of humanity: "the number of them which were sealed was 144,000." Just as a magnet singles out pieces of iron from heaps of metal and arranges them in figures, so a hidden power draws into a spiritual figure those of humanity who are of like nature with itself. The Christ who is approaching mankind anew is able to form a pattern in the midst of chaos, because all those in whose hearts the power of Christ is present now receive something from above which will preserve them from being sucked into the whirlpool of destruction. Nothing need be altered outwardly to begin with. Those men who are distinguished from their environment by their inner attitude to Christ continue to live and work where Providence has placed them. Seen from the Spirit, however, they appear as bearers of light amidst the dark and fluctuating confusion of Earth. The bud of a Christ-humanity of the future is formed. The number mentioned by the writer of the Apocalypse is not quantitative. As once the twelve tribes of the Chosen People were grouped in imitation of the stars in Heaven, and as later the circle of the twelve disciples formed the seed of a humanity grouped according to twelve prototypes, so in the midst of a vast humanity which thinks only in quantitative numbers a new archetype of community, a cosmically ordered, completely universal assembly is gathered. The sealed Book in Heaven contained the ground-plan and archetypes of our world. Now those who are sealed form the radiating core of a humanity in union with Christ: they are the "Book" which contains the seed and the blueprint of a new creation, a new cosmos. The end of the world may come; the beginning of a new world is present in embryo.

At last the Seer John is given the key to solve the riddle of the sealing. Full of questioning astonishment, he is absorbed in contemplation of the 144,000 shining in white raiment. One of the twenty-four Elders who sit in a circle round the Throne voices the question which stirs in the soul of John, so that the content of his own soul meets him as though from outside. He can only reply to him who asks the question, "Sir, thou knowest." And then, by the same Being the answer is imparted to him: "These are they which came out of great tribulation, and have washed their robes, and made them white in the blood of the Lamb." Only those who pass through the school of suffering can absorb the divine spark into their soul, the spark which will be sealed in them as the seed of a new cosmos. Those people who "have a good time", and to whom success comes easily, cannot so easily belong to the true bearers of the future. Neither does the inner light spring simply from suffering well borne. A new motif emerges which has been taken up and treasured through the whole history of Christendom: "The blood of Christ makes man pure and bright."

In the transition from the first to the second Seal, the first descent of Man took place, from the pure heights of the Spirit to the depths of his own blood. The gleaming white was replaced by the crimson colour of blood. Mankind lost the white robe of paradisal origin. Some day, however, this step must be retraced, from red to white. This will be possible when Man absorbs into his blood the power of the blood of Christ. The vitality of the sinful human blood—sinful since the "Fall"—is wearing out and coming to an end. The blood that flowed from the wounds of the Christ is the bearer of transformed, spiritualized forces of imperishable life. He who learns in the school of tribulation to open his being for the entry of Christ, to receive into his own blood the blood of Christ, obtains through Him Who dwells within his heart a share in the eternal life which bears the seed of the new world, and of which it can again be said, "The life is the light of men." From the white robes of those who bear the Seal of God in their forehead the light of a new Heaven and a new Earth begins to dawn.

V

THE FIRST TRUMPETS: COSMIC STORM

THE EIGHTH AND NINTH CHAPTERS

THE cycle of the seven Seals seems not to have reached its full development even at the end. The sphere of the Trumpet-blasts presses upon it as if unable to await its due time. The Seven Trumpets appear within the seventh Seal, thereby becoming visible at the stage of Imagination before they begin to sound at the stage of Inspiration.

As in the transition from the Seven Messages to the Seven Seals, so now between Seals and Trumpets a solemn pause intervenes. But its content is not quite so majestic as the divine figures who stood in the environment of the heavenly Throne before the Lamb unloosed the Seals of the Book. It seems as if the breathing space of the Gods is cut short. Indeed, instead of forming a genuine interval between the seventh Seal and the first Trumpet, the pause is antedated, as it were, within the seventh Seal. "When he had opened the seventh Seal, there was silence in Heaven about the space of half an hour." Now the Trumpet motif appears, though at first only as a quiet picture within the heavenly silence: "And I saw the seven Angels which stood before God; and to them were given seven Trumpets." We sense what is to come, and because of this premonition the silence is tense. We cannot see the Trumpets without the foreboding that presently they will sound, and that their blast will shatter the world.

Nevertheless, the order of events demands an interval. Archetypes of devotion and worship are revealed. The centre is formed by the Altar, which has made a prophetic appearance once before. We witness a solemn rite celebrated in Heaven: "And another Angel came and stood at the Altar, having a golden censer; and there was given unto him much incense, that he should offer it with the prayers of all saints upon the golden Altar which was before the throne. And the smoke of the incense which rose with the prayers of the saints ascended up before God out of the Angel's hand." The pause before the opening of the Seals was filled with the song of praise with which those on high accompanied the beginning of Creation. Now in the second pause a scene nearer to the human level is enacted. The figure of a heavenly priest advances to the altar to celebrate a ritual act.

68

The Revelation of St. John presents a sequence of significant focal pictures. Before the cycle of the Seven Seals, the *Book* made its appearance in Heaven. Since the Seals are attached to the Book, the picture of the Book becomes the source of the unfolding of all the following cycles of Seven. At the beginning of the Seven Trumpet-blasts, the *Altar* appears in Heaven. In the fifth Seal it has appeared once already, as if in the act of approaching; then the theme is developed as the Seals unfold. At the end of the opening of the Seals the Altar has become the sacred centre of all things. From it the forces issue which carry the development forward to the next stages. Just as the Seals were loosed on the Book so the Seven Trumpets sound from the heavenly Altar. At the last great cycle of Seven the golden Vials are handed out from the *Temple* in Heaven. This is the third structural picture of the Apocalypse. These fundamental pictures, the Book, the Altar and the Temple stand at the beginning of each cycle in turn.

The polarity of Book and Altar points to the basic order of all spiritual life. Even in Heaven the duality of doctrine and ritual exists. The supersensible worlds contain the thronging *thoughts* of God which, as they begin to move and become a world, appear in the picture of a sealed book. On the other hand, the Heavens declare also the unfolding *deeds* of God, the proceedings of the celestial Hierarchies, the actions of the Beings in the higher spheres. These are no profane transactions; every deed is an Act of Consecration. The proceedings and transactions of the Gods are nothing else but the celebration of a rite; and the centre of all heavenly proceedings and transactions can only be an Altar. Doctrine of the Heavens: the thoughts of God. Ritual of the Heavens: the deeds and actions of the heavenly Hierarchies.

If there is to be harmony between Heaven and Earth, the fundamental ordering of Heaven must be reflected on Earth. This is, in truth, the function of Religion. The "Book" must not be only in Heaven; on Earth also *the* Book must hold a central place. Likewise there must be—as a clear reflection and likeness on Earth—in the midst of all the busy doings and activities of men, the "Act of Consecration", the rite celebrated at the Altar. There must be no shortage of altars on Earth. One of the reasons why the Apocalypse was not adequately valued in the Protestant era may have been that the apocalyptic descriptions of the celebration of the Angels at the heavenly Altar was felt, if not "Roman" at least as something alien. Indeed, no purely human thought can ever produce a real altar. It is futile to "invent" a ritual, or put it together from traditional sources to make an aesthetic unit. Ritual, like doctrine, must be derived from the spiritual worlds. Earthly ritual must truly reflect Heavenly ritual. Then it can become a pattern for the sanctification of all earthly activity.

There is a book on Earth which, even by its title, claims to be *the* Book. "Bible," both in Greek and Latin, means "The Book". The Biblical Scriptures, rightly understood, are in reality not written like other books or documents, but are a transparent, near-to-Heaven reproduction of the Book in Heaven. But the vital impact of the Bible depends on our capacity to sense through the verbal text, written as it is in an earthly language and still more secularized and obscured by translations, the heavenly Word of God. A fundamentalist, clinging to the letter, is in serious danger of eclipsing the heavenly Book. The unique position of the Book of Books cannot be secured simply by dogmatic claims. But if the indwelling Spirit-word is kept alive it can work like a leaven for all other literature.

When the Book appears in Heaven, it is sealed. The unsealing causes the stream of images to flow. The Altar appears without seals but it is not without mystery. What process of spiritual release at the heavenly Altar corresponds to the unsealing of the Book?

We eagerly await the moment when the pictures will be replaced by the sphere of sound and tone, when the transition occurs from divine thought to deed, from divine theory to divine practice. How will the new stream of sacred activity begin to appear which will ultimately consecrate also our human activities?

During the pause in Heaven the smoke of incense ascends in silent celebration. When the waiting Angels prepare to let the blasts of the Trumpets sound, we expect also the priestly figure at the Altar to change his attitude. What will he do?

His action is quite different from what we expected. It startles us. "And the Angel took the censer and filled it with fire of the altar and cast it into the Earth, and there were voices and thunderings and lightnings and an earthquake." The "Act of Consecration" has its new beginning at the heavenly Altar through a cosmic storm. Thunder and lightning give the signal for the sounding of the Trumpets. The heavenly action cannot simply flow, blessing and sanctifying, into earthly action. Between the substance which issues from the heavenly Altar and everything earthly, a high tension, a contrast and difference in type prevails, so that at first contact only sparks and flames of fire are emitted. A terrifying secret is revealed which will remain effective through all the seven stages of the cycle of the Trumpets.

When, through the fire from the heavenly Altar, the cosmic storm breaks over the kingdom of Earth, we recognize the Angel who performs the priestly service. It is he who has already intervened twice at critical points in the apocalyptic events. With unpretentious words he is called "a strong Angel" (v. 2), "another Angel" (vii, 2; viii, 3; xiv, 15), or "another mighty Angel" (x, 1). At the climax of the Apocalypse, however, he is identified as that angelic being who is the only one mentioned by his own name: the Archangel Michael. We saw him first as a herald, calling for someone to open the Seals. His voice is heard at the beginning of evolution in time. Later, in the sixth Seal, when the continued descent of intelligence threatens to pervert the evolution of Creation, he calls a halt to the powers of destruction. By printing the seal of God on the foreheads of the chosen humanity of the future, he establishes ascent in descent. Now at the heavenly Altar we see him again; concerned that the pause in Heaven should not last too long, he gives the signal for the sounding of the Trumpets. He is always the Angel of Progress; he sets in motion that which stands still; he wrests the seed and promise of the future from the downward plunge. Now he pours out over the Earth the fire of the heavenly Altar and releases the cosmic storm which the Trumpets produce and sustain as they ring out one after another.

The inauguration of the new cycle at the high Altar sets the pitch for the first part of the Trumpet-blasts. The first effects strike terror; they demand courage and strength in those who wish to follow the writer of the Apocalypse. But courage and strength can only live in souls which trust that there is purpose, help and blessing in all that comes from the heavenly Altar, though the divine help may be masked by a stern outward appearance.

Just as the Seals revealed the successive *fall of consciousness*, so the Trumpets reveal a dramatic sequence of acts which constitute a *fall of being*.

But the composition of the Apocalypse makes it clear that the catastrophes and destruction of which we are to be spectators are nothing final as yet, but they must be passed through and overcome as necessary stages of transition. Towards the end of each of the great cycles of seven, the powers of goodness intervene to wrest domination from the power of evil; a new ascent breaks free from the downward move. Indeed, as in a parabola, the descending line should merge into the ascending branch of the evolutionary curve at the middle, i.e. the fourth stage; but the plunge projects beyond this. Here a law operates which is similar to that whereby the coldest hours of the night come only after midnight, and the coldest months of the year only after the time of the shortest day. The crisis comes at the fifth stage. In the apocalyptic alphabet, five is the number of crisis and of evil. Only in the sixth cycle, in the midst of continuing catastrophes, can the fruits of trials withstood ripen and become effective; then the powers of good wrest a new beginning from disaster and destruction.

This order in the composition of the Apocalypse emerged already in the sixth Seal, when the "strong Angel" who helped the unsealing to begin ordered a halt to destruction, and sealed with the Seal of God those who have stood the test. Similarly, in the midst of the sounding of the sixth Trumpet, the strong Angel who with the fire from the heavenly Altar gave the signal for the beginning of the Trumpet-blasts, will resist the evil through the power of good.

The Seven Trumpets are the centre and heart of the Apocalypse. In them the rhythm of its breath and pulse, the key-note of its soul can be felt. The voice of the Trumpets is heard continually in the background of the whole Apocalypse. Twice it was heard directly, if only for an instant. At the beginning John heard a "Voice as of a Trumpet" (i, 10); and again the Trumpet Voice arouses him and opens the great vision (iv, 1). When at the beginning of Chapter VIII the Seven Trumpets are given to the Seven Angels who stand before the face of God, we share in a cosmic moment similar to that suggested by the first words of the Bible, announcing the genesis of our world.

The Seven Angels with the Seven Trumpets stand in the very place where, in the first still motionless symmetry, the Seven Spirits of God appeared around the heavenly Throne, burning like lamps of fire (Chapter iv). They are the seven Elohim (cf. page 42) who appear at the beginning of Genesis and then again in the Apocalypse, first as the Seven Spirits of the Lamps, and eventually in and behind the picture of the Seven Angels bearing Trumpets. Each time the Seven Spirits of God achieve their purpose by uttering a mighty sound.

The sound of the Trumpets releases in rapid succession the stages of a cosmic conflagration in which one great collapse follows another. The fire thrown from the heavenly Altar, mingled with hail, falls upon the Earth and causes devastation. At the second Trumpet-blast, a burning mountain falls from Heaven. The consequences are similar: evil is spread over the Earth. At the third Trumpet-blast the fire retains its direction from above downwards. A burning star plunges from Heaven. Renewed devastation on Earth. At the fourth and middle Trumpet-blast, however, the fiery element withdraws and with it the direction of movement changes. Now evil invades the upper sphere: Sun, Moon and Stars are darkened in the sky. At the next stage the direction is completely reversed: the depths reply to the heights. The fifth Trumpet-blast: a star which fell from Heaven breaks through the closed door of the bottomless pit, and out of the abyss vapours and clouds of smoke rise and cover everything. They change eventually into gigantic swarms of locusts, to which all living things fall victim. At the sixth Trumpet-blast, the direction from below upwards is maintained: the upward thronging forces of the pit change into spectral warriors; horse-like beings rush madly over the Earth, trampling upon everything; at the same time their bluish steel-like armour makes them look like machines. Although, from the sixth Trumpet onwards the powers of good also come on the scene to wrest a new upward impulse from the downward plunge, it is not until the seventh Trumpet that the unfolding of evil is completed; the two-fold beast rises from the pit.

What meaning, and what divine purpose, can be hidden behind the flames of cosmic conflagration, behind the release of demons? Heaven wishes to bestow something new, but instead of being ready to receive the new gifts Man clings firmly to the old. He must learn by experience that the old world is doomed. Only thus can the way be made clear for the gift of the heavenly Altar, a new being and a new consciousness.

The cycle of Seven Trumpets reveals a principle of evolution which we can recognize in the large as well as in the small cycles of human history. Our present "small" cycle began at the end of the Middle Ages.* We can attempt to understand the revelation of the series of Trumpet-blasts which have followed each other in this epoch from the consciousness of the Angel who celebrated at the heavenly Altar and

---

* In his *Outline of Occult Science* (Anthroposophical Publishing Company, London) Rudolf Steiner describes a cyclical pattern in evolution. According to his description evolution is from time to time interrupted by planetary catastrophes. The last great global catastrophe, remembered in the many stories of the Great Flood, caused the submersion of the Atlantic Continent. A comparable catastrophe will occur in the future. Between these cataclysms which mark the big evolutionary cycles, seven sub-cycles or "cultural epochs" follow each other. According to Steiner we live now in the fifth "post-atlantean" epoch, which began in the fifteenth century. In this present period humanity develops a state of soul which is acutely object-conscious, and which Steiner calls "consciousness-soul".

The apocalyptic sequences of Seven, being archetypal, can be traced both in the bigger cycles and in the smaller sub-cycles.

released the subsequent events by pouring out fire. As said before the Archangel Michael obviously is hidden behind this Angel. He drives forward the wheel of history, and is concerned to see that the humanity of the future should voluntarily assimilate the forces which Heaven will bestow on it as new faculties and organs. He is anxious that human beings should be able to receive and to use for their good what is intended for them. Are not then the blasts of the Trumpets also warnings and admonitions of Michael? In the age of the consciousness-soul, Heaven draws the attention of human souls through the Trumpet-blasts to the dangers which are inherent in the necessary progress of civilization.

Since the beginning of the fifteenth century, European humanity has awakened to the clear perception, through the senses, of material objects. With this awakening a new enthusiasm for thinking has been born. Delighted with their discoveries, human beings have looked around them with new eyes. They really began to perceive the Earth itself for the first time. It has been an age in which the character of the first Trumpet has asserted itself. The icy hailstones of dead thought have been mingled with burning enthusiasm for the new science and philosophy. In the physical world fire and hail do not mix. The spiritual picture points to the danger which threatens all enthusiasm which is only directed towards earthly matters. It is inevitable that cold rationalism and calculations of earthly profit should be mixed with it. So all enthusiasm which does not embrace the opened worlds of Spirit must one day fail and end in disappointment.

A second phase of recent history has produced the astonishing development of Natural Science. It was in the age of Galileo and Copernicus that the second Trumpet sounded. Once more within our present small cycle the flame of new thought was kindled everywhere. But the more the physical world yielded its secrets, so much the more firmly was the door into Heaven and the supersensible world closed. The world became stony and opaque. It was as if a rocky mountain— even though burning with heavenly fire—had fallen from Heaven. This was the epoch in which Albrecht Dürer produced his classical engraving called *Melancolia*. The anxiety of the Archangel Michael, verging on resignation, could not be more precisely presented than in this picture. The figure of the Archangel, with weary wings, pensively supporting his heavy brow with his hand, sits beside a rock hewn in crystal form, recalling the mountain which was cast down to the Earth during the second Trumpet-blast.

If the world turned to stone for human consciousness when Natural Science gained ground, so in the following age of "Enlightenment"

Man himself became ever smaller in stature. The third Trumpet shows a burning star falling from Heaven, a star which bears the name Wormwood, because it is bitter and produces a lasting effect of bitterness. In this there are forces at work which, like all that is bitter, acts astringently and has a shrinking effect. Sated, self-satisfied bourgeois egoism seizes upon men, making them believe they are great, but in fact causing their souls and spirits to become weak and shrivelled.

Then came the days when, for a generation which was becoming increasingly clever, the glory of the Sun, Moon and Stars was extinguished. In the past the lights of Heaven had stimulated a feeling for the unseen world. But as cleverness took more and more possession of the human soul, the last organs and capacities for supersensible perception of the universe died away.

Then came the time when the bottomless pit reacted on the new soul-forces of humanity, when the depths sizzled and bubbled as if drops of water had fallen on hot iron. The spectral world of abstractions poisoned the nineteenth century. Through materialistic thinking, Man evoked forces of destruction which began to eat up his own life-forces, just as when swarms of locusts descend upon the verdant life of the countryside.

At the present time we are approaching the sounding of the sixth Trumpet. All this must be lived through; even the change of the locust swarms of the fifth Trumpet into spectral war-horses. While fulfilling all the earthly duties and necessities which the present moment continually demands from us, we should not cease to reflect upon what we have done with the forces poured out from Heaven, and to ask ourselves if, ultimately, the greatest amount of intelligence will not have been expended in discovering methods of reciprocal destruction.

In describing the devastation produced by the first Trumpet-storm, the Apocalypse makes use of a recurring numerical expression: the fiery hail sets alight *one third* of the Earth, and *one third* of all the trees; the burning mountain turns *one third* of the sea into blood, and causes *one third* of all the creatures in the sea to die; the burning star changes *one third* of all streams and springs into bitterness, to the ruin of mankind. The middle Trumpet darkens *one third* of the light of Sun, Moon and Stars. What is meant by this *third*? A quantitative reading of numbers here, as everywhere in the Apocalypse, cannot help us. It would be foolish to imagine that one-third of physical earthly existence will be annihilated. What about the two-thirds which would

75

then still be left? All apocalyptic numbers are to be taken *qualitatively*. When, in this context, one, two, three is counted, it would be just as true to say: body, soul and spirit. The number three expresses the threefold being of Man. Human beings, and in a certain sense, all earthly creatures consist of the body-third, the soul-third, and the spirit-third. To begin with, however, earthly creation including Man has only a Nature-given relationship with spirit. So long as his nature remains childlike, Man cannot count the spirit-third of his being as his own possession. If he wishes to grow up and become a free, responsible individual, the spirit-third which is only the dowry of Nature does not help him to do so. When destiny has once led him into the development of his "ego", he will lose this dowry. Man cannot live permanently on the capital of the forces he brought with him. And when the Trumpet-blasts ring out, the remainder of this capital is suddenly used up with alarming rapidity.

The spiritual third of the human being, as of everything earthly, falls a victim to destruction amid the cosmic storms of the Trumpet age. Inherited spirituality, given by God to the first creation to help it on its way, is coming to an end. And what are the forces which complete its destruction? The fire poured out from the Altar of Heaven. It is the new spirituality which, however, Man can acquire only through the inner activity of faith and the awakened consciousness of spirit. Heaven pours down flames of spiritual fire through the opening doors of the supersensible world. This fire destroys everything which is not of like nature with itself, even "natural" spirituality. Natural spirituality, inherited, not acquired, serves only the "lower ego" of man. The new spirituality—to which a man opens his heart when he makes St. Paul's words come true: "Not I, but Christ in me"—can contain the fiery flames of the Higher Ego.

Either Man opens his heart to Christ if, inwardly or outwardly, he erects an altar as a pure mirror of the heavenly Altar; then the fire from Heaven is for him benediction and fulfilment. *Or* humanity becomes more and more fettered to the material world. Then universal egoism, and the war of all against all, will be the order of the day, and the fire from Heaven will kindle one conflagration after another, and all that Man clutches and clings to will be annihilated.

VI

THE BEGINNING OF THE LAST
TRUMPETS
HUMANITY AT THE THRESHOLD

THE TENTH AND ELEVENTH CHAPTERS

WITH the Seven Trumpet Blasts the central core of the apocalyptic drama is reached. At the sound of the first four Trumpets four concentrated acts follow each other with solemn, equally measured pace. The fifth Trumpet is the summons to the decisive crisis. The fall of the cosmic fire from Heaven, the eclipse of the cosmic light in the heights is followed by the fateful rise of the powers of the abyss. At the sixth blast the Power intervenes who wrests a new ascent from the descent. But the demonic powers of the pit are not yet vanquished. The cosmic battle extends still further. Eventually the seventh Trumpet demands almost a separate apocalyptic book.

At the sound of the fourth Trumpet the sun is darkened, together with other heavenly lights. The sun ceases to be the giver of the forces which nourish our humanity, which in fact make us human beings. This turning point is the decisive test in the great education of mankind. Outwardly the sun may continue majestically to circle the sky, but Nature whose royal leader the sun is, no longer supports man. He is left alone. The natural riches of the world become uninspiring. Man grows lonely and is thrown back on himself.

But the twilight of the Gods which is manifested in the apocalyptic darkness of the sun is followed by a reassuring portent. The mighty Angel who arrests the destruction is said to have a countenance shining like the sun. The Sun of the Spirit is about to rise over the human race which is threatened with extinction in darkness. Christ Himself is the Lord of that spiritual Sun. He is not directly visible on the stage of the apocalyptic drama, but He stands behind the angelic Power through whose countenance His countenance shines. Will the human race be able to receive the gracious beams of the spiritual Sun when the material sun ceases to be effective?

At the seventh Trumpet the mystery is fully revealed. The woman "clothed with the Sun" appears. In heaven the image appears of that part of humanity which is able to receive the spiritual Sun into itself. But the woman who is about to give birth to her son is surrounded by battle. The "sun angel" Michael fights against the dragon. Later this war must be continued on earth when human beings themselves must fight against the beasts of the abyss.

Thus, the whole theme of the drama of the Trumpet blasts could be defined as the breaking through of the Spirit Sun. The old creation which once came into existence through the divine command "Let there be Light" is "running down". The Trumpet blasts are a call to a new creation. But first a challenge must be thrown down to the powers of darkness. The dawn of new light can only be assured by fighting until the victory is won over the mounting forces of the abyss.

What inner human processes reflect the macrocosmic drama of the replacement of the outward sun by the Spirit Sun? The corresponding microcosmic process consists in breaking through from the stages of earthly egohood to the life of the Higher Ego. The Higher Ego of Man, his true Ego, is sun-like in character. It is not only akin to the spiritual Sun; it is of the same essence. Yet this higher Ego never simply descends into earthly Man as it were by a natural process. What we normally acquire on earth is the semblance of an ego, an ego-*form*, by which we cut ourselves off from the world. It is only when we practise a new receptivity, when we absorb a higher content for this ego, rising above what is only earthly and personal, that the "Sun" breaks through into our soul. Then this experience is like a microcosmic parallel to the cosmic event pictured in the Trumpet blasts. If egohood *and* receptivity unite within the soul, the sunlit Higher Ego, the Ego Genius of Man, can enter into it.

In the Mysteries of the ancient world, and in the traditions which remained alive into the Middle Ages, the stages of the Path of Initiation were comprised within two main periods. The first stages together brought about *Catharsis*, the cleansing and purifying of human nature by passing through a succession of dramatic tests and trials. The human being was prepared as a vessel capable of absorbing the divine content intended for him. The last stages which were called *Photismos*, or Illumination, brought the instilling and imprinting of the Higher Being into earthly Man. In the succession of Trumpet blasts, we might call the first stages leading up to the great crisis, Catharsis; and the last two Trumpets, which open the prospect to the powers of salvation, Illumination, i.e. permeation with higher content.

When in the course of evolution humanity outgrew the childlike, receptive pre-ego stage and entered the epoch of the formal ego, men created for themselves the terrors of the Trumpet drama in infinite variation. When Man began to model and fashion the world around him by his own wits, although he seemed to make life easier and more secure, he gradually deprived himself of the bountiful home originally provided for him by Nature. Progressively he built an unnatural world, in which the forces of death dominate. And the world which he thus created frightened him back into himself. Advancing mechanization in all fields puts man on the defence. The threat to his existence is not only concentrated in the means of mechanical destruction which are let loose in war-time. There are other and subtler means which can be the more dangerous and soul-destroying the less they are recognized. An instructive example is the film. Since a film strip consists of innumerable separate photographs divided from one another, innumerable shocks continually issue from the screen and strike the human eye; but they succeed each other with such rapidity that they escape our perception, which functions more slowly. Whereas natural seeing enriches and strengthens us, because it offers us coherent reality, the "flicks" whereby we strike ourselves with millions of splinters as it were, frighten the soul into itself and weaken it.

The incessant rush and roar of city traffic on the large scale and the effect of electric radiations in their ever-increasing variety, in a subtle form, are other examples of the process of devitalization and destruction which eat into the human being. A false sense of values and absorption in false ambitions eat into the human soul. This is pictured at the fifth stage in the crisis of the drama where, for example, the smoke of the pit becomes a cloud of locusts. In next to no time locusts devour all green life; where they pass everything stands bare and dead. There are a thousand things in modern life corresponding to this process. When we have finished our day's work in the treadmill of civilization, we are not only tired, but affected in our very substance; we feel robbed of our vitality as a tree is eaten bare by locusts. Sleep alone is not enough to restore us.

In this process we become less and less sensitive to influences from above, but more open to influences from below. Before the Heavens open again one day, the star which falls into the depths forces an opening through the covering of the pit. It is a consequence of the prevailing blindness to the higher world, that Man should forfeit his inward calm. From the opened pit Spirits of restlessness invade souls and bodies. A wild hunt of spectres is let loose. Epidemic possession threatens us in reality.

The first period of the "ego Age" (i.e. the Age since the human race has begun to grow an ego), was characterized by the fact that no "content from above" was any longer received into the human soul. This is the microcosmic meaning of the first four Trumpets. From the fifth Trumpet onwards, influences also set in from below which "hollow out" the ego and eventually even rob Man of his individuality. This is the second period. The third stage of ego-evolution stands as a task before us: if there is to be a future, we must again become able, without losing the fruits of our wandering in the depths, to receive a content from above. The formal, fictitious ego must be overcome in that we receive into our souls our "genius" as our higher ego-content. This Higher Ego will prove to be the messenger of an entire spiritual environment whose light will shine into our souls in times to come. This is the sphere of the spiritual Sun, the sphere of Christ, Who is approaching mankind anew. In Man the break-through of the Sun is accomplished when he finds the strength to wrest inward peace from the restlessness which, rising from below, threatens to dominate his soul. Through devotion and composure of mind, and the practice of inner calm, the new receptivity for Heaven is prepared. Then the positive meaning of the Altar will be revealed which remains as a constant presence behind the Angels of the Seven Trumpets. Man will not be forsaken in his struggle for inward peace. When he sees the mighty Angel whose countenance is as the Sun appearing upon the scene in the midst of all the darkness and the spectral storms, he may read in the cosmic mirror of the apocalyptic drama that he can count on higher help. The change from evil to good which took place in the corresponding passage of the cycle of the Seals is now repeated in a form which implies a prophetic promise. At that time, the Angel who was strong enough to call a halt to the powers of destruction, carried the Seal of God in his hand, in order to print it on the foreheads of the men of the future who belong to Christ. Like every sealing, this too presupposes a valuable content which must be protected. Now, at the sound of the sixth Trumpet, the mighty Sun Angel, grown to cosmic dimensions, again intervenes in the wheel of evolution. He holds a little book in his hand which he desires to give to Man to eat. Will Man be in a position so to assimilate the divine content intended for him that it will become completely part of himself, in fact the substance of his Higher Ego? We surmise that then *his* countenance, too, would shine as the Sun, because when he has passed through the trials of purification, the sunlike seed of the Higher Ego will kindle the light of Illumination in him.

The herald of progress effects the change. Possibilities of Good appear in the midst of Evil, because a supporting power comes on the scene to help struggling humanity. The Apocalypse describes with extremely simple words the Being who effects this change. It may be an indication of enhanced power when now the heavenly herald comes forward with the title of "another mighty Angel", combining the simpler names of "the other Angel", and "the strong Angel", which he bore before. The prospect which he offers to the eyes of the Seer shows that a new and greater concentration of the will of God has taken shape in him. Once, in the heights of Heaven, this hierarchical Being voiced the question which the Lamb alone could answer. Later he intervened between Heaven and Earth, and rescued the men of God by sealing them. Now we clearly see him descending from Heaven to Earth. He stands with one foot on the ocean, and with the other on the mainland of the Earth. He is the messenger of God who is going before Christ to prepare His way. In the kingdoms of the heavenly hierarchies, this Being has a similar task to that which John the Baptist had on earth, before Christ's first coming. The heavenly herald prepares the way for Christ Who, in the supersensible world amid apocalyptic storms, comes ever closer to humanity. At the climax of the seventh Trumpet, the role of the Angel is raised to that of a warrior. Then he will no longer be called "the strong Angel", but will be given his full name as victor over the dragon.

"And I saw another mighty Angel come down from Heaven, clothed with a cloud, and a rainbow was upon his head, and his face was as it were the Sun, and his feet as pillars of fire. And he had in his hand a little book open; and he set his right foot upon the sea, and his left foot on the Earth." The two fire-footed pillars with which the Angel stands on the globe together form a gateway. This gate comprises the Earth in its entirety, its two pillars including the polarity of land and sea. To what country is this gate the entrance? What is the destination of him who sets foot across this threshold? We stand at the border between Spirit and Earth. All that went before was trial and preparation. Now the fulfilment possible in the future is indicated by a tremendous tryst with the Gods; the Angel herald offers himself as the gateway which leads into another world. Out of this world the Christ is to come to humanity. The Sun-countenance of the Angel lets us divine the rising and approaching of this Sun. This stage of evolution, to which all the suffering and loss of the Trumpet epoch has led, may be called "Humanity at the Threshold".

The experience of the Threshold and of the spiritual Being who is called the "Guardian of the Threshold", represents a decisive stage on the spiritual path which the individual man may tread.* This experience is communicated to his consciousness in many different ways. Mankind as a whole is also led to the threshold of the spiritual world through many stages of trial and discipline. A meeting of *Humanity* with the Guardian of the Threshold takes place. But the consciousness of individual men and women cannot attain, simply as a matter of course, the level on which this event can be observed and understood. Rather they will be lost in one perplexity after another when the spiritual world approaches. Only here and there a realization of the actual situation may flash through the soul.

It is precisely this tragic *dilemma of the human consciousness* which makes the apocalyptic character of the present age. Our souls are under the spell of materialistic habits of thought. For a long time the consciousness of humanity has been concentrated on the outside of the world. Now the spiritual world is reaching mankind; humanity is arriving at the Threshold; new realities overwhelm us for which no understanding is available. It must seem hopeless ever to grasp them with conscious thought. Yet everything depends upon whether humanity rises to that level of consciousness on which what is actually happening can be understood.

When the mighty Angel appears as the Guardian of the Threshold, humanity meets at the same time its own Genius. We see ourselves in the form of the Angel, as in a mirror. The cloud with which the Angel is clothed reflects the sphere of real Ideas into which Man rises as a thinking being. The rainbow with its sevenfold harmony of colours is a picture of the gamut of emotions of which Man is capable. The fiery feet, continued into flaming pillars, direct and inspire us to walk the Earth with energy and active purpose. The Sun-countenance reveals the nature of the Higher Ego, which will freely co-ordinate the trinity of Thinking, Feeling and Willing. We behold, in fact, a modification of the sublime vision of the Son of Man, which formed the beginning of all the apocalyptic disclosures.

In the above-mentioned book Rudolf Steiner describes how the human being, in approaching the threshold of the spiritual world, is faced with a growing independence of the three fundamental forces of the soul, Thinking, Feeling and Willing. When mankind as a whole approaches the Threshold a corresponding differentiation is effected. A regrouping of the human race is set in motion. Today its most conspicuous manifestation is the gradual

* Cf. Rudolf Steiner, *How to attain Knowledge of the Higher Worlds.*

disappearance of the earlier national units and the emergence of the great East-West polarity. The Angel of the Threshold with a countenance like the Sun represents symbolically the new ordering of humanity. The cloud with which he is clothed represents the element of spirit and thought which constitutes the world of Eastern Man. In the fiery feet of the Angel the predominant will-character of Western Man is signified. And the harmony of colours in the rainbow points to the task of harmonizing and balancing, set for the people of the Middle regions which lie between the two extremes.

At the present time, when the East becomes increasingly militant and may, before long, even outstrip the West in energy and practical efficiency, it will seem curious to say that "spirit and thought constitute the world of Eastern Man". But the attitude of the East towards the West has for a long time been a strange mixture. Because from ancient times the East has lived in spiritual realities as in a universally visible cloud, it was bound to look contemptuously on the harassed "busyness" of Western civilization, and its utilitarianism. The East has always known that the organizing and technical achievements of which Western peoples are so proud, have only been derived from materialistic forms of thought incapable of grasping real truth. Since, however, in its arrogant conception of the inferiority of other races, the West has extended its claim to political and cultural sovereignty over the East, the East could not but mobilize its own will to defend itself. Rivalry with the West began, and since the old Eastern spirituality had fallen into twilight and decadence, the East eventually absorbed its fill of Western mentality, which it yet felt as unspirituality. It was as if one man met another who wished to impress him with the retort: "Wait a moment; I will show you that whatever you can do, I will soon do better." But Western intellectualism, no matter whether it was concerned with technical, industrial or social questions, was bound to become something quite different in the East. There it was absorbed by the cloud of the old spirituality, which became charged with it, as if with electricity. Sinister thunder-clouds, from which at any moment lightning may flash and rolling thunder rumble, have been the result. The East is today engaged in demonstrating to the West the soullessness and inhumanity of intellectualism. While it may ultimately make a more radical use than the West itself of the thought-forms originally conceived in the West, it will furnish the West with ever clearer proofs that utilitarian cleverness is better adapted to falsifying the truth than to finding it.

Thus we are faced with a paradoxical situation. The West confronts

the problems of the modern world without ideas, because intellectualism is not equal to these problems. The West falls back on so-called
"practical" experience, especially in financial matters, although it is
precisely this "practical" experience which has failed and has created the
present chaos and tension. Against this, the East makes use of the
Western intellectualism which it has absorbed to maintain, with religious impetuosity, ideas and goals which, because they no longer
reckon with the true nature of Man, threaten to unleash cosmic conflagration. Even though another catastrophic war be avoided, we can
never settle down peacefully between the extremes into which East
and West are driving each other: on the one side, an attempt to
"manage" without ideas except belief in money and power; and on the
other, ideological fanaticism, aggravated by unchecked application of
the cleverness learnt from the West. What has become of the impulse
of the middle region? Will Christianity, which is supposed to know
Christ as the "Golden Mean" of the world, allow itself to be led astray?
Will it perhaps even throw in its lot with one of the two parties?

When the first Creation rose from the mists of the Flood, the miracle
of the rainbow was set in the sky as the sign of the covenant between
God and Man. The figure of the great Guardian of the Threshold
also contains this sign. When amid woes and catastrophes the second
Creation, within Earth and mankind, forces its way to the light, the
rainbow must shine above it, too. It is the sign of Man's strength of
heart, which is able to establish the golden mean between the element
of Will in the fiery feet and the cloud-like spirituality of Thought in
the head. Once more the rainbow is the sign of the Covenant.
Through the strength of the middle region the polar opposites which
would otherwise clash can find a way to co-operation and mutual
give-and-take. The "rainbow" men who can bring the peace of the
world are not confined to the geographical middle of the world.
Wherever the Christian apocalyptic impulse is active, the sign of the
Covenant appears. A warmth of heart not squandered in an egotistical
religious life as an end in itself, but penetrating the whole of human
nature towards both poles, can produce a harmonious triad: a Christ-
filled Feeling, between a Christ-filled Thinking illumined by wisdom,
and a Christ-filled Willing, inspired by love.

Mankind's Guardian of the Threshold was revealed to the Seer John
in picture, word and being, one after the other. After this cosmic
figure had risen before the Imaginative consciousness, the faculty of
Inspiration heard him speak. He "cried with a loud voice as when a

84

lion roareth" (x, 3). This resounding cry finds a sevenfold cosmic echo: seven thunders answer him. It is as though yet another sphere wished to join in the sound of the Trumpets. John understands the new word of revelation and prepares to write down what the seven thunders evoked by the Angel's cry have uttered. Then he is instructed to leave still sealed what is sounded in the cosmos as a secret for the future. The Angel of the Threshold can nevertheless calculate the result. That the thunders answered him in this way is to him a sign and proof that the time is now quite ripe. He now proclaims a solemn oath: "That there should be time no longer . . . that the mystery of God should be finished" (x, 6–7).* In Goethe's fairy tale of *The Green Snake and the Beautiful Lily*, an exact parallel can be found to the stern oath of the Angel. After three secrets have been revealed, and the Snake has whispered the fourth into his ear, the Old Man with the Lamp in the subterranean rock-temple, can utter the cry of liberation: "The time has come." Likewise, when the thunder has boomed out the revealing echo to his question, the Angel of the Threshold can give the password for the fulfilment to begin.

From Imagination and Inspiration the great encounter with the Guardian advances to the stage of Intuition: the Angel gives a share in the substance of his own being, and thus offers his contribution to the fulfilment he has solemnly proclaimed. The little book which he holds open in his hand he gives to John who, in obedience to a spiritual instruction, has asked for it. He accompanies the action with the words, "Take it and eat it up." And John experiences what the Angel foretold: in his mouth the little book tastes sweet as honey, but it "makes his belly bitter": it permeates his whole being with transforming force (x, 9 and 10). When humanity reaches the threshold of the spiritual world, Man has only one choice, of remaining behind and plunging into ruin, or of absorbing spiritual content into himself in quite a new way, which demands of him a transformation of his whole being, and precisely thereby gives him strength for inner progress.

How do we learn to assimilate into our being the Book offered us, in accordance with the purposes of the Angel of the Threshold? In the little open book, the first of the basic apocalyptic pictures reaches us in an altered form: the heavenly Book which was closed at first with Seven Seals. Now we are already in the realm of the second basic

---

* Literally, the beginning of the oath runs: "There will be no more time." This is a solemn and emphatic way of saying what in ordinary language would be expressed as: "There is no time to lose," "there is no more time."

picture: the heavenly Altar which forms a background to the Trumpet blasts. So in a sense it is before the cosmic Altar that the Angel gives us the Book to eat. Book and Altar meet. Everything spiritual that we accept as doctrine and knowledge will penetrate and transform our whole nature when we learn to combine thinking and devotion, inspiration and reverence, when the celebration at the altar becomes a source of our seeking for knowledge. The synthesis of knowing and believing, Book and Altar, flowing from the intuitive element of the great Angel, involves a severe test of sincerity both from science and religion. Side by side with Book and Altar; as if in anticipation of the Seven Vials of Wrath, the third basic picture appears: the Temple. The Seer is instructed to measure the Temple and the Altar, and to distinguish strictly between the Temple and the Forecourt: "There was given me a reed like unto a rod, and a voice spoke unto me saying: Rise and measure the Temple of God and the Altar, and them that worship therein. But the court which is without the Temple, leave out, and measure it not, for it is given unto the Gentiles."

Humanity cannot approach the Threshold without taking stock of its beliefs and drawing up a balance sheet of religious life. The relentless question must be faced with complete sincerity, how far mankind has outgrown the forecourt of pre-Christian times and traditions and advanced to the Temple building of real Christian life. It is not difficult today to see the golden measuring rod with which invisible hands are at work measuring Temple and Altar. The thin veneer of nominal Christianity is cracking, and paganism which has uneasily slumbered for centuries beneath the surface of so-called Christian culture, raises its giant head.

Confronted with a Western Christianity adulterated by intellectualism and materialism, the Asiatic continent remembers its own ancient traditions. And if every now and then a wave of Germanic or Celtic "renaissance" sweeps through Europe, one cannot simply dismiss these nostalgic attempts to revive the pre-Christian spiritual life of Northern Europe as foolish or childish. They reveal a longing for cosmic wisdom and cosmic spirituality which finds no satisfaction in ecclesiastical Christianity. Even within the precincts of the Christian Churches themselves pre-Christian content and method continue to stifle the seed of true Christianity, since the magic of Egypt and Rome has never been completely overcome in Roman Catholicism, nor the spell of the Old Testament in Protestantism. Will the "forecourt" ultimately prove itself mightier than the Temple itself?

The Revelation of St. John contains no illusory optimism. It knows that when the time for balancing accounts has come, there will be no occasion for self-satisfaction. The measuring of the Temple is the signal for the opening of a tragic Mystery Drama. In the hour of profoundest need, the king summons his two strongest heroes to fight for him, and lo, both fall in battle: "I will call up my two witnesses . . . the two olive trees and the two candlesticks standing before the God of the Earth . . . and the beast which ascendeth out of the bottomless pit shall make war against them and kill them. And their dead bodies shall lie in the streets of the great city" (xi, 3-8).

Where previously the two pillars of the feet of the Angel of mankind stood, two human figures emerge. In them the spiritual life of the whole world has taken on human shape. The human mind has applied itself at all times in two directions. From the pyramids of Egypt and Babylon to the universities and factories of today, *Science and Technology* has issued from the endeavour to understand and to master the forces of Nature. On the other hand, in *Religion and Art* man has cultivated his connection with the world of the spirit. The Genius of humanity carries in His hands two torches, one directed towards Earth, the other towards Heaven. Between the Tree of Knowledge and the Tree of Life stands the Lord of the Earth.

By slight indications the Apocalypse makes human countenances appear from these two trees of the spiritual life of humanity. In saying that the two witnesses are endowed with authority "to turn water into blood", it points to the figure of Moses; and by ascribing to them "power to shut Heaven", it calls up the figure of Elijah. When, in Egypt, Moses turned water into blood, he was not performing a gruesome miracle. Rather, through his agency the great change of consciousness whose threshold mankind had then reached was accomplished in awe-inspiring visions: the descent from the dream regions of cosmic oceans into the blood of its own inner being. Moses brought men down to Earth—the Egyptians by the Plagues, his own people by the stone tablets of the Ten Commandments. He was the leader into that mental condition in which the dreams and visions of the past were replaced by abstract thought and ego-consciousness. Neither was Elijah working miracles when, before Ahab, he shut up the heavens and announced the period of drought, nor, after the triumph over the priests of Baal, when on Mount Carmel he called up the rain-clouds. In the picture of drought and rain the speech or silence of higher worlds is indicated. Whether Heaven bestows revelations, or keeps its sluice-gates closed, is manifested through men of God like Elijah, who regulate the connection between mankind and Heaven.

Moses looks back into the past, and describes the Creation of earthly existence. What has come into being lies before his receptive gaze Elijah looks prophetically into the future; he is the minister of the divine evolutionary will. Moses is the guide to thinking and knowing, Elijah to believing and seeing. And when the disciples on Mount Tabor perceived the transfigured Christ between Moses and Elijah, they saw in Him the Genius of Mankind, between the polar currents of the spiritual life of humanity. They saw the Lord of the Earth between His two Witnesses.

The powers of the bottomless pit rise up against the two Witnesses. The drama of the martyrdom of the two Witnesses and their subsequent resurrection is compressed into a few verses of the Apocalypse. But the same theme has been amply developed in Teuton mythology in the "Völuspa" section of the Edda. Wala's Song of "the Twilight of the Gods" describes the same events. Only the names are different; the characters are the same. The trouble caused on the Earth by Loki's clan, the offspring of the pit, grows till it is unbearable. Finally, the strongest of the Gods themselves confront the enemy on the battlefield. Two pairs of Warriors come forward. The Midgard snake, the devilish many-headed monster, is opposed by the god Thor, wielding the hammer; but he is unable to conquer. The two opponents kill each other, and from their flowing life-blood leap the flames of the cosmic conflagration. Wotan, the Father of the gods, himself confronts the Wolf Fenris, the cold, satanic power of darkness. But Wotan fails to win the victory. He succumbs; and the Wolf, his teeth gleaming, is left triumphantly alone. Had Widar, the great unrecognized son of Wotan, not been there, the fate of the Earth and mankind would have fallen under the Satanic power for ever. Some day, however, so the Edda predicts, Widar will come forth from concealment and will avenge his father on the Fenris-Wolf. The important correspondence between the vision of the Apocalypse and that of the Edda is emphasized through other apocalyptic fragments of ancient times. In the "*Muspilli*"—one of the oldest documents in Old German from the time of Charlemagne—the place of Thor is taken by Elijah, through association with the prophecy that the Second Coming of Christ would be preceded, not only by Antichrist, but by a new activity of Elijah:

"This I heard the philosophers say—
That Antichrist with Elijah will fight.
The assassin is armed and the strife begins.

The champions are so mighty, the cause so immense . . .
Antichrist supports the enemy,
Indeed Satan who will destroy him . . .
And many believe, who are men of God,
That if Elijah is hurt in fight
And his blood trickles into the Earth,
The hills will burn down, no tree will escape;
In the glow of the heavens the sea will dry up,
The moon will plunge downwards, the Earth will be burnt.
No stone will remain."

The second pair of warriors is referred to again in the short New Testament Epistle of St. Jude, and indeed in such a way that here too we find the bridge from the Apocalypse to the Edda. As if in passing, we are shown an enigmatic, exciting scene: the Archangel Michael is contending with the power of Satan for the body of Moses. This is the moment when the Wolf Fenris triumphs over the body of Wotan, and yet must already defend himself from the power of Widar, son of the gods, who has attacked him from above. Whether the Apocalypse and the Epistle of St. Jude are speaking of the body of Moses, or the Edda is speaking of the body of Wotan, it is the same pictorial truth. Wotan, as giver of the Runes, corresponds to Moses as the author of the Commandments: both were inaugurators of knowledge resulting from thought. The body of thought is the subject of dispute between Widar and the Wolf, between Michael and Satan.

In recent times, drawing from the intimate familiarity of the Russian soul with the Revelation of St. John, the Russian philosopher Vladimir Soloviev, in his *Short Story of Antichrist*, has contributed to this theme a boldly prophetic vision of the future. In Europe of the twenty-first century, which has just shaken off a Mongolian government lasting ten years, a man rises to the highest position as leader. Equipped with great gifts of genius, and through a boundless self-love, he sees himself as the fulfilment of the prophecy of the Second Coming of Christ. In the thirty-third year of his life, he goes through an inner crisis and a strange outward experience, from which he emerges completely transformed. A spirit of uncurbed pride causes him henceforth to hate Christ, and to despise Him as profoundly inferior to himself. He is chosen as President for Life of the United States of Europe; eventually, however, all the continents of the Earth combine to pay him homage as the Emperor of the World. After the solution of the social problem by the "Equality of Universal Satisfaction", he turns to the religious question, and summons the Christians, who are very much reduced in number, to a general ecclesiastical council in Jerusalem. Assisted by his chancellor, the black magician Apollonius, he presides over the Council and demands from all three groups—Roman Catholic, Greek Orthodox, and Protestant—fantastic promises of never-failing recognition of his authority. The great majority submit to Antichrist; only a small handful resist. The aged Elder, John, the determined leader of the Eastern Church, requires of the Emperor that he should confess Christ. The magician, standing by the ruler of the world, causes a dark cloud to rise, and kills with a flash of lightning the first of the faithful Witnesses. When the Pope, in the name of the still steadfast Roman Catholics, pronounces sentence of excommunication against Antichrist, a stroke of lightning from Apollonius strikes him also to the ground. Filled with horror, the Christians encircle the two corpses. Ernst Pauli, professor of theology and leader of the Protestants, exhorts them to courage. Apollonius is installed by the Emperor as the new Pope, and inaugurates an era of ecclesiastical power and magnificence accompanied by the most incredible miracles. After a few days, an answer comes to the prayers of the little group gathered round the bodies of the Two Witnesses in the region of the Mount of Olives: the breath of life returns to them. Through the impression made by this miraculous resurrection the union of the Churches is consummated; they must now find their own way, apart from all secular power.

Although Soloviev confines the Antichrist to one man, and the Witnesses to the representatives of two concrete denominations, we can yet recognize something of the style and tension of the Apocalypse in this present-day eschatology. It is true of Antichrist, as well as of the kingdom of God, that one cannot actually say of it, Lo here, or lo there. It is an omnipresent world power, which appears in countless forms, not only where the name of Christ is combated or shunned. Similarly the work of the Two Witnesses cannot be identified with ecclesiastical movements. The picture of the two corpses in the streets of the city called "the spiritual Sodom and Egypt" reveals a much more fundamental and comprehensive tragedy: lifeless Science and lifeless Religion. Both the secular culture of Thinking and Knowing, which has long since outgrown the confines of ecclesiastical religious life, and also the sphere of Faith and Worship based on inheritance and tradition, are swept away: the former into a fictitious vitality of mechanism, which in reality spells death to the soul; the latter by the prevailing intellectualism of the age. The powers of the pit have extinguished the candles whose light once helped mankind to rise to the level of the Spirit.

One hope remains. The Apocalypse points to a time after three and a half days when the spirit of life from above will return to the dead bodies of the Witnesses. The Edda and St. Jude's Epistle speak of the decisive intervention of Widar—Michael. When humanity reaches the Threshold, when the great Sunrise dawns which the seventh Trumpet will bring with it, then there may come a cultural resurrection, a revival of Science and Religion. Science can be restored and redeemed through a "Science of the Invisible" which is alive because it enters into the supersensible realm which gives life to all things earthly. Thus the breath of life returns to the dead body of Science and the outward form of culture. Likewise, when the spirit-world draws nearer to mankind, endeavours will be made towards a religious renewal. Everywhere new reformations must be set on foot, whereby the spirit of life returns to the stiffening corpse of Religion.

The resurrection of Science has been given an impulse of great importance through the work of Rudolf Steiner. His was not a purely human brilliance. In him a man became the organ of a higher, helping power which desires to wrest the corpse of human Thinking and Knowing from the adversary, and to make it throb with new life. The "Spiritual Science" founded by Rudolf Steiner signifies an inroad into culture of the "Michael" powers. Already it has shown its living influence in many departments of knowledge and culture.

The victory thus won opens the way also to the resurrection of the second Witness. His death was indeed brought about mainly by the cold breath of rationalism and agnosticism. With Thinking, devotion can also rise from the dead; indeed, without the practice of devotion in freedom, knowledge itself can never rise above the material, external side of existence. The impulse to religious renewal which lives in The Christian Community offers a special contribution to the awakening of the second Witness. What The Christian Community presents is no new religious theory. As the bearer and preserver of a new ritual and sacramental organism appropriate to present-day consciousness, it regards itself as an historic *fact* in religious development. It would have been impossible to found it if human potentialities only had been at its disposal. A higher sphere collaborated and bestowed on it the spark of life.

Thus the hope of a new springtide and Easter, affecting civilization as a whole, mingles with the stormy trials and struggles which face mankind at the Threshold. Whether the path from Dying to Becoming is open will always be shown by the degree in which the polarity between the Two Witnesses has ceased to be an opposition. The separation of Knowledge and Faith was a symptom of decline and loss. Their harmonious collaboration would conjure up everywhere a shining reflection of what the three disciples saw on Mount Tabor: Moses and Elijah like the pillars of a gateway, through which Christ, as the central Sun, appears.

There are altars today which can stand the test of the golden measuring rod. The altars of the new Sacraments are like an omnipresent Mount Tabor, well-springs of cultural resurrection. As in ancient times, cult again produces culture. Every time the Sacrament is celebrated, the miracle is accomplished whereby the tragic Twilight of the Gods is turned into Salvation. At one side of the altar the Gospel is proclaimed which, newly understood, is an elixir of life for lifeless Thinking: we see Moses, the one Witness, rise to new life. At the other side of the altar, devotion rises up, like incense, as response to the divine word. Devotion and worship are aroused from a new source; and Elijah, the other Witness, rises from the Tomb. The risen Lord of the Earth reveals Himself, and the risen Witnesses stand, one at His right hand, and the other at His left. Civilization receives from the altar the seed of living Knowledge and renewed Faith.

VII

MICHAEL AND THE BEASTS FROM
THE ABYSS:
THE DOUBLE FACE OF EVIL

THE TWELFTH AND THIRTEENTH CHAPTERS

IT is not so very long ago that an essential claim of Christianity to superiority over the pre-Christian religions was based on the fact that Christianity was thought to be free from mythology. This attitude has greatly changed in recent times. And as a matter of fact the assumption is not true. The Christian religion is by no means without mythology. In a sense, Christianity is even the climax and consummation of all mythology.

True, the sphere of pictorial vision out of which mythology arises remains undeveloped and misunderstood so long as Christian thought does not broaden out and rise to the level on which it becomes apocalyptic, and can comprehend the Revelation of St. John as an organic part of essential Christianity. In this last book of the New Testament Christian "mythology" is developed in all its greatness and fullness. In their concluding document, the scriptures of the New Testament offer a key to the understanding of world and destiny for times such as ours which grow into mythological dimensions. Once the Revelation of St. John is discovered and mastered, there will be no longer any need to look back to the mythologies of long-past ages, at the expense of Christianity.

However, a fundamental difference must be observed between pre-Christian and Christian mythology. The Old Testament, the basic example of all religious documents of the pre-Christian era, begins with a myth. The pictures of Genesis, the Myth of Creation at the beginning of the Bible, are followed by the books of the Old Covenant, which as they continue, lead increasingly out of the realm of God into the realm of humanity. In the New Testament it is otherwise. The myth stands at the end. Mythology forms the peak, the crown of all that precedes it. All pre-Christian mythology, whether in the Old Testament, or among the Egyptians, Babylonians, Greeks or Teutons, is retrospective; it is the dreamlike memory of ancient

93

times, when the destinies of men and gods were intertwined. Far beyond the capacity of personal recollection, the Seers who gave life to the myths among their peoples, remembered to the very beginning of all evolution. They looked back to the times in which the Gods not only fashioned the world, but were still active among men and guests at their tables. In contrast to this, the Christian myth as it is revealed in the Apocalypse of St. John is prophetic, previsionary, future-bearing. Instead of dream-like retrospection, an active knocking at the door of the future is practised, a rending of the veil before the mysteries which are only to be fully uncovered and realized in future aeons.

There is another important difference between pre-Christian and Christian mythology. The myths of the past are the last fruits of the old vision which humanity possessed in its childhood stage. The mythologies of the pre-Christian era are in themselves a conclusive proof that thousands of years ago mankind was clairvoyant, and lived in a completely different consciousness, much more pictorial than the abstract conceptual consciousness of the modern age. At the beginning of time, men were able to perceive supersensible Beings in the realms of Nature. All ancient mythology issued from these gradually fading, dream-interwoven visions of divine Beings in the starry Heavens and in earthly Nature. After the final extinction of the old clairvoyance, an extinction essential for the development of a waking day-mind and the experience of freedom, an interval of intellectualism had to come, which considered itself superior to mythology as being synonymous with superstition. The lost visionary capacities of ancient times were no longer known. The Apocalypse springs from new faculties of the soul. St. John's power as a Seer represents a new beginning. It was the first fruit of a new vision at a higher, more conscious stage. Intimacy with the Revelation of St. John, in which for the first time the new vision appears fully developed, can become the most wonderful stimulus for the seed of a new consciousness, which is quickening in modern souls today, and is pushing chaotically towards the light. The spiritual Sun shining from the Apocalypse can ripen the new powers of clairvoyant perception in a healthy Christian manner.

At the apex of the book, at the seventh Trumpet, Christian mythology is revealed on a grand scale. As spectators of the drama in Chapters 12 and 13 we perceive the very heart of the myth of Christianity. In three figures in particular, age-old conceptions of the

Gods are collected, and reborn. The first portent visible in Heaven is a Woman clothed with the Sun, the Moon under her feet, her head crowned with twelve stars. She is about to give birth to a child. The second figure is the Dragon, who lies in wait before the Woman. The third figure is the Archangel Michael, who with his hosts conquers the Dragon and his train.

The vision of a Queen of Heaven, a great divine Mother who gives birth to her child (or already carries it on her arm), did not begin with the Christmas story. This picture is a universal possession of all the races of the Earth. In ancient Egypt men looked up to Isis, who bears the Horus child; the Greeks paid homage to Demeter, the great Mother in Eleusis; and when they represented the goddess with an ear of corn in her hand, signifying that all creation on the earthly globe is her child, then Demeter-Ceres appeared only as a variation of the heavenly Mother carrying the Child in her arms. Celtic Europe, too, had its Madonna. Thus in the Grotto of Chartres, which later became the crypt of the Cathedral, the picture of the *Virgo Paritura* has been venerated from pre-Christian times, the Virgin who is to bring forth a Child. Even in the Far East, the picture of the Virgin-mother with the Child is known everywhere. With unearthly tenderness the Kwannon-figures of Eastern Asia touch our souls.* In short, the pictures of the Christian Madonna by Raphael and other painters would not be fully understood if they were assumed to represent only the historic figure of Mary, and not also the cosmic archetype which is a universal constituent of the myth of humanity.

The second figure, which represents a quintessence of countless mythological motifs, is that of the Dragon, a formless horror in fiery red, at the feet of the Woman. He is eager to carry off and devour the child as soon as it is born. Again, all ancient races share this picture. The Babylonians in their myth of Creation spoke of the world-snake, Tiamat, which emerges from the abyss beneath all creation, threatening humanity new-born from the womb of the cosmic mother. Among the Egyptians this dragon-figure is called Typhon; by the Greeks Python. The dragon Python threateningly approaches Leto, who has conceived a child by the father of the gods, and is about to bring forth her son Apollo. The Revelation of St. John says that the Child is "caught up unto God and to His throne" in safety from the Dragon; and similarly, the Greek myth describes Leto being rescued from the Dragon on the rocky island Delos, where she can bear her divine

* A wealth of suggestive material is contained in *Maria im Fernen Osten*, by Richard Karutz.

Child. The Egyptians also relate that Isis gave birth to Horus in a remote solitude, to which she had been withdrawn as a protection from the dragon Typhon.

In the figure of the archangel Michael, the Apocalypse shows the radiant victor over the Dragon who was also familiar, under different names, to the mythological vision of all races. The Babylonians called the conqueror of the dragon Marduk; the Indians, Indra; the Persians, Mithras; the Greeks, Apollo; and finally in the Teutonic mythology the dragon-slayer Siegfried appears as a belated Michael figure, the last of the Nordic Initiates. Within the Christian tradition itself, the early Christian figure of St. George is venerated as a human reflection of the heavenly destroyer of the Dragon, and is therefore taken as the patron saint of all Christian knighthood.

But the most striking parallel to the dramatic myth described in Chapter 12 of the Apocalypse is not found in any mythology, but in the quiet historical human events of Christmas. When Mary gave birth to her Son in Bethlehem, and carried Him on her arm, the heavenly picture which was living in all ages as a cosmic truth was projected into the sphere of humanity. Even the Dragon, the adversary lying in wait, is contained in the Christmas story, and confronts us in human shape as Herod. He must be there because the Mystery drama, hitherto enacted in the Cosmos, now descends to Earth. As in the mythical drama the Dragon wishes to devour the Child when it is born, so in the historical drama Herod plans to kill the Child. And the flight into Egypt is the earthly, human parallel to the incident in the heavenly drama, when the woman flees into the wilderness to protect the Child from the devouring Dragon.

It is the *myth of the human soul* which is revealed here, in the heart of the Apocalypse. The Woman in Heaven, who appeared to the writer, was seen by the clairvoyant souls of the ancient peoples and described as the Heavenly Mother, because in this picture the World Soul itself appears. Our whole Cosmos, to which not only the Earth, but Sun, Moon and Stars belong, may be compared to a human being. Like a human being, the Cosmos also has a soul. We see the body of the Cosmos with our physical eyes, although we cannot survey it as a whole. We are, ourselves, too tiny a part of it to have a comprehensive view of its total form, and to recognize all the details as members of its body. The soul that dwells in this cosmic body, the World Soul, is not visible to our physical eyes. The intuition of the clairvoyant pre-Christian peoples once saw it in the picture of the Heavenly Woman, and eventually it appeared to the Seer John, the first to attain the new faculty of vision. In the Revelation of St. John, we divine the time when humanity, under the sign of the Heavenly Mother, will be able again to open the spiritual, supersensory eye.

The great gift and secret of human existence consists of the fact that every individual man, however tiny a part of the whole Cosmos he may be, bears in his human soul a copy of the World Soul. Every human soul is a microcosm corresponding to the macrocosmic divine Mother, the soul of the world. We look into this picture as into a heavenly mirror of our own being, and read from it what God thought when He called souls into existence, in the Cosmos as well as in Man.

The Woman in Heaven appears as a wonderful three-fold organism. Her whole being is illumined by the rays of the Sun, in which she is enfolded as in a garment. Under her feet is the Moon, and upon her head she wears the Stars as a crown. The World Soul has Thinking, Feeling and Willing, just as we men possess the triad of Thinking in the head, of Feeling in our heart, of Willing in the limbs. That the Woman in Heaven appears clothed with the Sun means that where the heart is, a Sun should be always shining. Materialistic observation of Nature would have us believe that the Sun which we see in the sky is nothing but a ball of glowing, burning matter, moving through the universe. But really the Sun is the visible indication of the heart of the world. If the Sun in the macrocosm corresponds to the heart in the human microcosm, it follows that our heart is ordained to be a Sun. However trivial and sentimental such words may sound, the advice, "Have sunshine in your heart" does, nevertheless—when set against a sufficiently large background—point to a truth. It touches on a cosmic secret.

The silver crescent of the Moon is the chalice in which the Sun rests. It is the symbol of the will which serves the heart. The Sun is the content; the Moon the vessel.

And the World Soul has thoughts too: the Woman in Heaven wears on her head the crown of twelve stars. When we look up to the stars in the night sky, the thoughts of the World Soul appear before our contemplative gaze. The stars are not just gaseous bodies, so many light-years away from us. They are the crown on the head of the World Soul.

Through reading the Apocalypse we cease to speak superficially of Sun, Moon and Stars. We begin to recognize in them the cosmic pictures of Thinking, Feeling and Willing. And we rise to the realization of our own mission when we recognize the connection of World Soul and human soul with Sun, Moon and Stars.

Dramatic tension now enters into the tranquil picture of the World Soul. The fiery red Dragon rises up, the powers of the pit lie in wait for the decisive moment of metamorphosis, for the birth of the Child. Out of the "eternal feminine" of the Cosmos, the male principle, the cosmic ego, is to be born. The Cosmos itself grows beyond that which is only soul, when it concentrates all that is spiritual into a kind of core in the soul. At this moment the Dragon stirs.

The pictures of the Apocalypse are arranged in large and small cycles, in macrocosmic and microcosmic proportions and relationships. The picture of the Woman clothed with the Sun, who gives birth to her son, also refers to phases of evolution. Whenever the world enters into a great new cycle, when a new aeon begins, the cosmic Mother in Heaven becomes pregnant, and out of the womb of her soul, amid birth pangs, the genius of a new Creation is born. On one special occasion in the long course of human evolution, a child was born in Heaven when the "ego" awakened for the first time in humanity. At that moment a fundamental transformation in the soul and spirit of humanity occurred.* At that time the soul-element, the primal feminine principle of humanity, was endowed with the primal masculine element, the ego-form, the potential of spiritual individuality. The masculine ego of humanity was born from the maternal womb of the soul. Then, however, something happened which can be better grasped in the pictures of the Christian myth than by definitions. When the human soul gave birth to the Child, when the soul contracted into a Self, the Child was separated from the Mother. For protection from cosmic dangers, the human ego was withdrawn from human souls. A cosmic "flight into Egypt" took place. The divine Guides of the World safeguarded the delicate Spirit Ego which had formed in the soul region of mankind. The Apocalypse says that the Child "was caught up unto God and to His Throne". At the same time the Woman in Heaven, who has become a mother, is directed to flee into the wilderness. The Child is transferred to the heights of the Spirit; the Mother must forsake the heavenly sphere to which she has hitherto belonged, and descend into the wilderness of life on the physical Earth.

The Apocalypse teaches a profound secret about the human being when it speaks of the cosmic flight into Egypt and the wafting of

* According to the teaching of Anthroposophical Spiritual Science this took place in the middle of the "Atlantean" epoch. c.f. footnote on page 73.

the Child to the Throne of God. When the ego formed itself, it was not immediately left in the place where, later on, it was destined to be. As a protection against the powers of the pit, it must be withdrawn for a time to the spiritual spheres. Thus the evolution of an ego has indeed begun; but our true egos hover above us, they are not yet present in us. What mankind has been able to achieve is the ego-*form*. We are no longer merely buoyant souls; we have received the stamp of stability. Each of us has begun to acquire the imprint of his own personality, his own ego. Today, however, the stage of forming and concentrating has passed its zenith. We are beginning to suffer from the feeling that we are confined within strict frontiers, within the stiff armour of our egohood; we *suffer* from self-centredness. Hence we can estimate what the third figure in the central apocalyptic drama, the Archangel Michael, stands for.

Just as the Woman in Heaven is the picture of the eternal feminine, so the figure of the Archangel Michael represents the eternal masculine principle in cosmic evolution. The male Child which the Woman brings forth is a spiritual seed. In him appears the masculine principle of the spiritual human ego. But it is not yet fully grown; it cannot yet go its own independent way. A divine Spirit acts vicariously for it. The Archangel is the representative and deputy of the future human ego. To follow him means contact with the spheres in which our own true ego dwells.

The trials of the soul are not ended through Michael's victory over the Dragon. On the contrary, not until then do the tests really begin. The pictures unrolled before us are the archetypal tragedy; the very principle of tragedy is revealed. How is it that Michael contends against the Dragon *in Heaven*? How does the adversary come to be in Heaven? The old shallow, dualistic conception maintains that God is in Heaven, and the Devil is in Hell; but this is a very serious error. At the beginning of the *Book of Job*, which we may call the biblical *Faust*, we witness a conversation between the Lord God and Satan concerning Job: "Now there was a day when the sons of God came to present themselves before the Lord, and Satan came also among them." The Lord asks Satan: "Whence comest thou?" The adversary answers: "I have wandered over all the countries of the Earth." "Then have you not come across my servant Job?" Then Satan comes forward eagerly as the accuser of Job; he cannot say enough to disparage him. Finally he asks and obtains permission to torment him to the utmost, to strike him down and persecute him.

To our intense astonishment we must perceive that God has faith in men and therefore gives the Devil free scope, as though to say: "Only try; you won't succeed!"

Goethe adopts this idea in the introduction to his *Faust*, the *Prologue in Heaven*. The sons of God come on the scene: the Archangels Raphael, Gabriel and Michael. Mephistopheles is there, too, in the midst of them; we see the Adversary also as a dweller in Heaven. A similar conversation ensues. The Lord allows Mephisto to persecute Faust with all his strength. God has faith in Man.

> "Then very well, it shall be left to you!
> Divert this spirit from his fountain-head . . .
> And stand ashamed when then you must admit:
> A good man in his worst distress,
> Is fully conscious of the proper path."

That God has more faith in Man, that he has greater confidence in him than the Devil has—this is the hidden basis of all tragedy. The Gods concede that the greater a man is, so much the harder the trials, sufferings and losses into which he is plunged; they are certain that he will only come forth from them riper and richer. With the consent and will of the Godhead, Man has to face the powers of evil.

When the Dragon first makes his appearance, he belongs to the company of Heaven. But it is in Heaven that he and his hosts are overthrown and cast out by Michael and his Angels. The powers of the Adversary are removed from Heaven and cast down to Earth. The Heavens rejoice because the Dragon has been thrust out. On Earth, however, there is lamentation. "Woe to the inhabiters of the Earth and of the sea, for the Devil is come down unto you, having great wrath." The Earth is the wilderness into which the Woman in Heaven had to flee. The Child is caught up and rescued, but what becomes of the Mother who has fled to Earth? The same divine will which at first protected the Mother and Child now permits the soul to be threatened and opposed by demonic powers. The confidence of the Godhead in the soul of humanity takes effect, and the archetypal tragedy is worked out. The seventh Trumpet, in which this drama is enacted, is at the same time the third Woe. In consequence of Michael's victory the human soul must now fight with the powers of the pit. The age of tranquillity is past: the adversaries are arrayed against Man, with the permission of the Gods. But in all difficulties and struggles which have to be faced on Earth, there is the consolation that the opponent has already been vanquished in Heaven, that his back has actually been broken. Nevertheless this consolation makes sense only if it is coupled with an increase of courage and readiness to fight. On Earth the victory must still be won by Man.

For approximately 70 years we have been living in a characteristic "Michael" age. In about 1500 the learned abbot Trithemius of Sponheim and his disciple Agrippa of Nettesheim published an "Archangel Calendar" which in its principal content has been confirmed by Rudolf Steiner as a result of spiritual research. In regular cycles seven archangels follow each other as leaders of historic periods: Gabriel, Michael, Oriphiel, Anael, Sachariel, Raphael, Samael. Each period lasts approximately as many years as a year has days. Each archangel makes his imprint on humanity during his reign. In 1879 Gabriel, the Archangel of the Moon, was replaced by Michael, the Archangel of the Sun. From about the middle of the nineteenth century actual fighting took place in the spiritual world. This fighting cast its dark shadows into life on earth, because the vanquished armies of the Dragon fell to the earth and continued their fight in the sphere of human life. (This is the supersensible background for the catastrophic descent which, for example, the cultural life of Central Europe suffered, when it dropped from the sunlit heights of the Goethean age to the dark planes of gross materialism.)

It is of great importance in the general structure of the Apocalypse, that at the apex of the book, in its exact centre and heartpiece, at the sound of the seventh Trumpet, the name of the archangel Michael is mentioned. Here the Apocalypse surrenders its central secret. It discloses itself as a Michael book. Although he is not called anywhere else by name, Michael moves through the whole book. He is the producer in the cosmic drama, its moving spirit.

The sequence of the seasons of the natural year offers each autumn a wonderful introduction into the quality and mood of the archangel. At the threshold of autumn we celebrate the Festival of St. Michael and all Angels. It is a revealing moment. September is still filled with the afterglow of summer. The mature beauty of harvest-time surrounds us. In that month the sun passes through the sign of the Virgin. At that moment the apocalyptic image of the Woman clothed with the Sun is realized in the sky. Later, in November, the sun passes into Scorpio. The world has become bare, homeless, cold. The colours have vanished. In the sky the sign of the dragon rules. The season of Michaelmas lies in between. Then the sun is in the Scales. The archangel, holding the scales, intervenes between Virgo and Scorpio, between the Woman and the Dragon. The Michael power of balance prevails in the battle between angels and demons. A conscious crossing of the threshold of autumn every year makes us partakers of the drama which the Apocalypse depicts in the 12th chapter.

When Evil appears first, it is concentrated in the figure of the Dragon. Subsequently, however, it rises up in the form of *two* beasts (Chapter xiii). The Dragon cast out by Michael returns from the abyss twofold. The Seer stands at the boundary of the two worlds, on the shore between land and sea. There he sees a monster rise out of the sea, a beast with seven heads and ten horns. Out of the solid land he sees another beast come up. It seems insignificant and could be mistaken for a lamb. It is the two-horned Beast, hard as steel. The apocalyptic pictures are conceived as in constant movement; one arises from another just as, in a kaleidoscope, a new pattern is formed by movement and transformation out of the preceding one. The transition from the picture of the Dragon in Chapter 12 to the twofold Beast in Chapter 13 is similar to the way the pictures of the fourfold heavenly Beasts in Chapter 4 led to the picture of the Lamb in Chapter 5. When we beheld the Four Living Creatures we were witnesses of a synthesis: the four became one. The Lamb appeared as a concentration and aggregate of the Four Creatures. Now, when we see the demonic beast rise out of the abyss we are, inversely, spectators of an analytical transformation: a transition takes place from unity to duality. Evil appears in its double character. If we are prepared to continue the struggle on Earth, of which the first Act was fought out in Heaven by the hosts of Michael, we find ourselves engaged in a war on two fronts.

The duality of the animal figures is significantly connected with the pictures of Chapter 10. There, in the midst of cosmic storms, the great Angel appears whose countenance shines like the Sun, and whose strong feet span like pillars both land and sea. We mentioned that this vision appears when mankind reaches the threshold of the spiritual world. A gateway is then formed which must be passed through. Now, at the very place on which the Angel stands with his feet, the two Beasts rise out of the abyss. Where the foot of the Angel stands on the ocean, the snake-like monster with the seven heads and ten horns appears; and where the Angel sets his foot on dry land, the grim and gloomy two-horned Beast arises. Mankind cannot reach the threshold of the spiritual world without meeting the two demonic adversaries at the gate; the dual face of Evil is immediately seen. The powers on both sides which prevent mankind from crossing the threshold are revealed. Hence, at the beginning of new supersensible experience, a clear knowledge of the dual nature of Evil is imperative. The Apocalypse gives this knowledge in the form of pictures.

The twofold Beast is another piece of ancient mythology reborn. Greek mythology knew the double face of Evil. It describes the journeys of Odysseus as the wanderings of a human soul, and shows us how ultimately the hero must find his way between Scylla and Charybdis. He must face the dangers of the shattering rocks as well as of the treacherous maelstrom. But Scylla and Charybdis are not merely cliffs and whirlpools; they are supersensible hostile forces which avail themselves of external dangers to destroy the traveller.

The Old Testament calls the two Beasts in which the dual figure of Evil appears, Leviathan and Behemoth. In the apocryphal writings of the Old Testament, we find exact parallels to Chapter 13 of the Apocalypse. In the sixtieth chapter of the Book of Enoch, handed down in Greek and Syriac, we read, "And on that day were two monsters parted, a female monster named Leviathan, to dwell in the abysses of the ocean over the fountains of the waters. But the male is named Behemoth, who occupied with his breast a vast wilderness named Dûidâin . . . and I besought the other Angel that he should show me the might of those monsters, how they were parted on one day and cast, the one into the abysses of the sea, and the other on to the dry land of the wilderness." The twofold Beast appears also at the end of the Book of Job. Job has withstood all the trials of suffering, and thereby has eventually reached the portal of the spiritual world. Here he is told: "Behold now Behemoth . . . his bones are as strong as pieces of brass; his frame is as bars of iron." So the two-horned Beast is described here as a cold demonic machine, a soulless form, crushing and mangling all creation with its claws and teeth. Then Job hears the words, "Knowest thou Leviathan? Out of his mouth go burning torches, and sparks of fire leap out. Out of his nostrils goeth smoke, as out of a seething pot or cauldron. His breath kindleth coals . . . his heart is as firm as a stone, yea, as hard as the nether mill-stone." In the same degree as Behemoth is cold, so is Leviathan hot and glowing. The most puzzling part of it is that, concerning Behemoth, Job is told, "He is the beginning [A.V. "chief"] of the ways of God." This can surely only mean that where these two Beasts appear, there is the threshold. Here the ways of men cease, and the ways of God begin.

The Beasts, however, wish to hinder Man from setting foot over the threshold.

Teutonic mythology recognizes the same duality in the powers of the Adversary. It describes the Midgard snake and the Fenris wolf—the hot and the cold Beasts. In the New Testament, too, this important distinction is implied. The powers of Evil are referred to by two different names. The power which, in the Apocalypse, comes up out of the sea, is in the Gospels named Diabolos, the Devil, while the Beast that rises from the land is called Satan. It is therefore only a restatement appropriate for modern days of an earlier well-established knowledge, when in the Spiritual Science of Rudolf Steiner the distinction is made (utilizing old names) between the "Luciferic" (diabolos) and the "Ahrimanic" (satanas) principles. This agrees with the pictorial wisdom of the Apocalypse: the seven-headed, ten-horned Beast is the Luciferic power; the two-horned Beast, the Ahrimanic. And from the pictorial detail we learn that the Luciferic danger threatens us in the sea of emotions: the first Beast comes up out of the ocean; the Ahrimanic danger threatens from the environment of earthly life: the second Beast rises from the dry land. The relationship then is this: the temptations of the hot, Luciferic demonry assail us in the inward personal life of the individual, whereas the cold Ahrimanic corruption operates more as social evil in the impersonal relationships of civilization.*

The Luciferic power which comes up out of the sea affects an air of superiority. It bears seven heads and ten horns. It lives in the passions of vanity, ambition, pride and lust for power. Wherever the soul is not governed by the ego, or controlled by the Spirit, Lucifer rules: this is the danger of *soul without spirit*. All moral aberrations have their roots here. The Apocalypse describes how the whole world "wonders after" this Beast, and gives credence to its bombastic words. People under Luciferic influence easily make a great impression on the world around them. Many are willing to fall on their knees at once before "the tall, dark stranger" who promises excitement when life has become monotonous and dull. Before the scintillating brilliance of Luciferic greatness, they imagine they have at last met real Life among so much that is dead. Lucifer is usually very "successful"!

This Beast, we are told, has names of blasphemies upon his heads. Clever mockery and cynicism are natural qualities of the Luciferic character. Lucifer causes Man to feel himself a god; humility and

* Cf. also footnote on page 58.

religious devotion are thrust into the background. Religion in particular is too unassuming, not nearly brilliant enough. The splendour of superficial "genius" prevents quiet contemplation of the deeper strata of existence, and life is wrapped in a fog of illusion and fantasy.

Now an enigmatic detail is added: one of the seven heads of the Beast suffers a deadly wound; but this is healed. What subtle secret is hidden in this picture? May it be this, that if someone has "a good conceit of himself", he is usually a weak soul? Behind Luciferic ostentation, the poverty of the inner life is hidden. A strong character can afford to go his unassuming way; but the weak character must always advertise himself. Lucifer thrives on the inferiority complex: this is the wound which the Beast has on one of its heads!

How is it that the wound is healed? The inferiority complex is, to use a fashionable expression, repressed. It seems to have disappeared; but has it really? Repressed complexes, the left-over, unused parts of rejected experience, the tasks left unfulfilled; these continue to give trouble in the hidden depths of human nature. They are, so to speak, thrust down into the physical sphere. This causes those outcrops of our nature which the Apocalypse describes as *horns*; they represent conditions of tension leading in the end to sclerotic and cancerous diseases. True, the wound may appear to be closed within the soul, but the effects of Luciferic impulses appear in the bodily system. Leviathan-Lucifer takes over from the Dragon the preponderance of horns over heads. Everything immoral, since it is based on unacknowledged weakness of the soul, must poison human nature with the hardening that prevents real spiritual development.

Against the imposing external successes of the followers of the Beast stands the principle of those who overcome the Luciferic temptation: "Here is the patience and the faith of the saints. If any man have an ear, let him hear." Those who quietly go their way, sustained by an active faith in the Spirit, can afford to have patience. They can maintain their confidence when they have fallen into tribulation or are facing death. "He that leadeth into captivity shall go into captivity; he that killeth with the sword, must be killed with the sword." That the mere wielding of power invariably recoils on him who wields it, is a cosmic law which, sooner or later, is always fulfilled. Luciferic methods have a boomerang effect. But he who shapes his life patiently and faithfully out of inner strength need not fear setbacks. He moves forward, and though the steps may be short each step leads nearer to the spiritual goal.

The Ahrimanic Adversary which rises up from the solid land is much more dangerous than the Beast that rises out of the tossing sea. It gives itself no grand airs; it is unassuming, and appears as innocent as a lamb. But in its two horns it carries a deadly weapon. The first Beast is the archetypal figure of *soul without spirit*; the second Beast is the archetype of *spirit without soul*. It is the greatest danger of our age. It could almost be described as the distinctive feature of our epoch.

The "Ahrimanic" forces dominate today. They have replaced the predominance of the "Luciferic" forces of earlier times. They work in the cold, machine-driven mentality of our age of mechanization. It would be foolish to ignore the achievements of technical science; but only with what we may call the incorruptible, apocalyptic eye can the Ahrimanic forces be recognized and so adjusted that they are beneficial and not destructive to human progress. Life teaches through bitter experience that we cannot remain truly human without advancing as much inwardly as we have progressed outwardly.

In the materialistic conception of the world, which is supposed to be scientifically guaranteed, and which, even in the Churches, has been accepted as a matter of course as the foundation of life, the power of Evil most characteristic of our time is active. Therefore we can only come to terms with the Ahrimanic power through the liberation of Thinking, through a break-through to a fully human, spiritual thinking which takes into account supersensible realities. Time will show that the work of Rudolf Steiner has been a unique contribution to this end, a "Michael" achievement of the highest rank, a spiritual victory whereby the errors of the materialistic picture of the world have been uprooted and overcome. A world-picture which does not include supersensible reality is a lie. The Ahrimanic power has successfully managed to hypnotize us into accepting the outside of the world as the whole world. Under this hypnosis souls have become morally weak. Following on the track of Ahriman, Lucifer richly finds his prey. A materialistic world conception undermines the conscience of men. Within the great collective streamlined "systems" into which human society has been forced, according to the principles of mechanization— the "total state", "total war", etc.—human life has lost its value. Eventually, it is not even noticed when life is bestially destroyed.

The Apocalypse tells us that the second Beast does not itself come fully into sight, but remains prudently in the background, the better to betray mankind to the first Beast, the Luciferic moral evil. The two-horned Beast throws dust into the eyes of men. By the display of intellectual brilliance which yet grasps only the material structure of the world, it builds up a great Luciferic illusion. The world-conception of materialism is itself the image of the Beast, because it regards Man himself as an animal. Thus Man is cunningly alienated from his true being and destiny. The dogma of Man's animal origin and of the predestination of his character through heredity must eventually lead to men losing, even in their faces, the nobility of the human being, and to bearing on their brow the mark of the Beast. It is then only one step further that the mark of the Beast shall be imprinted on Man's right hand. Not only theory but practice falls prey to Ahriman. When we read that ultimately no one who does not bear the mark of the Beast may any longer buy or sell, the terrifying perspective of an economic system completely under the power of Ahriman opens before us. All that is left of genuine humanity and brotherliness is suppressed by the vast technical coercion of super-organizations, and the brutality of utilitarianism and unrestricted egoism.

At the very end, the Two-Horned Beast is distinguished by a secret number, the naming of which is expressly prepared for by the announcement of a particular mystery: "Here is wisdom. Let him that hath understanding consider the number of the Beast; for it is the number of a man: and his number is 666." This apocalyptic hieroglyph has been much puzzled over. Commentators have often thought they have found a solution when they discovered that the name of the Roman Emperor Nero, if spelt with Hebrew letters, could be read as the number 666. But this number, too, has a spiritual, qualitative significance. The seventh Trumpet sounds: a cycle according to the number Seven comes to an end. This suggests reading the number 666, not in the decimal system, but in a system of Sevens. In the system of apocalyptic numbering, a new group of numbers begins, not at every tenth, but at every seventh number. 6 is followed by 10, 66 by 100. So, instead of six hundred and sixty-six, we must read 6-6-6. The figure which stands in front according to the decimal system in a number with three digits, indicates, in the rhythm of Seven, the place which is reached within the large cycle. The middle figure gives the position of the middle, and the last that of the small cycle. Thus the number 6-6-6 signifies that everywhere, in the large and also in the middle and the small cycles, the last stage before the Seven is reached—the stage of completion. It is only necessary to count a single unit further in the small cycle, to make the first of the largest cycles complete. Thus the number stands directly before the great completion, which in the decimal system is called a thousand. So the number 666 occupies in the system of Seven the same position as the number 999 in the decimal system. It is the number of the last moment. It says: Listen, it is one minute to twelve o'clock; there is only one moment more before it is too late. Thus understood, the number 666 is part of Ahriman's satanic cunning: the Two-horned Beast generates in mankind the illusion of desperate hurry. The whip cracks, the hunt is up: No Time! Not an instant to lose! Today we pride ourselves on being votaries of "Tempo" and look down scornfully on those who have not yet allowed themselves to be drawn into the fierce speed and pace of modern life. But in reality, this crack of the whip is a monstrous lie. It can easily be proved that in ages of quieter living much more was achieved, even quantitatively, than is usually the case today. The suggestion of breathless hurry is a specially crafty trick of Ahriman's. In no more effectual way can people be held back and led away from spiritual interests. If one gives way to it, there is no time left for inward quiet and peace to commune with oneself. "Having time" is not a question of the clock, but of inner tranquillity. If a man loses his spiritual tranquillity, he loses not only time, but his real connection with life, and in the end, himself. Only through citizenship in the quiet kingdom of the spirit is it possible to escape the Ahrimanic seduction and self-robbery expressed in the number 666.

If we take seriously the knowledge of the twofold aspect of Evil, as the Apocalypse teaches it in Chapter 13 in continuation of the picture of the war in Heaven, we realize the misleading nature of the traditional dualism which simply places Good and Evil in opposition to each other. Evil does not stand opposite to Good, but opposite another Evil. Where then do we find Good? We find it as the Golden Mean, the balance between the extremes of the two Adversaries. That is why the Archangel Michael is often represented with the scales in his hand. The formula of the Golden Mean, coined by the ethical teaching of Greece, is more than an expression of expediency; it is the key to the mysteries of morality. We must be *served* by Lucifer—without the Luciferic power we should have no artistic gifts and no art—and we must also be *served* by Ahriman, for we need material science and technology. But Man must stand in the middle, holding by the bridle, so to speak, the Beasts from the abyss in both directions. The problem of Evil, too, requires for its understanding a "trinitarian" approach. The divine secret of the Three in One, once grasped in its significance, will solve all the riddles of existence, including that of Evil. What is the Power that stands in the middle, and shows us the way between the Devil and Satan, between Lucifer and Ahriman? The phrase of the "Golden" Mean is itself worth its weight in gold: in the middle is the Sun of the Spirit, the Golden Heart of the world, Christ Himself. And Michael is the Archangel of the Sun, and of Christ, because, as servant of the Golden Balance, he helps to overcome the Beasts.

What, then, can the drama in the twelfth and thirteenth chapters of the Apocalypse teach us who live in the midst of the spiritual conflict of the present age? We must enter into the rôle of the Woman who goes into the wilderness. In the wilderness of solitude and reflection the help of Michael will be granted to us. The wings of the Eagle will be given us. It is not without reason that the Eagle is the sign of John, the Evangelist and Seer. The eagle-wings of the apocalyptic vision carry us to high watch-towers, from which we obtain a comprehensive view of our age, and a knowledge of the spiritual aspect of world events. Thus we are enabled to triumph over Lucifer's *soul-realm-without-spirit*, and Ahriman's *spirituality-without-soul*. We can aspire to a spirit-filled soul and an ensouled spirituality, and can attain to inward sovereignty in both directions. This is the religion of tranquillity in the Golden Mean, the sphere of Christ. It is at the same time the sphere of Michael. Although it appears paradoxical, to cultivate tranquillity is the most effective way of combating Evil. We must not always be aggressive when we fight the spiritual battle. Out of a soul filled with peace a new morality is born. At last we can do what we have resolved to do; we no longer lag behind our purposes. Our souls have become weak through Ahriman; through tranquil living in the Golden Mean they can become strong again. This is the battle which has to be fought today. Before the description in the Revelation of St. John of Michael's fight with the Dragon, we read in the last verse of Chapter 11, "The Temple of God was opened in Heaven and there was seen the ark of his Testament." Before the Altar of the open Temple the battles are waged whereby victory is won over the powers of Evil. With the sphere of the Altar behind us, we shall be able to deal with Evil in the spirit of Christ.

VIII

TRUMPETS AND HARPS:
THE DIVIDING OF SPIRITS

THE FOURTEENTH AND FIFTEENTH CHAPTERS

THE seventh Trumpet has brought us to the peak of the apocalyptic drama. As it dies away, new vistas open. The key of the symphony changes completely. Where the devilry of the twofold Beast from the abyss has just been displayed, now a beneficent prospect opens before our souls which breathe freely once more.

The seventh and last Trumpet has always been linked with the Last Judgement. This is largely due to St. Paul. Using the apocalyptic vocabulary as a matter of course, he says of the seventh Trumpet: "In a moment, in the twinkling of an eye, at the last trump: for the trumpet shall sound, and the dead shall be raised incorruptible, and we shall be changed" (I Corinthians xv, 52). It has been supposed that the seventh Trumpet is the finale of world history. When it sounds, the Judge of the world will appear and, through His final verdict, not only will souls be destined to eternal bliss or eternal damnation, but our whole world will be brought to an end. Is it true that the Last Trump means the end of all evolution? Does it usher in the "Day of Judgement" in the sense of the "Last Day"?

The Revelation of St. John answers this question through its architectural structure. Evolution by no means comes to an end with the seventh Trumpet. The Apocalypse goes on, and the prospect opens on to a still wider cycle of epochs: the outpouring of the seven Vials of Wrath and all that is released through them. In the cyclical course of world evolution many "Judgement Days" occur. Our rigid ideas of dogma and tradition must be melted in the living stream of the Apocalypse. The Revelation of St. John teaches us to think in terms of cycles and thus to take part in the constant movement of its pictures.

However, although the seventh Trumpet does not signify the end of the world, it is nevertheless accompanied by a "Last Judgement". In the midst of the stream of time it leads mankind to decisions which assume an ever more final character. The sixth Trumpet has already introduced the motif of the Threshold. The pillars on which the

Angel stands form the gateway which has to be passed through. At this Threshold begins the great divide. Mankind is divided into the one section that succeeds in crossing the Threshold, and the other which evades the Threshold, thus binding itself all the more closely to the material world. Then, when the seventh Trumpet sounds, when the dawn of the spiritual Sun which the Trumpet heralds with cosmic music hastens to its fulfilment, a further duality is added to the duality of the two pillars. In Chapter 11, the two Witnesses, who are also called the "two Candlesticks", make their appearance. Two spirit figures with the characteristics of Moses and Elijah appear as living gate-posts at the Threshold of decision. Finally, we saw how the two Beasts from the abyss rose up at this same spot, and tried to hinder those who were crossing the Threshold. At this point the Apocalypse could say, as in the Book of Job, "Here is the beginning of the ways of God." Where mankind arrives at the Threshold of the spiritual world, the Day of Judgement dawns for human ways. Mankind must acquire strength to set foot on the paths of God beyond the Threshold. In the midst of things temporal the daybreak of eternity appears. That section of mankind which is able to stride victoriously past the demonic guardians of the Threshold finds eternity in time; the other section enslaves itself to increasing corruption.

From this point, then, the change of key and mood can be understood which characterizes the transition from Chapters 12 and 13 to Chapters 14 and 15. We enter a sphere which is not empty of dramatic events, yet is at the same time filled with divine peace. We gaze into the land beyond the Threshold.

At this point we should more than ever avoid reading the Apocalypse in the usual theological or ecclesiastical style. We must yield to the transmutation of images, to the changing nature of their cosmic art; we must read pictorially, or better still, musically. We have heard the thrilling symphony of the Trumpets. Each Trumpet blast has released visions of evolutionary phases and trials. Finally, with its powerful strains, the seventh Trumpet rends the veil before the drama of Michael's conflict in heaven, which must be continued on earth after the Adversary has been hurled down to it. With this the crescendo has reached its height. The apocalyptic symphony of the heavenly trumpets, resounding when accounts are to be presented to an old world—so that all that is rotten crumbles away and leaves room for the building up of a new world—all this can be enhanced no further; a significant diminuendo begins. In the second verse of Chapter 14 we read: "I heard a voice from Heaven as the voice of many waters, and as the voice of a great thunder; and I heard the voice of hárpers, harping with their harps." The Trumpets have played their part in the great world orchestra; the conductor beckons them to retire. For a little while they are still heard in the distance. Thunder rolls through the cosmos like an echo dying away. But no silence follows. Enchanting strains are heard. As quiet undertones they were already sounding before, but they had been drowned by the noise of the Trumpets. It is the sound of harps. By its very wording the Apocalypse describes the cosmic lyrical element of the strains of the harp so musically that the human words seem to imitate the sound. In a half sentence, the harp motif occurs three times in succession:

". . . as of harpers harping with their harps."

The continuous gentle undertone in the music of the Cosmos now penetrates to our ears. We share in the creative counterpoint which sounds while the Gods are building and weaving the world. The world is for ever being produced out of the Logos, out of the Word of God. In the inmost centre of the universe, the cosmic Word speaks like the music of a harp. The Voice from the inmost world becomes audible when the Trumpets withdraw. Nature offers a parable of this music when we hold a sea-shell to our ear. The murmuring undertone which we hear gives us an idea of the harp-like tones in the cosmic shell which we call our world. The humming of the loom of time, whereby the world comes into being as the robe of the Godhead, is pictured in the Apocalypse as the music of harps.

How misleading are the all too human ideas which are commonly adopted of the creation of the world by the "Word of God"! From the fatherly First Cause of the world, the creative Word rings forth into eternity. The Logos, the Word of God, is Himself a Being who from the very earliest beginnings has filled cosmic space with the sound of creation. As late as the Greek epoch, the ancient Mysteries taught their disciples to listen with the ear of the soul to the music of the spheres, to the harmony of the starry spaces. And when, in the Prologue of *Faust*, Goethe makes the Archangel say,

"The sun-orb sings, in emulation,
Mid brother-spheres, his ancient round . . ."

he continues to express the wisdom of the ancient world. The murmur of the sea-shell can charm us like a lasting echo of the primal sound, penetrating from the inner hearing to the outer.

In his lectures on *Egyptian Myths and Mysteries*, Rudolf Steiner traces the knowledge of the archetypal creative sound in the Vedas. It was known to the disciples of the Indian Mysteries as the "Primal Word Wha": "When the disciple rose into the higher spiritual world, he heard the Primal Word, for that world is a world of sound. There he heard the music of the seven planets. By means of the music of the spheres and the word of the spheres he perceived how the primal Spirit, Brahma, was articulated, through evolution, into the sevenfold chain of the planets; and this he heard from the *Primal Word Wha.* That was the name of the original note of Creation."

Just as sand is dispersed into the wonderful harmonic Chladnic figures if the plate on which it lies is made to sound, so in the primal beginning the planetary evolution of the earth was formed out of chaos, through the Word. Out of the pregnant silence the world came into being and, gradually, created beings dared to imitate the primal speech of the Creator. To the Word of God was added the word of Man. Then gradually the voice of the Creator was drowned by the voice of Creation. Noise began to stifle the persistent whisper of God.

If a speaker addresses an audience which listens quietly, he can say what he has to say quietly; he is speaking his own words. If, however, his hearers interrupt, and eventually many speak at the same time as he does, and raise their voices in order to drown his, then, if he is still determined to make himself heard, his speaking assumes a different character which emanates not from himself, but from his opponents. Thus in the evolution of the world, God's softly murmuring words of Creation have become the rolling thunder of the *Trumpets.* In them the voice of God is also to be heard. The soft stirring of the wind is changed into the crashing sounds of thunder and lightning. But behind and beneath the loud, penetrating word of warning, the word of Creation continues to sound. When the notes of the last Trumpet have died away, the music of the *Harps* becomes audible. The surviving prat of mankind shares the experience of Elijah who, after the noise of the earthquake and the fiery storm, heard the still small voice in which the inner word of the world was revealed to him.

Before the sound of the harps is introduced, a prospect is revealed at the beginning of Chapter 14 which is clearer and more hopeful than any other in the Revelation of St. John: "I looked, and lo a Lamb stood on the Mount Zion, and with him a hundred forty and four thousand, having his Father's name and the name of the Lamb written in their foreheads." Then the reference to the music of the harps is made, and the Seer John continues: "And the 144,000 sang as it were a new song before the throne, and before the four beasts, and the twenty-four elders, and no man could learn that song save the 144,000."

The cosmic tempests have passed. Lightning has cleared all impurities from the air. Open expanses shine in the distance. We stand at the Threshold and look through the Portal. Even a first glance is only possible after all the preceding trials have been withstood. The section of humanity which has kept pace with evolution is gathered on the top of the holy mountain, because it has been able to cross the Threshold. For the second time the Lamb is active. The first deed of the Lamb was the opening of the Book with the Seven Seals. Only one single force in the universe was capable of setting in motion the process of Creation: the power of sacrifice and love. It was the Christ Himself who, as the "Lamb of God", started the wheels of Creation by means of a first cosmic sacrificial deed. The second sacrifice of the Lamb took place on Golgotha: through the Death on the Cross, the Lamb of God—the highest Divine Being who has walked on Earth in human form—intervened in the destiny of Creation, which was in danger of sinking into the abyss. The destiny of mankind was given an upward direction. Now as the sound of the seventh Trumpet dies away we stand at the Threshold of the spiritual future; we are permitted to see the birth of a new aeon. In this decisive moment of world-history, a divine sacrifice is again essential. A new intervention of the Christ in the course of Man's destiny must ensue through the sacrificial gift of His own Being, in the image of the Lamb. Can this be done? What sacrificial deed of Christ comes to the help of humanity, when it reaches the Threshold of the spiritual world?

The 144,000 assembled round the Lamb on Mount Zion are the future humanity whose hearts are turned to Christ. This humanity of the future is gathered round the Christ in a pattern of twelve times twelve. Every community of Christians should possess that cosmic comprehensiveness which characterized the fellowship of the twelve Apostles, in which each one was different from the others, each as it were an envoy from a different realm at the court of the King of Kings; a representative of one of the twelve cosmic potentialities of human nature, symbolized by the Zodiac. Whether a community is small, or whether it consists of a large number of members, speaking spiritually it numbers 12,000—that is, it bears within it the number of universal humanity which unites individual freedom with the spirit of community. When the separate communities unite into one combined assembly, which respects and maintains the individual character of the sections and itself attains universal completeness, remaining under the sign of the number 12, then the number becomes twelve times 12,000. The number 144,000 is the mathematical symbol of the community of all communities, built on the twin law of freedom and universal comprehensiveness, and hence filled by the spirit of Christ.

When it is said that the 144,000 gather round the Lamb on the summit of the holy Mount Zion, it is, of course, not the earthly hill in the south-west of Jerusalem that is meant, but the high plane on which the foundations of the heavenly Jerusalem are laid. Nevertheless, the nature and history of the earthly Mount Zion can familiarize us with the spiritual landscape of the heavenly mountain lying beyond the Threshold. It is not accidental that an earthly locality should appear as the picture of a spiritual place. The place of worship which in days of old crowned the now long overgrown or built-on heights of Zion, was an important central sanctuary, one of the very oldest Mystery centres of mankind. The site of the Temple which on Mount Moriah, the eastern hill, has for 3,000 years dominated the skyline of the city of Jerusalem—the centre of the world for Jews and Mohammedans—is also sacred. But infinitely more venerable is the second of the twin peaks, Mount Zion. The wide rocky plateau of the site of the Temple represents the lunar pole of Jerusalem. Mount Zion, surrounded by the atmosphere of age-old Mysteries, represents the pole of the Sun. The solar Mysteries of the earliest days, long before the history of Israel began, had their home on Mount Zion. From the grottoes of Mount Zion the priest king Melchizedec came to meet Abraham and to bestow on him bread and wine, the sacred elements of the solar Mysteries. It was here that David later built the first sanctuary of his people. And on the same spot, over David's tomb, the building was eventually erected which acquired such great significance for the birth of Christianity—the Coenaculum, where on Maundy Thursday Christ washed the feet of the disciples and dispensed bread and wine; where after Easter, for forty days, the disciples were vouchsafed intimate fellowship with the Risen Lord and where, on the morning of Pentecost, they received their apostolic charge. The Hall of the Last Supper on Mount Zion took the place of the Holy of Holies in Solomon's Temple. No longer the Ark of the Covenant behind the veil, but the Table bearing bread and wine was henceforth the place of the Throne of God, which John saw in the centre of the heavenly figures set in a new order. Hence the Hill of Zion, once the home of the oldest Sun Mysteries, and eventually the solemn scene of the foundation of the

Christian Mysteries, appears quite rightly in the Apocalypse as the earthly symbol of the spiritual place where the bearers of the future must assemble. On the summit of the holy mountain, irradiated by the crimson dawn heralding the Heavenly Jerusalem, those souls come together who recognize in Christ the holy Spirit of the Sun, Who offers Himself for us, just as the outward sun continually offers its warmth and light and life. The 144,000 on Mount Zion derive their life from the forces of the Sun of Christ. In the sign of the Lamb they have reached the maturity which has fitted them to become bearers of the future.

The Apocalypse describes the 144,000 as those "redeemed from the Earth" as "Virgins", and hence "first-fruits unto God and to the Lamb". They are those who have not escaped from their earthly tasks but have won through to a new purity and spirituality. The new Christian humanity appears to the apocalyptic vision as an immense choir. They sing the "new song" which no man could learn but themselves. They take part in the music which becomes audible when the Trumpets are silent. To the sounding of the cosmic Harps, the musical revelations of cosmic inwardness, they add the musical revelations of human inwardness. A two-part song of creation is intoned. Out of the music of the Harps, and the New Song, the new world is woven. The "New Song" not only contains but creates new life. It makes all things new. And for this it needs no special effort. The interplay of souls in the human race of the future, purified in Thinking, Feeling and Willing, is itself music. Their very Being is song. The thoughts which they think, the feelings which flow from their hearts, the resolutions formed by their will, are potential creations even before they are transformed into outward reality. In this Community, the creative power of the Word, possessed by the Word that was in the beginning, is born anew.

But while the Seer John discloses the vision of the founders of a new aeon, he does not refer us only to hopes of a distant future. Unless the seed is sown now there will never be any fruit. In the midst of a fear-ridden world, starved of ideas and spiritual nourishment, we must even now be on the way to the mountain-top. We must begin to tune in with the choir of singers who sing the New Song, which is the share of humanity in the "Let there be . . ." wherewith the Godhead creates the new world.

No sooner has the vision of the summit of the sacred Mountain faded, than the dramatic element again intervenes. Three Angels come forward, one after the other; they have a stern message to deliver.

The first Angel seems to begin by continuing the mood of redemption. He flies through the heights of Heaven with a Book in his hand: the *evangelium aeternum*, the "Everlasting Gospel". What does this indicate? We are to realize that at periods of great crisis, independent of outward changes, the atmosphere around human souls is changed. There is "something in the air". In the supersensible worlds, above the heads of men, a light is kindled and radiated to mankind. We recognize it as unwritten Holy Scripture. The "Everlasting Gospel" begins to take the place of the written Gospels. The letter of the Gospel loses its importance and becomes unessential. Traditional circles, which cannot imagine a genuine Christianity without the tangible book of the Bible, will feel very uncomfortable. They regard it as an irreparable misfortune that even in the churches familiarity with the Bible is rapidly decreasing, and that young people often no longer get to know the Gospels at all. The Apocalypse offers consolation for this, startling though it may seem. It shows that a time will come in which souls will be able to find, and must mature to the point of finding, the real Gospel, and this independently of the literal Bible; they will be able to read it, so to speak, directly out of the spiritual sphere.

For many it may be difficult to imagine that some day it will be possible to live in the Gospel without opening the actual Bible. Of course the wording of the four Gospels, as we have them today, will not be immediately legible in the spirit. But there will be a sphere of progressive spiritual perception. And if we may say it without being misunderstood, the Holy Scripture appearing in the spirit will be revealed backwards. Where the written New Testament ends, the "Everlasting Gospel" begins. The first book of the New Testament whose substance and meaning will be sensed will be the Revelation of St. John. This is "in the air" even today. Fundamentalism makes heavy weather of the Apocalypse. In its strange, unusual and difficult language it is an apparently insoluble problem. Nevertheless the Apocalypse is that part of the Everlasting Gospel which the Angel pours into the human sphere first of all. In a sense, all supersensible knowledge is part of the Apocalypse. In the long run spiritually receptive people will be quite at home in the realm of the supersensible. The events of our time, the destiny of the present age, will cause men to accustom themselves increasingly to supersensible matters, and thus to become familiar with the Apocalypse. It may be that different names and expressions will be used, but the number of those who are in living contact with the sphere of the Everlasting Gospel will increase. In this way many a man may meet the Christ, independently of traditional teaching. Perhaps at first he will not call the Being whose influence and presence he experiences by the name of Christ. He may even imagine himself to be an opponent of Christianity, because he knows traditional Christianity only in distorted forms. Nevertheless he may have made a genuine contact with the sphere of Christ. The times in which the Everlasting Gospel reaches mankind do not lie only in the distant future. The first beginnings are already here, only the scales of materialism still blind our eyes, and the platitudes with which even good people think stifle the tender seeds of the spirit in the depths of the soul. But the Angel with the Everlasting Gospel has already begun to fly through the heights of the Heavens, to make the Gospel message immediately alive through reviving it from within.

The Angel with the book in his hand offers comfort, but at the same time speaks very stern words. He cries, "The hour of his judgement is come." It seems that at this point in the Revelation of St. John, the idea of the "Last Judgement" appears after all. But precisely here it can be shown how far the Apocalypse is from the rigid dogma according to which the Last Judgement represents the catastrophic end of the world, establishing eternal unchangeable duration both of damnation and salvation. The original Greek of the Angel's cry leads to a more correct understanding, for the Greek word used is "crisis". The Angel announces the great Crisis.

This phrase has become very familiar today in the sense in which it was first used in medical language. The "crisis" in an illness is the decisive point at which it becomes apparent whether the patient will recover or not. Thus the "Judgement" is not the end, but the crisis for the world and mankind. It leads up to the crucial decision. All decisions assume a more definite character when the sphere of the Everlasting Gospel begins to influence human affairs, when the spiritual world comes so near that it can be read like an open book. With the approach of this sphere, the division of mankind takes place. It will bring to light who they are who refuse to heed the unmistakable message which is "in the air". Thus the crisis works itself out by its own momentum.

The second Angel now flies through the heights of Heaven. In him severity is the prevailing characteristic from the outset. He announces only one tremendous verdict: "Babylon is fallen, is fallen, that great city, because she made all nations drink of the wine of her fornication." For the first time the contrast to those who gathered round the Lamb on Mount Zion is clearly revealed. The dividing of spirits is at hand. The one section of mankind is carried up to the sacred summit, the other plunges into the depths of the abyss. A perspective is shown which acquires its final clarity at the end of the Apocalypse. Two great cities appear as pictures of the grouping of mankind. On the holy mount the city is built which comes down from Heaven. It is built by those who draw their nourishment from above, who so ally themselves with the forces of the Spirit that they can penetrate and transform with it all earthly things, even the material body. The heavenly Jerusalem is called the "Bride" because it represents that part of humanity which weds Spirit to Matter in purity. The other city sinks into the abyss. It is called the Whore of Babylon because it mingles, in a manner which is impure, the bodily element with soul and spirit. Instead of matter being transformed by the spirit, the spirit is defiled by the untransformed bodily element. The darkness over Babylon is the shadow cast by the light which dawns round the summit of the holy mountain.

When the third Angel flies through the heavens, the tension increases. This Angel pronounces an even severer judgement: "If any man worship the Beast and his image, and receive his mark in his forehead or in his hand, the same shall drink of the wine of the wrath of God . . . the smoke of their torment ascendeth up for ever and ever, and they have no rest day nor night." We should be mistaken if we regarded such pictures of the Judgement as only to be fulfilled in the future. The beginning of them is already here. We have said that the worship of the Beast, and of the image of the Beast, does not only occur where coarse moral offences are committed, but that the materialistic conception of the world itself is the Image of the Beast; for indeed, it understands the human being himself only in so far as he is akin to the beasts. It is generally assumed that through technical progress which, of course, is the fruit of material science, we shall be able to live more "human" lives. The reverse is true. We are in danger of dropping to the animal level. If we are honest we must admit that with the magnificent progress of technical science, we have really increased our trouble and decreased our time. Our technical achievements have begun to recoil on us—to begin with, on our nerves. What was intended to alleviate life, in fact compels us to live in sub-human, mechanized conditions—eventually indeed in a form of hell. Our civilization is magnificent in its control of natural laws and in the treatment and use of raw material, but it does not reckon with the true nature of Man. Man is run over by his own machines. This synthetic civilization must recoil upon us, because we are beings with soul and spirit, and need a truly human environment to live in. Mechanization extends the animal principle, for it turns men into automatic animals. The all-powerful machine tends to reduce Man to the level of the Beast, to print the Mark of the Beast on his brow and hand. When the Apocalypse says that the men with the Mark of the Beast will have no rest day or night, it prophesies a state of affairs which has largely come true already. Restlessness and nervousness are the firstfruits of a materialistic civilization. Thus the "Last Judgement" has already begun. It has already become an exceptional achievement if anyone succeeds in maintaining a state of inner peace and concentration. But only by wresting inward peace from the turmoil and pace of our civilization, and through achieving a union with the powers of a higher World, can we preserve our humanity.

Now follows another vision of supreme grandeur: "And I looked, and behold, a white cloud, and upon the cloud one sat like unto the Son of Man, having on His head a golden crown, and in His hand a sharp sickle." Suddenly the picture of the Second Coming of Christ appears. He comes on the clouds of Heaven, as promised in the Gospels, and He shows Himself in the form of the Son of Man, the Spirit-Man. The Second Coming of Christ takes place under the sign of the Ideal Man. His coming signifies both the salvation and the advancement of the spiritual nature of man.

This answers the question, what divine sacrifice is meant when for the second time the Lamb enters actively into the drama of the Apocalypse? The secret of the third Sacrifice of the Lamb is now revealed. The first Sacrifice of the Lamb was offered at the beginning of our earthly Cosmos, when the Son of God set Creation in motion through the sacrifice of His own Being. The second Sacrifice of the Lamb occurred when Christ died on the Cross. In the Apocalypse this is no longer explicitly referred to; Golgotha is taken for granted throughout. Now the third Divine Sacrifice is made. The world has again reached a point where it cannot find its future without intervention from above. This time the Christ does not again intervene in a physical incarnation, as He did two thousand years ago. The third Sacrifice of the Lamb occurs when, through the offering of His Divine cosmic nature, the Christ comes spiritually close to humanity. The Second Coming of Christ in the supersensible sphere—the sphere of the etheric life and formative forces symbolized in the picture of the cloud —is the outcome of the third great Divine Sacrifice.

And now it seems again as if the Revelation of St. John would confirm the traditional opinion that Christ returns as Judge of the world. The Christ who approaches mankind in His "etheric" form bears on His head the golden crown, and in His hand the sharp sickle. He brings the illuminating thoughts of God anew to mankind, but He is also prepared for the reaping of the world. Again three Angels come flying through the heavens. The composition of the chapter observes a wonderful symmetry: the summit of Mount Zion; then the three Angels flying through the heights of the heavens; again a great picture, Christ on the white cloud; then again the three Angels. The first Angel calls to the Son of Man on the cloud: "Thrust in thy sickle and reap, for the harvest of the Earth is ripe." And He who is enthroned on the cloud thrusts in His sharp sickle, and the Earth is reaped. Then the second Angel comes out of the Temple of Heaven. He carries a sharp pruning-knife in his hand. And the third Angel comes and calls to the second Angel: "Thrust in thy sharp knife, and gather the clusters of the vine of the Earth, for her grapes are fully ripe." And the second Angel cuts the grapes, and the blood flows forth over the Earth, and rises "even unto the horse bridles" so that the human armies on horseback have to wade through blood.

The Second Coming of Christ does indeed signify the Judgement of the world; but Christ Himself does not come as a Judge in the sense in which medieval dogma pictured Him. The Sun of Christ brings to light what is ripe and genuine on Earth, and what is of no use. In the pictures of the great Harvest the symbols of bread and wine are used. First the "earth" is harvested, the wheat is cut; that is, outward achievements are tested. Then the vine of humanity is harvested; that is, the inward achievements of Man are also brought to the test. The spiritual side of human civilization is judged. Only that is of value which the spiritual Sun has ripened, and which can become the bread and wine of eternal life. When progress is put to the test by invisible powers of Heaven, blood flows on Earth. For it is fundamentally men themselves who carry out the Judgement of the world. When the seventh Trumpet has sounded, a double realm of spiritual reality approaches mankind; the sphere of the Everlasting Gospel, and the sphere of the Second Coming of Christ. Both bring about decisions, and these become increasingly final. The great division proceeds apace. When the opened Book of Life confronts humanity, it will be shown who can read it, and who cannot. And when the Christ Himself approaches humanity, it will become clear who feels and sees Him, and who does not. Our attitude towards these realities in the super-sensible world decides our future, and these decisions make destiny and cannot be reversed.

In the middle of Chapter 14 it is said, "I heard a voice from heaven saying unto me, Write—Blessed are the dead which die in the Lord. Yea, saith the Spirit, that they may rest from their labours, and their works do follow them." We ask about the meaning of this passage. The next verse offers the solution: "I looked, and behold a white cloud, and upon the cloud one sat like unto the Son of Man." We begin to understand: the dead who are united with Christ are blessed for evermore, because the first dawning rays of Christ's Second Coming are already becoming visible in the realm of the dead. Among the souls of the dead who are now themselves in the spiritual sphere of the "cloud", in which Christ comes, the sunrise of His approach is perceived earlier than it can be by men incarnated on the Earth. Just as the watchman on the tower sees the sun rising above the horizon sooner than do those in the valley, so the souls in the kingdom of the dead obtain their share in the miracle of the Second Coming before people on earth can do so. From this passage we may surmise that the new Coming of Christ brings crisis and a dividing of spirits also into the realm of the dead. Only those souls which have died in the Lord, that is, those who have brought into the other world the fruits of a Christian life, are able to see the rise of the Sun which is Christ. What has been won and experienced on Earth of the nearness of Christ becomes, after death, the organ of the soul, the eye whereby the light of the Christ can be seen. Souls absorbed in materialism cannot see Christ, however near He may be. They are blind and groping in darkness. They are without light because their lamps are lacking oil. But the souls of those who in this earthly life have cared for the Christ will be blessed "from henceforth" at the dawning of Christ's Second Coming. They can begin to gather round the Lamb on the bright summit of the Holy Mountain, as the human race of the future. Paul also points to this secret: "For this we say unto you by the word of the Lord, that we which are alive and remain unto the Coming of the Lord shall not prevent (i.e. go before) them which are asleep. For the Lord Himself shall descend from heaven with a shout, with the voice of the Archangel, and with the trump of God; and the dead in Christ shall rise first. Then we which are alive and remain . . . shall meet the Lord in the air, and so shall we ever be with the Lord." Not until after the Sun of the Second Coming of Christ has made itself felt in the realm of the dead will its beams gradually find entrance also into the souls of men incarnated upon Earth.

Not only the dawn of redemption, but also the twilight of doom reaches first the realm of the dead. The addicts of materialism who close their eyes to the supersensible realities and mock at them, will at death enter into the very world the existence of which they contemptuously denied during their earthly life. Suddenly the foundation of their being fails them, since they had thought that on Earth they already knew and possessed the whole of existence. It is no longer so very difficult to imagine that a time is approaching when terrible suffering in the life after death will be the result of such materialist faith. Such souls will be tormented by a persistent sense of deprivation. They can no longer rest in matter as their accustomed element for life, and yet they are not extinguished as spirit among spirits; they suffer constant suffocation. The greater and more magical the power of materialism becomes on Earth, the more must life after death become a dark place for those souls who have lost themselves in it. The souls who, through the fruits of a Christian life, are able to see and receive the light of the new nearness of Christ, form their future destinies side by side with those who are not only incapable of any perception of light, but as a consequence of their estrangement from spirit in the life on Earth just finished, fall deeper and deeper into the strangling curse of darkness. The hell of materialism, however, does not exist only after death. It merely appears with more relentless clarity; whereas in earthly life it can still remain cloaked by self-deception and illusion.

In Chapter 15 a comforting glimpse into the sphere of Redemption is offered once more. The picture of the Holy Mountain is further developed: "And I saw as it were a sea of glass mingled with fire: and those that had gotten the victory over the Beast and the image of the Beast . . . stood on the sea of glass, having the Harps of God in their hands; and they sang the song of Moses, the servant of God, and the song of the Lamb." Once more the picture of a choir is presented: the Singers at the Sea of Glass. Yet the song sung by future humanity, as we now see it, no longer rings out only to the strains of cosmic harps played by divine Beings. The Singers at the Sea of Glass themselves carry harps in their hands.

The motif of the harp make its appearance in the Apocalypse three times. The harps first sound in the hands of Divine Beings at the beginning of earthly creation. When the Lamb opens the seals of the book of evolution so that the heavenly archetypes may flow from it and begin to solidify in earthly images, "the four beasts and the four and twenty elders fell down before the Lamb, having every one of them harps and golden vials full of odours . . . and they sang a new song" (v, 8 and 9). In sight of the Sea of Glass (iv, 6) into which the creation begins to crystallize out of the cosmic ocean, the Gods themselves cause the strains of the harps to sound. They sound for the second time when the Trumpets fall silent, and the music of the harps becomes audible as the divine undertone of the Cosmos. It is the 144,000 who then sing the new song to the accompaniment of the harps. Mankind of the future sings to the harps of the Gods. Now in the third passage it is Man himself who unites in his own being the musical instrument and the song. The strains of the harps and the new song both sound from the being of Man, just as, in the very beginning, both proceeded from the Divine Beings.

A dramatic element is interwoven however into the song of the new Creation which men may now sing. The Apocalypse indicates this by naming the hymn of the Singers at the Sea of Glass the "Song of Moses". An important event in the Old Testament is recalled. Moses led his people before the hostile armies of the Egyptians through the ford of the Red Sea. They could safely tread the path to the Promised Land, whereas their pursuers were engulfed by the waves. After their miraculous rescue Moses raised the song of thanksgiving. It is the first psalm in the history of the Old Testament. A dividing of spirits, on a small scale, preceded this "new song". Now the song of the Singers at the Sea of Glass sounds in the background of the great cosmic dividing of spirits. Those who are fit to join in the song pass safely through the ford, but waves have plunged into the abyss the section of mankind hostile to the spirit. Later, it will be said of those who have been thus overthrown that in them word and sound have died. The curse of animal dumbness lies upon them. "The voices of singers and harpers shall be no more heard in the great city" (xviii, 22). The song at the Sea of Glass is the cosmic octave of the psalm at the Red Sea.

It is a striking feature in the composition of the Revelation of St. John that the Sea of Glass appears here a second time. As the gaze of the Seer turned back to the primal divine womb of Creation—in the first picture of the Sea of Glass—he saw the sphere of the Earth just crystallizing out of Heaven, still possessing its virgin purity and transparence, not yet sunk into material density. Now, to the eye of the Seer looking into the far distant future this picture appears again. He perceives the new planetary condition into which the Earth will one day pass when it undergoes its great "dying and becoming". The new Earth, too, will spring like a pure crystal sphere from the ocean of becoming. But the sea of glass of the future differs from the one at the beginning; its pure crystals are mingled with fire. What the Apocalypse portrays here is poetically described by Novalis in his apocalyptic fairy tale.* He describes how, in the city of Arkturus which consists of milky blue ice-crystals, a mysterious reddish glow begins to illumine the alleys, and gradually emits ever brighter and stronger rays. The crystalline sea of the new Creation is not a cold world. It contains the whole warmth of the force of Love which human souls have practised and accumulated throughout the earthly cycles of time. The Love of Men is the blood circulation which warms the new planet.

The reddish glow which shines through the Sea of Glass confirms the earlier revelation of this beatific vision. Through the music of the harps in the hands of men, through the notes of the hymn which is sung from their hearts, the Sea of Glass comes into being. The magical power of the notes which no longer issue from the Gods as in the beginning, but now proceed from men, creates the new Earth. When, in the future, men reach the level of weaving and moulding the new Earth and the new Heaven through the music of their souls, then the warmth, the fire of love in hearts glowing for God, will be interwoven with the crystallizing process of evolution.

The lectures on the Revelation of St. John given by Rudolf Steiner in Nuremberg in 1908 contain concrete suggestions about the creative participation of the human spirit in the formation of the new world. In explaining the Seven Seals, Rudolf Steiner describes the future evolution of mankind as a progressive unsealing. Less and less will men be able to hide their true nature by dissimulation. Even in his outward physiognomy Man will bear the mark of the Beast or the sign of Christ. We are approaching an epoch when all that is within will lie open to the light of day. "Everything material will bear the stamp of the spirit; nothing, nothing at all, will then be such that it can be in any way disguised. Already in the preceding epoch nothing can be concealed from him who has the eye to see it. It will then no longer be possible to conceal thoughts either. Thought will no longer be a silent thought which can be hidden. When the soul thinks it will also cause the thought to sound outwardly" (Lecture 8). Thus when the Revelation of St. John speaks of the sound of the harps after the seventh Trumpet, it is pointing to the music of the spirit which will one day issue of itself from the advancing section of mankind.

* Cf. page 45.

We men have full authority over the word, but how sadly we misuse it! How often do we debase it to gossip, or indeed to lies. We forget that this is only possible because we cannot yet *see* thoughts. The more a new supersensible perception is born in humanity, the more fraud, dissimulation and lies lose their power. Mankind will begin to be divided into those who are smitten with animal dumbness on the one hand, and the "bearers of harps" on the other. The harp of spirituality will be the word-bearer of the future. We prepare our souls to become the harps of God by practising in our speech the music of silence. Whether a man is musical or not depends more on the ear than on the voice, and so we shall attain to the inner music the more we practise the art of listening. If we train our inner ear to hear the singing of the Angels, our own soul will itself become a harp on which the Higher Beings will play, and in our speech the "new song" will rise. It is our task and privilege, amidst the rolling Trumpet blasts of our age, to cherish in our souls the divine music of the harps.

IX

THE VIALS OF WRATH:
ANGER AND LOVE

As the Apocalypse prepares for the seven stages of the next cycle, the profound solemnity of the scene continues. Both before the opening of the Seals and before the sounding of the Trumpets a majestic pause was observed. But an urgent question was bound up with the silence before the Seals, and the stormy onrush of the new fundamental force ushered in by the Trumpets threatened to cut the second pause short and to take one's breath away. Now, however, the way is clear to fulfilment and perfection, and so the persistence of the solemn mood raises our hope of Salvation. The Temple in Heaven opens, with the Ark of the Covenant, the tabernacle of divine Self-witness; and out of the open Temple seven Angels proceed, clothed in pure white shining linen, their breasts girded with golden girdles. One of the Four Beasts gives the Seven Angels seven golden Vials, and the Temple is filled with the smoke of the incense of the glory and power of God (xv, 7 and 8). The seven angelic priestly figures carry the sacred vessels of the Temple out from the innermost Holy of Holies, ready to shed their contents over humanity. Surely blessing upon blessing must flow out over earthly existence from this divine activity. What else could issue from within the Temple but the overflowing gift of the Love of God? But just as our expectation was abruptly disappointed when the peaceful celebration of the Angel at the heavenly Altar released the blast of the Trumpets, so now we are thoroughly startled and cast down from the heights of blissful expectation; for the Golden Vials prove to be Vials of Wrath which only bring more appalling trials and disasters to mankind. As we come in this last great cycle, after Picture and Sound, to the outpouring of Divine Essence, we face the deepest, most poignant mystery of existence. An immense paradox, an apparently incomprehensible contrast between cause and effect needs to be deciphered. The cause is of Heaven; the effects seem to be of Hell.

The background of this profound mystery begins to be revealed when we consider that the trinity of focal pictures in the architectural structure of the Apocalypse is now complete. After the Book and the Altar, it is now the Temple from which the Seven Golden Vials are brought. In its dramatic Time-architecture the Apocalypse is built on the same ground plan as that which underlies the secret Space-architecture of Solomon's Temple. The builders of the Temple in Jerusalem copied its structure from the same archetypal sphere in which the Seer John beholds the apocalyptic drama. Book, Altar and Temple characterize the significance of the three chambers of the sacred building on Mount Moriah. The eastern portico (Elam) formed the passage from the forecourt to the interior of the Temple. This was the place of *teaching*; the wisdom of many centres of learning flowed together here as into a central sanctuary, and thus assumed the character of a sacrifice offered to God. In the vast middle chamber, the long house (Hekal), the *ceremonial* had its home. In the centre stood the altar on which the sacred fire burned and the incense was offered. Besides the seven-branched candlestick, the ceremonial fittings included the trumpets of the Jubilee year which were sounded every fifty years for the sacred Jubilee (from Jobel, meaning "trumpets"). The third and innermost chamber, the Holy of Holies (Debir), enshrined behind the closed curtain the very heart and being of the Temple: the *Mysteries* of the Presence of God; the divine answer to the sacrifice offered by Man.

Book, Altar and Temple which the Apocalypse presents as projections of the Picture, the Word and the Essence of the Higher World, are the constituent elements of all true religious life on Earth. Preaching carries the thought and the word of God, the content of the heavenly Book, into the thinking and speaking of mankind. Ritual makes all human activities receptive for the gracious and creative collaboration of higher worlds, by linking them with the mood and meaning of sacrifice at the Altar. But Religion is only complete when it includes Mysteries. Only through them does it reach beyond our world, and unite Earth with Heaven. But since on Good Friday "the veil of the Temple was rent in twain from the top to the bottom", they can no longer be actual "mysteries", in the sense that their content is kept secret. They are now "open secrets"; that is, access to them is free and no longer the privilege of a priesthood, or of a high priest. Since, however, they possess a divine spiritual content, which can at first only be surmised by Man's consciousness, they are at the same time always "in secret". In traditional Christian language the Greek word *mysterium* is rendered by the Latin word *sacramentum*. Ceremonial becomes Sacrament when in it "transubstantiation" answers to the "offertory"; when that which Man cannot achieve by his own strength is taken up, in reality, into the process of redemption. The Sacraments are the real Temple Mysteries, the gifts from the Holy of Holies in Heaven.

Here, where the Revelation of St. John fully attains to the sphere of Intuition, the Seven Angels bring out the Golden Vials, the sacramental vessels of the Holy of Holies. But how is it possible that the Seven Vials should prove to be dispensers of Wrath? Are the words of the first Epistle of St. John, "God is love, and he that dwelleth in love, dwelleth in God, and God in him," no longer valid in the sphere of Intuition? Should not the Seven Vessels, taken from the innermost dwelling-place of God, contain love upon love? Is it not, indeed, the angry God of the Old Testament who sends His messengers on their mission? With disconcerting force this problem insists on a solution.

We need to form fundamentally new ideas concerning the intercourse of Man with the Beings of a higher world. When a supersensible encounter is described in the New Testament, the Being from the spiritual world invariably addresses the human being first with the words, "Fear not!" So Gabriel speaks to Mary when he appears to her in Nazareth. So the angels speak to the shepherds at Bethlehem. Christ hailed the disciples with it when He appeared at night walking on the sea. Even the risen Lord had to say this first when He joined the group of disciples. And the figure of the Son of Man, before whom the Seer on Patmos falls to the ground as dead, accompanies with the same words the gesture with which He raises him. Why is this? Spiritual Beings do not appear externally to those who are permitted to meet them. Such meetings can be experienced only in the inmost soul. In most cases, when a Being from the spiritual worlds approaches we are not aware of it. But if we do become aware of it, the experience begins by being a severe trial, because we do not possess the strength simply to face the essential reality of the spirit. A first touch of the spirit always excites fear and awe; and it is not until we summon the inner courage which is at the same time the strength of faith, that the encounter becomes real. This strength is called upon by the words, "Fear not." But what happens when the supersensible world approaches and we do not notice it? It is very important for our age, in which relations between the supersensible and earthly world are changing so fundamentally, to realize that it is impossible to escape or shirk the effects of the approaching spiritual world. This will be just as impossible as to remain dry when out in the rain. When we understand this, we begin to understand the secret of the so-called Vials of Wrath.

To begin with, the New Testament text does not say "wrath" in this passage. It uses the word *thymos*, which means an impassioned movement of the soul. If we describe someone as having an impassioned nature, we generally mean that he has a choleric temperament. But we could just as well say of someone whose temperament is loving that he has an impassioned nature. Thus the apocalyptic word which describes the content of the Seven Golden Vials implies something exceedingly intense and full of warmth, which proceeds from God, but is not necessarily "wrath". It is one of the most profound Christian truths that the essence of God is Love. The Love of God, however, has nothing of the sentimental softness which is often linked with it in Christian circles. In the sense of the apocalyptic word *thymos*, we might say, Love is the passion, the vehemence of God. When, therefore, at the outpouring of the Seven Golden Vials unheard-of punishments are inflicted on mankind, this does not mean that God's Love has been changed into wrath. The Love of God remains identical in its essential force.

A brief survey of the stages of human evolution can illustrate the variations of the mystery of divine Love. In primeval times, when even the very first traces of personality were not yet awakened in the human being, the life of the nation, as of the individual, was lived in the realm of the divine Will and formed part of the destinies of the Gods. The fortunes and misfortunes of men followed the variations in the life of the supersensible Group Spirits which led them. Severe punishment was meted out only for transgression of the tribal laws. A new era began when, not yet for individual but for national life, a new principle made itself felt.

The significance of the Old Testament lies in the fact that it records the evolution of the race which became, in classic purity, the first bearer of this new principle. Freedom and egohood were to be developed in a special way, and thus the destiny of the race assumed prophetically the form of an "ego-destiny", such as that which the individual Ego-Man would assume later. At that stage of human evolution the race of the Old Testament became the "Chosen People"; it moved into the centre of spiritual world history and became the instrument of God's progressive Will, the object of God's love. This, however, was shown paradoxically in that the nation was led from one trial to another. In its early days it suffered the Egyptian exile, and at the peak of its spiritual evolution the Babylonian captivity. No longer does all go smoothly with the people who are under the guidance of the good Gods. From a definite moment in time, the saying held good for the life of the *nation*, "Whom the Lord loveth He chasteneth," while in the life of the *individual*, the *ancient* law of divine Love still remained largely in force. That can be clearly read from the commandment of Moses, "Honour thy father and thy mother that it may be well with thee and that thou mayest live long upon Earth." Only in the *national* destiny did that divine Love proclaim itself which wills that freedom should enter into human relationships. Trials and suffering result from the new form assumed by the love of God when it concedes and entrusts freedom and self-dependence to mankind.

Evolution reached a third stage when individual human beings also became mature enough to fight their way to freedom and the ego. Job, the great martyr of the Old Testament, is the first-born of the new law of destiny. The endless series of painful afflictions does not strike him as a series of punishments inflicted by an angry judge; the love and confidence of God are revealed in them. Henceforth many difficult destinies will be experienced in the lives of individuals as well as nations as a consequence of the love of God. Divine Love is revealed as severity, although in itself it is nothing but love. It is a far-seeing love. It does not bestow benefits which would keep men in a condition of immaturity; it aims at Man's freedom, and therefore releases him from the protective rule of direct guidance. Now the saying "Whom the Lord loveth He chasteneth" gains force for the individual also. But it must not be misunderstood as though God were a patriarchal father of a family who chastises his children when his love turns to wrath because of their bad behaviour.

The Revelation of St. John requires us, more than any other of the Biblical scriptures, to think of the love of God as a cosmic force and substance and not in terms of a human emotion. The sevenfold love of God is poured out as a heavenly flame, a burning fire. If this consuming fire meets with something that does not itself also burn with the fire of love, conflagrations arise, both great and small. Everything must burn to ashes which is not akin to the nature of divine Love. This secret of the self-giving of God is expressed in the words of Pater Ecstaticus at the end of Goethe's *Faust*. They are a striking expression of intuitive experience:

"Endless ecstatic fire,
Glow of the pure desire,
Pain of the pining breast,
Rapture of God possessed!
Arrows transpierce me,
Bludgeons so batter me,
Lightnings so shatter me,
That all of mortality's
Vain unrealities
Die, and the star above
Beam but Eternal Love!"

Divine Love can come to Earth thus as intended; but it needs souls able to receive what Heaven sends. At least a spark of the same fire of selfless love must glow in them. This glow is then strengthened and enhanced by the overflowing love of God. Otherwise the love arrives on Earth transformed into its opposite, becoming judgement of wrath, although there is no wrath in the nature of God.

This mysterious law gives an important key to the destinies of our own epoch. One might think that mankind is serving today the sternest sentence in world history, and yet it is simply the case that a division has arisen between the divine and the earthly world, while Intuition is flowing through the Cosmos as actual force and substance. Conditions on Earth are not ripe for its reception, and thus what is meant as divine Love reaches the Earth in the form of catastrophe; conflagrations of cosmic wrath are exactly what *men* make of the love of God. If we would understand the signs of the time apocalyptically, we could see—however incredible and paradoxical it may sound—that the love of God is being bestowed on mankind with tremendous power in a quite new fashion. Thus indeed it is no wonder that mankind should not immediately be able to accept what is intended for it.

The true Being of God dwells beyond the Threshold. The seventh Trumpet leads mankind to this Threshold. Under the law of the "Last Trump", the paths of men, coming to their end, must find the transition to the paths of God. The Being of God as He really is can be received by those who can cross the Threshold, ushered over by the Genius of Mankind who stands there as Guardian. To them the Seven Golden Vials, guarded by priestly Angels in the Holy of Holies of the Temple, are offered as the Vials of divine Love. But blindness and alienation keep mankind this side of the Threshold, although the veil is rent and the Temple stands open. Because Man will not come to God, God comes to Man. An age is dawning in which the super-sensible world will flow into the human world. In any case, the contents of the Seven Golden Vials are poured out, revealing the boundless generosity of God. But that part of their content which is spilt must turn into its opposite. In our day the world trembles beneath the forces which press in from the world of the supersensible. The more powerfully the love of God approaches, the more infinite must be the sum of trials and afflictions arising from its perversion, the changing of its intention into the reverse.

How can the content of the heavenly Vessels poured out among mankind by the Angels be received on Earth in the right way? In the midst of an unprepared humanity, possibilities of accepting this content in such a way that it remains what it is—the sevenfold Love of God—must be provided. It is the most important task of com-munities of Christians to protect and cherish those means by which the Seven Golden Vessels of Heaven are reflected on Earth. A Christianity appropriate to the Age, and a match for the dynamics of present world events, must be sacramental. The Seven Golden Vials of the heavenly Temple are the archetypes of the Seven Sacraments. Rightly understood, the Christian Sacraments correspond on earth to the Vials in heaven, and can absorb their celestial content into them-selves.

As we advance through the Seals and Trumpets to the Vials of Wrath, ritual and sacrament become more and more concentrated. It is not in conformity with the Cosmos, with the sphere of real archetypes and the will of the Creator, if the nature of the Altar and the Temple is not fully realized on Earth. Christianity, as the religion of the open Heaven, means life with the Altar and the open Temple in Heaven. In the circle of those who gather round the new altars* a sphere may evolve in which the deepest longings of our age may find fulfilment because super-earthly substance in its pure form, corresponding to the purpose of God's Love, may be present in it. Here the inner tranquillity, devotion and equanimity which have been lost among people of this Age can be acquired again. It will be combined with a new sense for the secret of sound, of the Word, and hence for the world of Inspiration, and moreover with an ability to experience the essential presence of the Love of God. Through this ceremonial and sacramental training, patterns of human relation-

* The altars founded by The Christian Community are referred to.

ships can be born which produce as in embryo new social organisms on Earth which can develop into mirrors of heavenly organisms.

Through representing the heavenly Temple on Earth, the Sacraments regain their power of inspiring social and cultural life. But if the content of the Seven Golden Vessels is wasted, if the sacramental blessing of life is neglected, anti-sacraments will come into being. The blessing will be turned into a curse. The Apocalypse describes the anti-sacramental desolation which, in consequence of the overturning of the Seven Heavenly Vessels, will visit a humanity found guilty of this profanity. The sevenfold revelation of cosmic wrath appears as a perversion of the Seven Sacraments.

The first of the Seven Angels pours out his Vial on the dry land. The result appears on "the men which had the mark of the Beast, and upon them which worshipped his image"; "a noisome and grievous sore" attacks their body. The province of human existence to which the first Vessel refers is, both in its divine intention and in its perversion, the sphere of the material body. This is shown in the figure of the dry land. A carcinoma, a cancer-like sore appears which is, as it were, a concentration of all possible diseases, revealing a fundamentally wrong relationship of man to his body. For a time, it was possible for materialism to remain academic theory. Up to the middle of last century thinkers could skilfully advocate a materialist view of life without much practical consequence for moral conduct. In the long run, however, it could not remain purely theoretical. It was bound to become practical in its effects. When Man, a being of soul and spirit, gave himself up to the philosophy of materialism, he misunderstood his own being. Losing sight of his soul and spirit, he overlooked the fact that within the human body the same material substances become completely different from what they are outside, in mineral, plant and animal. It was inevitable that a radically wrong attitude to his own material body should be the result. Man is no longer really at home in his own body; he feels himself, as it were, in ill-fitting clothes. As said before, the picture of the Universe and of Man presented by the materialistic faith is in terms of the Apocalypse "the Image of the Beast", because it can conceive of Man only in terms of his animal nature. It regards him as "a tailless ape". The Latin Bible uses, instead of the word meaning "mark" or "sign", a significant expression: "character bestiae". Man gradually assumes the stamp and "character of the Beast" because he pays homage to a philosophy which understands only his animal nature and is blind to his real humanity. Basic "dis-ease" is the result. Instead of mastering his body by his spiritual nature, Man is tyrannized and tormented by it. *Sickness* is the first of the seven anti-sacraments. It cannot be denied that today diseases make their appearance which have no individual causes, but are diseases of the Age. Materialism makes us ill; and so we might call, quite technically, the concentration of illness which appears in the apocalyptic picture the "cancer of materialism".

A true relationship to our material body must begin with childhood. The secret of progressive Incarnation, which is an observable fact in the growing child, can direct our thoughts to the truth. It is the spirit and soul descending from the Spiritual World which "in-form" the body.

> "For of the soul the body form doth take,
> It is the soul that doth the body make."

The innocent vitality of childhood derives from a wonderful agreement and congruence of body with soul and spirit.

The *Sacrament of Baptism* should be the means by which these sacred facts of our manhood are taught and revealed. If they are grasped and appreciated, the foundations for a right relationship to our body at every stage of life would be laid.

The second Vial is poured out over the sea. From the plane of the material body we turn to the sphere of the life-forces, signified by the picture of the ocean. When the adolescent grows from childhood to youth, he goes through a second birth. This might be called the real *secret of youth*. After twice seven years the physical body is fully developed and matured. The moulding forces of the soul can now turn inward; the spiritual man is born in the human being. This is part of the charm of Spring which youth possesses. The forces of life are seized upon and set in motion by the budding spiritual centre of the soul. At this stage Nature herself lends wings to enthusiasm, which vibrates not only through the soul but through life and body as well.

We continue to enjoy today the bloom of early life; but we have all but lost the art of preserving the secret of youth, in a changed form, for the later stages of life. The content of the second Golden Vial is wasted. Even young people pass carelessly through the most graceful stages of life. In fact, many of them are no longer really young today. They have little capacity for wonder or enthusiasm. Children are brought up in such a way that at the transition from childhood to youth they have long known all there is to know. Values are depreciated by premature anticipation; and instead of being warned by them, adults take delight in symptoms of precocity which are in fact symptoms of universal neurasthenia. So it is no wonder that the anti-sacrament of blasé *boredom* should take the place of the freshness of youth in human life. The Apocalypse describes how, through the pouring out of the second Vial, the water of the sea is turned into blood, and indeed not living but putrefying blood. Children reaching the threshold of youth receive very little help in entering the wonderful time of life which is opening to them. They are left to the mercy of the maturing bodily nature. True, "the voice of the blood" which begins to speak, opens a new world of experience. But this is soon robbed of its magic when the light of Heaven is extinguished above it.

The threatened loss of the content of the second Vial can be averted by the *Sacrament of Confirmation*, with everything that belongs to it. In The Christian Community the Confirmation Festival is linked with Easter. Youth and Easter belong together. New life awakens in boys and girls when the spark of the Spirit awakens. At the threshold between childhood and youth Christ and the Holy Spirit come close to young people through what may be called a natural law. The awakening spiritual individuality is like the rising of a spiritual Sun above the horizon of the soul. At its moment of birth, the human ego still betrays its original sun-like character, and is therefore akin to Christ. Afterwards, the blind rigidity and self-assertiveness of the earthly ego will obtain mastery, and there may be much suffering and painful discipline before eventually the sunshine of the Higher Ego can break through. But if the Easter Sacrament has blessed the spiritual bud, if the strengthening of the inward man—which is the meaning of the word "confirmation"—has taken place, then Ariadne's golden thread of eternal youth is handed to the human being for his way through the labyrinth of his whole life on earth.

The scene changes when the contents of the third Vial are poured out. The broad surface of the sea no longer appears in the picture. The sphere to which the content of the third Vial refers is shown in the image of "rivers and fountains of waters". The life-forces are individualized. This occurs in mankind through the evolution of a *personal inner life*.

The water of the rivers and springs is changed into blood under the influence of what the Angel pours over them, and the stern judgement is pronounced: "for they have shed the blood of saints and prophets, and thou hast given them blood to drink." The path of personal spiritual development demands that the blood should cease to be the carrier of purely earthly desires, and become the bearer of the ideals of morality and religion. In his efforts to attain to this discipline, the disciple can see a link between the purification of his own blood and the blood of the saints and prophets, the great spiritual messengers of human history whom he chooses as models. The symbol of the Holy Grail stands for those inward efforts through which ultimately the blood of Man receives into itself the power of the blood of Christ, an experience to which saints and prophets bear witness.

The mechanization of modern life runs counter to the development of a personal inward life. Figures like the prophet Elijah, John the Baptist, Bernard of Clairvaux or Francis of Assisi have ceased to be the ideals which we endeavour to emulate. We are fascinated by the successful business men, the practical men of affairs, who dominate every sphere of life. They are the cause of countless martyrs, even without actually shedding blood. The great martyrs of the past die again, and with them all those who have ever walked the Earth as torchbearers of the spirit. Their blood is shed again spiritually because it is made to appear that they have lived in vain. They are pushed aside as ascetic sentimentalists from whom the modern man, who strives after cleverness and success in life, can learn nothing.

What does it mean, then, that those who have shed the blood of the saints and prophets should be given blood to drink? Whoever thinks he can grow a personality without the ideals of a higher world is turned back to his own blood, pulsed through by carnal impulses and desires. The level on which the individuality unfolds is lowered to the level of sensuality. Epidemics of *sexuality* make their appearance as symptoms of the third anti-sacrament. The betrayal of the sanctuary of the personal inner sphere leads ultimately to a degenerate civilization. In an epoch in which there is no living religion sexuality begins to run riot in social life.

The loving sacramental purpose of God which is the original content of the third Golden Vial can be received in *the Sacrament of Confession*. This sacrament has become more problematical than the others for many centuries, because it must take into account the growing sense of individual freedom and moral responsibility among men. The Reformation was justified in its day in throwing overboard the misuse and degradation of the Sacrament of Confession. And today any form of Confession which still contains remnants of an authoritative tutelage is rightly rejected by the adult section of mankind. The modern Christian ought to be able to settle for himself much which, in earlier times, the Father Confessor decided for his penitents. Today the "Sacramental Consultation"* which is the modern form of Confession is chiefly intended to provide a sanctuary where the soul can freely raise its most intimate personal concerns to the supersensible guidance and grace which come from higher worlds. It has long been one of the ominous signs of our time that so many people flock to the psychoanalyst. It can, however, only have the effect of an anti-sacrament if the subconscious complexes underlying some difficulty of soul or body are raised into consciousness without spiritual help. For the patient is thereby turned back to the instincts and desires of his unregenerated blood. The Sacramental Consultation conducted in freedom has a healing effect. It is a Psycho-synthesis, because it unites the soul with its own Higher Ego, and consecrates the human blood with the blood of Christ.

The fourth Vial is not poured out on to the earthly sphere, but it changes the influence exercised by the Sun on the Earth. From now on, men and women will be scorched and burnt by the fiery glow of the Sun as if by the flames of hell. The great heat sends men out of their minds and hardens them all the more firmly in their detachment from the divine, so that eventually they are only moved by a burning hatred of that which is divine.

Our attention is drawn to that province of human existence in which Man is united to the *divine forces of Nature*. We receive the rich gifts of Nature through our senses as well as through our breathing and through food. The Sun is the majestic heart of Mother Nature, who bestows these gifts upon us. We are fed in body, soul, and spirit by what the Sun evokes from the earthly cosmos. The true character of the gifts of Nature offered to us through the Sun lies beyond the comprehension of materialistic science. A loving Cosmic Entity, disguised in the visible exterior of the Sun gives us of its own body and blood. According to the accepted scientific view, the Sun is a gaseous body radiating light and heat according to physical laws. Could Nature be such a productive, loving and generous being if this usual conception of the Sun were the whole truth? What the purely physical effects of the Sun are like can be seen in unmitigated measure at the Equator. In those latitudes the physical Sun engenders no life, but seems to scorch every living thing like a devouring beast

* As practised in The Christian Community.

of prey. But are the blessings of the temperate zones only physical? Certainly, the denser atmosphere reduces the purely physical impact of the Sun. But the most significant fact is that through this filtering of the physical light, the concealed etheric and spiritual effects proceeding from the Sun are released. When once the charm of materialism is broken we shall become aware with astonishment to what extent we in our temperate zones have to thank the supersensible *spiritual* Sun for the manifold gifts of Nature. It is one of the tragedies of our Age that a one-sided way of thinking, if it has controlled Man's consciousness long enough, eventually becomes a practical truth. We have increasingly impoverished our own relationship with Nature because we have overlooked the soul and spirit in Sun and Earth. Nature, as seen by materialism, is bound to destroy Man instead of nourishing and building him up. Before long even the most lavishly fruitful parts of the world will become sterile. We shall soon search in vain for unspoiled country. In our desire for quick profit we have already exhausted vast areas of the globe. Soil erosion, which increases year by year (for example, in the U.S.A., to an alarming degree) is a clear indication of what will happen if only the parching effects of the physical Sun remain, because Man deceives himself about the true character of Nature as a whole.

The Sacrament of which the perversion appears at the outpouring of the fourth Vial of Wrath is the centre of all Sacraments. It contains the Sun Mysteries of Christianity. It is the *Sacrament of the Altar*, in which bread and wine are dispensed, in which all the gifts of the spiritual Sun are concentrated. Through the process of Transubstantiation, the secret of the Sun of Christ is united with the secret of the natural Sun which is contained in bread and wine; in the Sun-steeped earthly elements the Risen Lord is at hand and close to those gathered round the altar, as though He were present in His own Body and Blood. The Sacrament of the Altar sanctifies not only the personal element in the individual; it affects also the whole relationship of Man and the human community to Nature and to the whole world. From this source, blessings can flow to wherever our place in life may be.

The anti-sacramental effect of a Nature materialistically thought of, and thereby ultimately *made* material, imprisons man in purely material existence. The more greedily he snatches at the gifts of Nature, the less do they give him. He becomes like a fish out of water. The *anti-sacrament of inner desiccation* eventually hardens Man completely within the shell of the body. His very existence is a denial of God, a blasphemy against the true state of the world. The loss of religion must ultimately turn into hatred and enmity against everything spiritual. But bread and wine, the blessed gifts of the Sun and of the Risen Christ, can raise the soul again out of its frustration and isolation, and integrate man again into the whole of God's Creation. This is Christianity regained, with its all-embracing cosmic character, which has been forgotten and lost since the days of early Christendom, in the triumphal progress of the material conquest of the world.

The fifth Vial seems at first not to refer to the human kingdom at all. It is poured out upon the Beast, and causes a terrifying darkness in its kingdom. The consequences of this darkness, however, show themselves immediately among mankind too. They are tormented so that they "gnaw their tongues for pain". Their hardening and hostility towards all that is divine develop into the utmost bitterness. But where is the "Kingdom of the Beast" to be found? The phrase has a double meaning, and refers at first to the sovereign domain of a demonic power. But it also has the simple meaning implied when we speak of the different "kingdoms" of Nature—the mineral, vegetable, or animal kingdom. The Kingdom of the Beast is presented to us as a kind of "animal kingdom", which, however, is not identical with the kingdom of our earthly animals, but consists of men who through neglect of their true human nature have fallen below its level. It is that section of mankind which through worshipping the image of the Beast has degenerated spiritually and sunk to another kind of animal kingdom. The essential ingredient of the human kingdom— if God's purpose for Man is not already thwarted—is love and fellowship. Wherever the image of the Beast, that is, of Man as a purely natural being, governs the intercourse of human beings, social life declines and ultimately dies. This is the real cause of the "social question". What was formerly taken for granted instinctively as a fact of life becomes a problem, and this problem can never be solved by organization. Souls will plunge more and more deeply into isolation, separation and egoism. Through fear for his existence, Man will snatch at whatever he can reach; but the result can only be total impoverishment and a war of all against all. When love dies, cheerfulness and joy also die. All sense of humour is lost, too. Bitterness and depression become widespread. Total isolation and haunting fear stand at the end of the road.

This *bitterness* is nothing but the perversion of another sacramental mystery. The health or sickness of a society are reflected in the respect or otherwise with which marriages are treated. *The Sacrament of Marriage* which blesses the union between two persons does not only concern those directly involved. It involves the higher spheres, where every true union between human souls is continued in an alliance between the Angels of those souls. The idea that a marriage is only a personal concern of the married couple is one of the fundamental errors which are bound to arise as understanding of human nature and of the mysterious laws of human society dies away. The social significance of marriage is not exhausted by the newly-established family and the procreation of the race. The most important effect of the Sacrament of Marriage is the fact that it releases a whole heaven of higher, superpersonal forces of life which can flow into human communities and civilizations. Where this sphere is active, darkness begins to light up; the burden of life's cares becomes endurable; the torments of bitterness are healed through divine sources of joy.

At the very beginning of the outpouring of the sixth Vial, our attention is drawn to a sphere in which good could come out of evil. We anticipate that, at the sixth stage of the last cycle of Seven, a turn for the better might take place, similar to that shown in the sixth Seal and the sixth Trumpet. The river Euphrates is mentioned. It is obviously not the earthly river which is meant, but one of those ancient spiritual streams, called by the Old Testament the "rivers of Paradise". It signifies in the realm of archetypes the channels through which the forces of higher spheres enter the life of mankind. We recognize as the realm of the sixth Vial the *inter-relationship of humanity with the supersensible world*. True, we learn that the sacred stream dries up when the Angel pours out the contents of his Vial. Thus we have entered into a time when Heaven can no longer bestow its blessings upon Earth as a matter of course. We learn further that in the river-bed now lying dry a way is prepared by which the "Kings of the East" may come. Does this mean that a new Christmas event is approaching? The kings who now travel from East to West do not bring gold, frankincense and myrrh. Their journey is accompanied by sinister phenomena. Demonic powers in the form of disgusting frogs and toads emerge from every direction and bewilder the world by the arts and "miracles" of black magic. One of the Egyptian Plagues seems to be repeating itself. At that time, the decadence of the Egyptian priestly rites was thrown into relief by the clear spiritual aim of Moses. When the priests of Egypt tried to oppose Moses and Aaron with their magic skill, the Plague could only become worse—

the number of the frogs became greater than ever (Exodus viii, 1–7).

The sixth Vial operates in the same way as the rod of Moses. It demands an account of the supersensible forces which Man still has at his disposal. The result reveals a dangerous advance of the demonic legions. A decision is inevitable; a battle must be fought. The Apocalypse calls the place of this battle Armageddon—that is, the "Mountain of the Threshold". Here the gates of Heaven and Hell are open. Great armies press forward out of the regions of Hell. Will there be enough Servants of the Good to oppose them victoriously with forces drawn from the open Heaven?

The light of a mighty Sun rises above the horizon and illumines the battlefield. The great "day of God Almighty" is breaking. The dawn of the Sun of Christ's new revelation seems to be coming to the rescue of the faithful little flock. But the motif of the Second Coming is presented from its sternest side. "Behold, I come as a thief," He cries. These words have a still greater significance here than in the Seven Messages. Man is again threatened with the great impoverishment which will overtake him if he sleeps through the spiritual events which might enrich him. But the new nearness of Christ is still more two-edged and dangerous within the Vials of Wrath. God's law of magnanimity, which is active in the pouring out of the golden Temple vessels, is also revealed in the mystery of the Second Coming. The vessels of the Love of God are poured out over mankind, regardless of how they are accepted, as Sacrament or Anti-Sacrament. Man has at his disposal the fatal power of being able to turn the Love of God into its opposite, indeed, finally even to misuse it and place it at the service of the opposing powers. When the Son of Man appears on the clouds of Heaven, the greatest possible powers of blessing and consecration will indeed flow into human life, but these gifts can also be misused and turned into the contrary. But the impoverishment of those who shut themselves off from the approaching Christ is not the worst consequence. At the Coming of Christ the way is open also for Antichrist. Precisely at the time when Christ approaches mankind, men will manage to suspend the Laws of Nature, and to perform miracles with the forces of the pit.

To which secret of God's love is *black magic* the antithesis? The Temple of Heaven from which the Seven Golden Vials are brought out would be meaningless if from thence the white magic of life and *an influence from the good divine forces* were not possible on Earth. The secret of the sixth Vial is realized, according to the loving purpose of God, in the existence of a genuine priesthood on Earth. In the words and actions which are spoken and carried out in the spirit of a true Commission, given in *the Sacrament of Ordination*, superhuman forces flow into the life and civilization of mankind. The orbit of this Sacrament embraces the ideal of the universal spiritual priesthood of all men and women in every aspect of life and work. In this priesthood Christ Himself opposes Antichrist on Earth by strengthening His disciples so that they will stand their ground victoriously in the Battle of Armageddon.

When the seventh Vial is poured out into the atmosphere, a voice says, "It is finished." (A.V. "It is done.") A cosmic Good Friday seems to have dawned. Through thunders and lightnings and earthquake a great cosmic death overtakes everything. The first act of a tragedy is unrolled before us which later will extend far beyond the cycle of the Seven Vials of Wrath. The great city of Babylon, in which that section of mankind is concentrated which has completely abandoned itself to material existence, breaks into three pieces and plunges into the abyss. Mountains and islands vanish. The last possibilities for inward effort and meditative withdrawal disappear. The cities of men sink in ruins. The colossal death of a civilization swallows them up.

Humanity thinks that through its own activity it has created a world which will live and escape death. Since, however, it has not understood the secret of life, which extends beyond the level of the material, it has failed to grasp the mystery of death. Through fear of death, it has clung more and more closely to material existence and to purely earthly, animal vitality. It has failed to see that it thereby abandons itself still more to the forces of death. The transitory world has become a tyrannical though unacknowledged despot. The sum total of the dead and of the power of death has been infinitely increased by mistaken activities which only seemed to be serving life.

Not until Man knows the secret of life can he look death calmly in the face, and obtain its blessing. The most valuable fruits of human existence are gained if a man knows how to live with death. Without a measure of sacrifice, Man cannot promote true humanity either in himself or in others. No consciousness, no single thought is physiologically possible without death having its share in the processes of the human body. Only when men see through death, when they accept death as a friend, and pass bravely through the trials of death, will mankind as a whole attain once more to a civilization which is really alive. Death can and will be the great teacher and educator of mankind.

One of the most important tasks of religion is to teach men how to die. Even in Christian circles it is often regarded as a kindness not to tell a man that he is about to die. Here we enter the sphere of that Sacrament which by its very existence can effect a great change in this. When the priest brings *the Last Anointing* to the dying so that the facts themselves speak their clear message, the courage and not the cowardice of the soul is taken into consideration. And lo, a power is revealed from deep within which disproves all theories of the essential weakness of the human being. It is only on the surface that Man is cowardly and weak. In the inmost eternal core of his being, which is disclosed at the approach of death, a heroic *readiness for death* is present. When this is reflected in the eyes of a dying man, eternity is revealed in the midst of transitoriness. If human beings were trained to lead their lives in accordance with this fountain-head of faith which lies dormant within the eternal core of their being, all human existence would assume a different aspect. The purpose of divine Love which forms the content of the seventh Vial will place death at Man's side as a friend. If it is changed to the contrary, the anti-sacrament of *total death* will spread over the whole Earth.

Mankind cannot be simply without sacraments. Protestantism could afford to give up sacraments for theological reasons, because it arose in centuries when the spiritual legacy of Mankind had not yet reached its lowest level. Today it is different. The anti-sacraments of the Vials of Wrath are a fact. They are actually invading human life, and ultimately there only remains the choice, either to remain at the mercy of the anti-sacraments, or to cherish the sacraments which reveal the true form of the love of God. The anti-sacraments are present everywhere: disease, boredom, sexuality, desiccation, embitterment, black magic and the universal decline and death of civilization. They are the seven spheres of Divine Love perverted into Wrath. In the seven Sacraments: Baptism, Confirmation, Sacramental Consultation, the Sacrament of Bread and Wine, Marriage, Consecration of Priests, Last Anointing—we have sacred golden Vials on Earth for bestowing on mankind the unadulterated content of the Seven Vials of God's love.

X

THE FALL OF BABYLON

THE monumental last act of the apocalyptic drama follows directly from the pouring out of the Seven Vials. We recall once more the architectural structure and movement of the whole. The Book begins with the central vision of the Son of Man. By presenting the image of Spirit-Man first, the Apocalypse gives us to understand that Man is its concern. At the end Man has become the World.

To the unity of the picture with which the Apocalypse begins, there is a corresponding duality at the end, the vision of a humanity which breaks up into two units. Two cities appear, Babylon and Jerusalem. The one eventually falls into the abyss as dross; the other, drawing form and substance from above, rises towards the future and gives a glimpse of the new planetary condition towards which our earthly cosmos moves.

This progress from the One to the Two determines the fundamental law of the apocalyptic path. We have, however, pointed out earlier that, so long as we consider only this duality, we perceive only the tension and opposition in the drama. The full apocalyptic conclusion is formed by a trinity. Between the pictures of Babylon falling into the abyss and Jerusalem coming down from Heaven, a celestial warrior advances: the Rider on the White Horse. He is none other than a metamorphosis of the Son of Man, whose form appeared at the beginning. Now Spirit-Man, the Genius of Mankind, is fired to the greatest activity as the final cosmic decision is at hand. Before this radiant, determined Being, the fate of the world is decided. It divides into two halves, one rising, the other falling.

Here and there, during the Trumpet blasts, the visionary picture of the two cities was already to be seen. The "great city" which fell away from the spiritual spheres appeared repeatedly at the sound of the Trumpets, and assumed an increasingly distinct form as the pouring out of the Vials of Wrath accelerated its destruction. The seventh of the Golden Vials makes the fall of the "great city" irresistible and final.

The concluding drama, wherein the dividing of the spirits assumes cosmic proportions and issues into a cosmic duality, clearly results from the pouring out of the Vials of Heaven. Both pictures, of the "Whore Babylon" and the "Bride Jerusalem", are revealed by one of the Seven Angels who brought the Vials from within the Temple of Heaven and poured them out. "There came one of the Seven Angels which had the Seven Vials, and talked with me, saying unto me: Come hither; I will show thee the judgement of the great *whore* that sitteth upon many waters; with whom the kings of the Earth have committed fornication; the inhabitants of the Earth have been made drunk with the wine of her fornication. So he carried me away in the spirit into the *wilderness*, and I saw a woman sitting upon a scarlet-coloured beast . . . having seven heads and ten horns" (xvii, 1–4). "And there came unto me one of the seven angels which had the seven vials full of the seven last plagues, and talked with me saying: Come hither; I will show thee the *bride*, the Lamb's wife. And he carried me away in the spirit to a great and high *mountain*, and showed me the holy city Jerusalem, descending out of heaven from God, having the glory of God" (xxi, 9–10).

Both Babylon and Jerusalem appear on the one hand in the picture of a city, on the other in the figure of a woman. When the apocalyptic Babylon is mentioned, usually the idea of the female picture, the "scarlet woman", prevails. The fact is easily lost sight of that the "great whore" is also described as a city, i.e. as a representative part of humanity and of the earthly creation. Conversely, the heavenly Jerusalem is in the first place mainly imagined as the image of a city; that it is also a "bride" does not so readily enter into the symbolic pictures called up by the name. In the image of the city, the body of a section of humanity is seen; in the figure of a woman, its soul.

When the mythical consciousness of earlier ages looked back to the origins of our world, they also spoke of a woman. Mythical retrospection saw the picture of the Great Mother of all beginnings, "Mother Earth". The Apocalypse adds the double picture of the Whore and the Bride: *Mother Earth; the Whore Babylon; the Bride Jerusalem.* Half way between Mother Earth and the double vision of the final goal there belongs the picture which also marks the middle of the Apocalypse: the Woman clothed with the Sun who, at the moment she is to bear her son, is threatened by the fiery red Dragon. Mother Earth becomes a mother in a special new way when in the soul of mankind and in the soul of individual men, the ego is born. The peace and harmony of early ages is over; the dangers appear immediately which will eventually lead to the cleavage in mankind. The tragedy into which the heedless section of mankind is drawn is underlined by the metamorphosis of the supplementary picture.

The Whore Babylon is described as sitting on a scarlet red beast with seven heads and ten horns. We recognize the Dragon which once threatened the Woman who was to give birth to a child. The Woman whom we now see is no longer at such a safe distance from the Dragon that the Archangel could, as formerly, come to her assistance. She has entangled and associated herself with the Dragon. And when we are told that the Whore is clothed in purple and scarlet, it is clear that the Dragon has tainted her with his colours; she has been absorbed into the kingdom of the Adversary. The threefold adornment which the Woman wears—gold, precious stones and pearls—is the heavenly Trinity of Sun, Moon and Stars, debased into earthly ornamentation. While the Mother in the heights bears the golden heart of the world radiating from within her, the debased figure completely abandoned to this world adorns herself with the glittering material gold which is the materialized earthly shadow of the Sun. And just as the Woman in Heaven has the stars as a crown about her head, so the Whore adorns herself with precious stones, which are like the thoughts of the stars imprisoned in matter. Not until we consider the heavenly Jerusalem, in the fashioning of whose body gold, precious stones and pearls also play a part, shall we recognize fully what infamy lies in the fact that the Whore Babylon also adorns herself with pearls. Pearls are not minerals. They grow through the reaction of living beings to pain. In the overcoming of pain caused by the incursion of a foreign body, the oyster develops the pearl. Thus the pearl is a wonderful symbol of pain overcome in the soul. In the language of apocalyptic symbols it is equivalent to the conquest of the dark and oppressive forces of the night, which the Heavenly Woman masters when she keeps the Moon under her feet. In the spiritual-physical body of the heavenly Jerusalem, pearls as well as gold and precious stones are tokens and results of inner discipline and spiritual victories, tokens of *inward mastery*. The Whore Babylon has not herself suffered the pains whose results she hangs about her as ornament. She is the antithesis of the Woman who has the Moon beneath her feet. Gold, precious stones and pearls in her are tokens of *outward show*, unearned and unintegrated. The Woman and the Dragon are not clearly distinguishable; the glaring red of passion and greed envelops both in equal measure. Out of the golden cup which she holds in her hand, "full of abominations and filthiness," the Whore Babylon dispenses an unclean wealth, which binds those who accept it to the dark depths and forces of the world. It is often said of a man that "two souls dwell in his breast". This is true also of mankind as a whole. Since the Woman in Heaven, the higher soul of humanity, bore her son, Man has had the choice between his higher and his lower ego. The free decision between above and below, maturing during the ages of the life of the Earth, must lead to a parting of the ways. In the picture of the Whore that part of humanity ultimately appears in which the lower soul, earthbound and heavy, has arrogated all power to itself.

Where do we meet with the "great whore" in human life? Although in the history of Christianity only scanty use has hitherto been made of the last book of the Bible, the picture of the Whore Babylon has nevertheless often played an important part. Reformers and revolutionaries have often used it to describe the organized ecclesiastical power from which they endeavoured to break away. Although Martin Luther said of the Apocalypse that his mind could not adapt itself to this book he again and again made use of the picture of the Whore Babylon in his struggle against the papal Church. Emanuel Swedenborg did the same thing later with even greater heat. Those who saw in the Roman Church the great Whore Babylon thought that they could appeal to a distinguishing mark which the Apocalypse mentions: "Here is the mind which hath wisdom. The seven heads are seven mountains on which the woman sitteth. And there are seven kings" (xvii, 9). It is tempting to think that these hieroglyphs are so easy to decipher. A city which stands on seven mountains—can that be anything but Rome, the classical "city of seven hills"? And so it was argued by theological scholars that the first Christians, among them the author of the Apocalypse, which was conceived as a polemical treatise against heretics, saw the Whore Babylon in the Rome of the Caesars. Commentators thought they found further guidance in the passage which says that the seven heads of the Beast, on which the Woman is sitting, are also seven kings: "Five are fallen, and one is, and the other is not yet come; and when he cometh, he must continue a short space" (xviii, 10). This passage was thought even to indicate the date of the Apocalypse. The succession of the Caesars was calculated somewhat like this. Five, i.e. Augustus, Tiberius, Caligula, Claudius, and Nero, have already fallen; their lifetime was past. After the assassination of Nero there was a short interval filled by the government of the three soldier Emperors; Galba, Otho and Vitellius. It is supposed that these three can be grouped together as *one* of the seven kings of whom the Apocalypse speaks. Then the seventh, whose coming was still impending, was Vespasian, whose accession was awaited with great Messianic hopes, and whom the Jewish writer Josephus indicated as the longed-for Messiah. So it seemed indisputably established that the Revelation of St. John came into existence in the time of the three soldier Emperors, i.e. between about 65 and 69 A.D. If this somewhat trivial interpretation were correct, it would still remain very puzzling why the writer of the Apocalypse should emphatically describe the words "seven mountains" as being comprehensible only to a "mind which hath wisdom".

It is our conviction that such interpretations lead in a wrong direction; they misunderstand the nature of the Apocalypse. They assume that our present non-visionary consciousness is the normal and only possible one. Within the limitations of present-day consciousness, the Apocalypse can only be regarded as an accumulation of allegorical pictures representing material events. But the truth to which we shall always return again is that the Apocalypse has its origin in a higher consciousness. It is written out of a first-hand perception of supersensible realities, and supersensible chains of events. The pictures used to describe the spiritual world are indeed borrowed from the material world. But simply to read historic personalities or earthly events of the past, present or future into the apocalyptic pictures is to remain below the level of the book. Only a search for the supersensible facts and principles which appear in these pictures can lead further. Such research, pursued with unwearying persistence, reveals the cosmic artistry, the breadth, scope and grandeur of the Apocalypse. An alphabet of apparent hieroglyphics becomes transparent for spiritual forces and rhythms with which every age has to deal in its own way.

The picture of the *mountain* occurs so often in all the Biblical Scriptures that it points unmistakably not to an earthly, but to a spiritual sphere. For example, even Christ's words about the "faith which can move mountains" may become a truly apocalyptic expression. Of course, this does not mean that faith can do the work of the spade. The mountain before which I stand blocks the view behind it. Not until I climb to the top of it can I see the view again. The magic of faith consists in moving those mountains which shut out the view into the world of the spirit from the human soul. The faith which moves mountains raises the soul to a level where nothing obscures the horizon. We recall that at the sound of the second Trumpet a burning mountain fell from Heaven. At that stage Heaven itself caused men to "come up against a brick wall"; they fell into a kind of consciousness wherein they lost sight altogether of the spiritual sphere: the mountain of materialism towered up in front of them.

According to the book of Daniel (Chapter 2) a similar vision seized upon the soul of Nebuchadnezzar. An invisible hand broke off a stone and hurled it against an image. As the stone fell it grew into a gigantic rock. It was a prophetic vision of the fact that the human race which once saw into the sphere of the Gods with innocent forces of clairvoyance, had to descend into the dark valley which is surrounded by nothing but mountains. Physical sense-perception is the mountain which no longer allows a view into the inner realms of existence.

In Grimm's fairy tale of Snow White, the apocalyptic motif of the Seven Mountains occurs in a characteristic context. The proud queen, Snow White's wicked stepmother, stands in front of the magic mirror to be assured that she is the most beautiful being in the whole country. But at a certain moment the mirror answers, "Your Majesty, you are the most beautiful here. But Snow White, across the seven mountains, with the seven dwarfs, is a thousand times more beautiful than you." The world in which Snow White lives is not the same as the world of the stepmother. The queen is in the world of matter and of the physical senses; but Snow White moves in the world of the elements and of the elemental beings, which are not of a physical nature. In the picture of the seven mountains the towering boundary zone appears, which must be surmounted by anyone who wishes to pass from the world of the senses to the world of the supersensible.

Thus the Seven Mountains of which the Apocalypse speaks are also a frontier range between this world and that. Obviously the fact that a city like Rome is built on seven hills is not coincidence. And indeed, Rome is not the only town which has had similar mythological scenery for its foundation. Prague, which is also a city of seven hills, has frequently been called the Eastern Rome. Apocalyptic motifs can, as it were, stray into physical geography when world history turns cities into symbols causing them to spring up in places where, through nature and destiny, special possibilities of a connection between the two worlds exist. As regards Prague, the secret of the seven hills is brought out by the name of the city, which means the "Threshold". Such places and centres, however, are also danger points. The enchantment of a magnificent material civilization seduces human souls until eventually the Seven Mountains and the apparent glory of this world blind the eye for the world beyond. When the Apocalypse shows us the proudly adorned Woman sitting on the Seven Mountains, it is placing before us a Power whose will is that mankind shall be separated from the spiritual world. It is to the interest of this Will that Man should remain imprisoned in the earthly world until he is either convinced that there is no supersensible world, or else submits to the dogma that it is not given to Man to cross the Threshold into that world.

This Power is known in the Gospels, too. Christ Himself opposed it when He hurled denunciations against the Scribes and Pharisees. In the Gospel of St. Matthew, the series of denunciations begins at once with words which strike particularly at the spirit of hindrance revealed in the Apocalypse: "Woe unto you, Scribes and Pharisees, hypocrites! for ye shut up the kingdom of heaven against men; for ye neither go in yourselves, neither suffer ye them that are entering to go in" (xxiii, 13). Christ lashes out against a degenerate priesthood which does the opposite of what it should. The priest should be a *pontifex*, a bridge builder, who helps mankind to traverse the boundary zone and to acquire citizenship in both worlds. When those who are entrusted with the care of men's souls are themselves no longer capable of crossing the Threshold of the Seven Mountains, they slip all too easily into the tendency to keep those entrusted to them also on this side, and to enjoin them not to strive after the world of the supersensible. Thus the leaders of religious life themselves become the power which holds mankind back from the spiritual world.

The decadence against which the woes were pronounced is the misuse of power in the priestly office. In the times before human souls began to grow an ego and were still childlike and immature, the priesthood exercised with full justification an authoritative guidance of souls. But when the seed of egohood and individual spiritual endeavour began to stir—and at the time of the Gospels this had already been active for some centuries—the "magic" of the priestly office had to cease. The symbol of the shepherd became the new ideal of a priest-hood which reckoned with the growing freedom of human souls and ministered to it with kindness and understanding. The old authoritative relationship could only be maintained by force. And in fact this mistake has not been avoided in the history of Christianity. On the contrary, it was practised to a high degree after the persecutions of the Christians had ceased and Christianity had become the established religion of the Roman Empire. Christian spiritual life was threatened by an appalling relapse into the principles of Egypt and Babylon.

Were then Luther and Swedenborg right when they identified

the Whore Babylon with the Roman Catholic Church? It will always be wrong to apply this apocalyptic picture only to others or to historic events and not also to oneself. The Whore of Babylon represents a danger which threatens the spiritual life of mankind at all times and places. Wherever spiritual and religious groups are so formed that the interests of the community are placed above the value of the individual, the Christian principle is supplanted by the Babylonian. Where the Church becomes an end in itself, where the individual is led only to loyal obedience to a Church instead of to the deepest inward freedom and to individual experience and knowledge of the spiritual world, it is threatened by the Spectre of power which sits upon the Seven Mountains. This Spectre also influences theology. Especially the old theoretical division between faith and knowledge paralyses and stultifies the free spiritual endeavour of the individual and his research into the unseen. Confinement to "simple faith", the denial and renunciation of a free, conscious relationship with the divine spiritual world, will become more and more the watchword of that type of religious leadership which was so severely censured in Christ's first denunciation in the Gospel of St. Matthew.

In the Gospel of St. Luke this battle-cry of Christ (which in Luke concludes the series) is formulated still more sternly. "Woe unto you, lawyers! For ye have taken away the key of knowledge: ye entered not in yourselves, and them that were entering in, ye hindered" (xi, 52). Here a priesthood is denounced which not only has become bigoted, representing the narrow doctrine that there can be no knowledge of the supersensible, but such groups of leaders who continue esoteric traditions and methods of knowledge within their own circles, but strictly avoid sharing them with those whom they lead. By maintaining secrecy, they make spiritual knowledge a means to authoritative pre-eminence and power over men. It is true that in pre-Christian times it was fully justified to restrict esoteric knowledge only to the very narrow circle of Initiates, because humanity in general had not yet developed the ego-centre of the soul. But this antiquated division between priests and laity cannot be transferred to the sphere of Christianity without an Egyptian-Babylonian falsification.

The danger which the writer of the Apocalypse indicates in the picture of the Whore Babylon is, however, still more comprehensive. It is not concerned only with errors perpetrated by the leaders of men. In every soul the Power is active which attempts to block the way of the true Self when it prepares to cross the Threshold. The nearer a man comes to the spiritual world, the more will a kind of claustrophobia take hold of him. The "faith that moves mountains" does not exist of its own accord in the soul; it must be wrested from a thousand attacks of fear and cowardice. On the inner path of the soul countless excuses may only too easily be offered, but they are promptings of the Power that sits, also within us, on the Seven Mountains, and which tries to chain us more and more firmly to earthly things, instead of letting us press forward to the spirit.

Throughout the whole of the Bible the theme "Babylon" plays an important part. In its first pages the "Tower of Babel", in its last pages the "Whore Babylon" is described. The story of the Babylonian Tower records the collapse of a magic culture of the past which had degenerated. The Tower was built from below upwards. The Heavenly City (as we shall see in the last chapter) descends from Heaven to Earth; it is built from above downwards. In the heavenly Jerusalem everything depends on the flow of divine grace from above. Babylon erects a towering sign of human arrogance, from below upwards, in defiance of the Gods.

Before degeneration set in, the pre-Christian religions were centred on a principle which indeed implied the direction from below upwards; for all true religious experience in pre-Christian times was based on *ecstasy*. The Gods were worshipped and approached in worlds high above mankind. Communion with God was only possible when the soul rose out of the physical body. Only ecstasy could lead from the Here of Man to the Beyond of God. The imposing wealth of the pre-Christian religions and temple-cults was the product of the ecstatic approach to the sources of divine inspiration. But in the course of time human nature changed, and souls were absorbed more deeply into the more hardened and unyielding bodies. Forcible means were more and more needed to loosen the soul from the body, and to lift it into a condition of ecstasy. Babylon was the centre where decadent means of effecting this condition through orgies of drunkenness and uncontrolled passion set the tone and influenced civilization and society. From the third pre-Christian millennium onward, the orgiastic rites were symbolized in monumental buildings, which soon found corresponding parallels in Egypt. The Tower of Babel described in the Old Testament is not just a myth; it has an historic background. The kind of tower known as a Ziggurat, examples of which have been preserved to this day, was one of these visible symbols of the Babylonian religion. Men thought they could compete with the Gods by erecting colossal buildings when the earlier and purer union with the spirit could no longer be practised. The pyramids of the Babylonian temples were explicitly called "Mountains of the Gods". Because souls could no longer attain to the Mount of Vision as they used to do, mountain-like towers were built in defiance of fate. They only emphasized the growing gulf between humanity and the Gods.

The Old Testament records how these practices horrified the upholders of a pure spiritual life. The Old Testament Apocrypha, supplementing the Old Testament itself, says that Abraham's refusal to join the Babylonians in their arrogant tower building compelled him to leave his Chaldean home with his family. The decadent Babylonian cults carried the purely material and animal forces of earthly existence into human relationship with the Spiritual World. The principle of spiritual fornication came into being. Instead of Man raising his soul nearer to a pure union with the Spirit, he mingled earthly sensuality and passion with his intercourse with the world of the Gods. Thus, in the precincts of the Babylonian temples in particular an organized practice of sexual rites arose, in which religious fervour went hand in hand with sensuality. Prostitution did not originate in a secular setting; its origin is entirely ritualistic. It was in Babylon that the "temple slaves", who were prostitutes, made their first appearance among those serving in the temple. All vices which aim at ecstatic intoxication have their origin in such pre-Christian cults, into which the Babylonian principle was introduced. Educated by the Old and New Testament, we regard today orgiastic passions and religious life as radically incompatible. But we should be aware that wherever people give way to a kind of intoxicating "possession", whether it be through drugs, or the gambling mania, or through an uncontrolled lust for money, success or power, a misguided longing for real contact with higher worlds may lie at the root of it. People wish to escape by physical means from the deadly round of daily life, and become thereby only more entangled with this world.

It would be wrong to suggest that the degenerate Babylonian rites could no longer lead to a union of human souls with supersensible beings; but instead of the higher Gods, lower Gods and eventually demons, gained the ascendancy. A religious life came into being which, instead of opening Heaven, unleashed the powers of the pit. In particular, a lust for autocratic power entered mankind—again, not through the secular side of life, but through the degeneration of religion. Leaders and rulers eventually laid themselves open to possession by demonic powers, which prompted them to declare *themselves* as Gods, and to claim divine homage and automatic obedience.

So the two passages referring to Babylon, which enclose the whole Bible, are closely connected. The degeneration of Babylon continues throughout the whole of human evolution. On the one hand the curse of the Whore Babylon causes widespread immorality. But it also continues to influence the sphere from which it originally sprang, religious life itself. It induces the leaders of religion to lord it over the faithful, and thus to set themselves and the Church between God and mankind. And with the rank and file of Church people, it appears in many forms of religious egoism.

Under countless masks and disguises the Whore Babylon walks among mankind. No mortal is quite free of her. If therefore her picture is used to characterize historical or contemporary conditions, it should at the same time be recognized as a mirror for self-examination.

A completely new foundation has been laid for religious life with Christianity. When people were no longer able to rise to the sphere of the Gods as had once been possible, in the fullness of time a God came to men on Earth. A new dynamic relationship was established between God and Man; a force working no longer from below upwards, but from above downwards. The way of ecstasy was replaced by that of indwelling. The religious life founded on the Incarnation, Death and Resurrection of Christ can no longer have its being in an invasion of the spiritual world through ecstasy; men must open their hearts, in the sense of St. Paul's words, "Not I, but Christ *in* me." And the grace pouring down from above is not confined to the personal spiritual life. Christianity can and must attain to the intensity and authority through which it penetrates and transforms not only the soul, but also the body. Thus the principle of building from above downwards comes into being. The architecture of the Tower of Babel is replaced by that of the heavenly Jerusalem, which comes down from Heaven to Earth.

When the Apocalypse says that the Seven Mountains on which the Whore Babylon is sitting are at the same time Seven Kings, of whom five have already fallen, the sixth is still living, and the seventh will only enter into his kingdom in the future, it uses hieroglyphs which can only be deciphered by the reading of spiritual realities. The spatial picture of the Seven Mountains is transposed into the picture of a succession in time. Seven great cycles of evolution appear, threatened by the danger of the Babylonian temptation. Five of these belong to the past. The sixth is the present—that is, the period in which the way is cleared for the final split into the two sides: Babylon or Jerusalem. The seventh is still in the lap of the future. Each of these epochs has its dominating principle, in which mankind has to develop new forces and enter upon new fields of experience. Five harvests have been gathered in, the sixth is in the process of growth, while the seventh is still in embryo.

Will Man devote the five forces he has gained by working under the five kings of the past to the service of the material sphere or to that of the spiritual and divine? And what will he do with the sixth and seventh products of evolution, which for the time being are not yet fully at his disposal? Achievements won in the past, and possibilities promised by the future, will either become organs of mankind for the spiritual world, and of the spiritual world for mankind, or they will become fetters chaining human nature to matter, which is itself doomed to destruction. In the picture, the fetters appear as the Dragon with seven heads and ten horns. The deadly weight of matter turns the wealth of potential organs for the spirit into limited bodily instruments, and leaves vulnerable places open to attack from the powers of the pit—instead of organs developing by which Man could grow so as to unite himself with the hierarchies of Heaven.

A scene recorded in the Gospel of St. John throws some light on the apocalyptic picture of the kings who are in danger of becoming victims of the great Whore. In the fourth chapter, Jesus rests at midday by Jacob's well in Samaria. A Samaritan woman comes to draw water. After Jesus has said, "Give me to drink," a conversation ensues between Him and the woman. It is as if in the midday heat a universal picture appeared behind every word that is spoken. In the second part of the conversation, which may at first seem puzzling, Jesus says, "Go, call thy husband." The Samaritan woman answers, "I have no husband." Thereupon Jesus says, "Thou hast well said, I have no husband, for thou hast had five husbands, and he whom thou now hast is not thy husband; in that saidst thou truly." The woman feels that He has seen right through her, and suddenly she becomes profoundly receptive for the words He is speaking to her. Now Jesus can tell her deep secrets of the future of mankind. No doubt the words which made the Samaritan woman feel she had been seen right through have also a simple human meaning; but what concerns one human being concerns also the whole human race. Samaria, the province between Judea and Galilee, was abominated by the Jewish race because at the time of the Babylonian exile, Babylonians settled there and intermarried with the Jewish inhabitants. The Jews avoided all intercourse with the Samaritans, because they felt the latter to be the bearers of Babylonian customs into Palestine. Samaria was regarded by them as another, smaller Babylon. So behind the conversation at the well there may have been the fact that the Samaritan woman had played a part in certain sexual rites of her people. Here is a strange parallel to the Apocalypse. In the Apocalypse we are told that five kings have already ruled; in the Gospel the woman has had five husbands. Behind the apocalyptic picture, as well as behind the words of the Gospel, that section of mankind emerges which has already developed five of its primary forces, but through the temptation of the great Whore has devoted them exclusively to the service of the earthly sphere. One can see in the five senses a reflection of the five primary forces, developed in the five evolutionary cycles of the past, now we have already entered upon another, sixth stage of evolution. A sixth sense must be acquired by mankind, but precisely for this reason Man is faced with a decision. The sixth primary force must work in a sense-organ directed to the supersensible world, just as the five senses refer to the earthly world. The need for an extension of the number of the senses is evident from the degree to which mankind has become imprisoned in the material world of the five material senses. In the scene at the well, the Samaritan woman suddenly seems to open her heart to the pure sphere of the Spirit, under the influence of the words which Jesus spoke to her. So, at the parting of the ways between the collapsing city of Babylon and the New Jerusalem descending from Heaven, humanity must now find the strength to free itself from the bonds of the senses, and to prepare itself for a true union with the higher powers which overshadow it.

Now movement enters into the picture of the great Whore, sitting enthroned at the place where she bars the way to the Spiritual World. A savage war flares up. The Beast on whose heads and horns the Woman is sitting, gathers the Babylonian section of mankind belonging to him. With superior numbers the army of the Dragon fights the Lamb. Passions, earthly desires, egoism, unlimited lust for power grow immeasurably at the expense of sacrifice and love. Human civilization assumes a form in which there is no longer room for the quieter virtues shown in the picture of the Lamb. The dominion of the great Whore captures one province of human life after another.

Nevertheless, in the unequal battle between the Dragon and the Lamb a day will come when the Lamb will carry off the victory. How is this possible? Just as in the fairy tale the giants are eventually overcome by their unseen opponent because they begin to quarrel among themselves, so the gigantic powers which fight against the Lamb are urged by the sight of Him to the greatest efforts, but in the end destroy themselves. All at once the Beast turns in hatred against the Whore Babylon, whom he has hitherto carried from one triumph to another. "The ten horns which thou sawest upon the Beast, these shall hate the Whore and shall make her desolate and naked, and shall eat her flesh and burn her with fire" (xvii, 16). Some day the monstrous effects of materialism must become noticeable. At first it seems profitable to form part of the Dragon's retinue. All the wealth which the Earth can provide is available. Successes are achieved which give ground for overwhelming pride. Some day, however, the false calculation must be exposed. Man is not only a being of the Earth. The world of matter lends him his body for a short while. In his true being he belongs to the worlds of spirit. None of the earthly treasures which he has gathered with such zeal and pride can benefit his true being. At last, in the hour of his death, he will become aware that all this must be left behind. Now he is overtaken by the terrible fear that he has absorbed too much earthly weight to be able to spread the wings of his true spiritual being freely.

The Fall of Babylon, however, will not only be experienced individually by those passing through the gate of death: it must also happen one day to civilization on a large scale. In spite of its magnificent triumphs, an entirely material civilization is based on a tragic miscalculation. The purpose of civilization can only be to serve and help forward the true being of Man; but in all the calculating and planning this has been forgotten. The Tower of Babel of a purely material civilization is fundamentally rotten, and must one day collapse. In our present day it is quite obvious that the materialistic way of thinking is carried *ad absurdum*. The Beast controls everything in which the true nature of Man is ignored. For a time Man may believe that he controls the forces with which he builds his world, and is making them his obedient servants. At last, however, they unmask themselves as the many-headed, many-horned Beast from the pit, which in the end is their own destruction too. Thus the Whore Babylon allows herself to be carried proudly by the Beast, which then turns against her and brings about her downfall. The wrong way of reaching for the heights can only lead to a plunge into the depths.

There are three groups of men who are drawn into the fall of Babylon. These see the smoke of the universal conflagration rising and shout their lamentation over the downfall of the great city in which their own doom is also sealed: they are the kings, merchants and sailors. The evil has entered into three main departments of everyday life. The kings represent the sphere of the social order in which initiative, leadership, spiritual enterprise is at home. It is the field of freedom, which is only gradually emerging from the restrictions of the past. How easily does the shadow of the great Whore fall across the field of freedom! This happens wherever the leaders are not intent on leading others to freedom, wherever freedom is an aim in itself, and hence becomes dominant and domineering.

The merchants represent the economic sphere. Trade can only thrive in the long run if it is governed by brotherliness and reciprocal service. If money-making becomes the dominant aim, Babylon takes the lead.

In the image of the sailors, the human being himself is shown. Man is fundamentally a traveller. Once upon a time an outward journey was also a path of inward experience. Today outer and inner paths no longer coincide. It is no longer a matter of course that we grow more mature by seeing the world. Those who have not gone far afield, but understand how to tread peaceful spiritual paths, are often gaining more real experience. It is alarming to observe how early in life people begin to become set in their ways, and yet remain emotionally immature. Some never seem to grow beyond the age of twenty-one or twenty-eight. This has a disastrous effect on human relations. Neurasthenic busy-ness robs man of his dignity. In all the frantic to and fro, perpetually increased by the speed of transport, human life ceases to be a true journey. Mutual respect and esteem, which are the foundations of law and justice, disappear. The shadow of the Great City which will collapse appears in the fact that power and utility are set above Justice, one of the most sacred possessions of mankind.

Work goes on; but it loses its meaning when Man becomes no more than a machine. "No craftsman shall be found any more in thee." It grows dark in the world, not because there is no longer light or means of outer illumination, but because the *Mystery* of Light itself is extinguished: "And the light of a candle shall shine no more in thee."

Finally we read, "And the voice of the bridegroom and the bride shall be heard no more at all in thee." In the realm of the Great Whore, the secret of the Bride is lost. When the soul is no longer wedded to the Spirit, it becomes impossible to weave community between soul and soul. The countless outward conquests of the Babylonian illusion are offset by the loss of the real values of human existence. The loss of these values, depending ultimately on an objective sanction by the World of the Spirit, must eventually cause the extinction of earthly existence.

Judgement is confirmed. A hierarchical power intervenes: "a mighty angel". Once more the figure comes forward whom we have seen repeatedly in the course of the Apocalypse, intervening in human destiny at crucial moments or diverting ultimate evil. "And a mighty angel took up a stone like a great mill-stone, and cast it into the sea, saying: Thus with violence shall that great city Babylon be thrown down, and shall be found no more at all." The heavenly mill-stone is thrown down upon Babylon, and it sinks in the vortex of the sea. The stern words of Christ find their fulfilment: "Whoso shall offend one of these little ones which believe in Me, it were better for him that a mill-stone were hanged about his neck and that he were drowned in the depth of the sea" (Matthew xviii, 6) (Luke xvii, 2). There can be no more classic picture than this of the mill-stone dragging its victim into the depths, to represent the dead weight of matter upon life.

Another of Grimm's fairy tales offers an illuminating parallel. In the story called "Machandelboom" the wicked stepmother has killed the child. As the boy was bending over the apple chest to pick out an apple, she shut down the lid, so that his head rolled among the apples. But the soul of the boy then goes through the story as a singing bird. Eventually justice is done: " 'Nay,' exclaimed the woman, and jumped up, her hair standing on end like flames of fire. 'It seems to me the world is coming to an end. I shall go outside; perhaps I shall be better off there.' But as she stepped out of the door, crash! The singing bird threw the mill-stone down on her head, so that she was completely crushed. The father and little Marlene heard this and went out. Then fire and flames and smoke came up from the town. And when that had passed, the little brother was standing there. He took his father and Marlene by the hand and they were all three very happy. They went into the house and sat down to dinner."

The fairy tale shows in a drastic picture how the Whore Babylon sins against the budding higher Ego in Man. She will not allow it to grow up; she is intent upon its death the moment it stirs, just as the Dragon in Heaven lay in wait for the child which was about to be borne by the Woman clothed with the Sun. But one day the world will flare up and the end will come. The power which employed the dead weight of Earth to paralyse the Spirit is ultimately itself cast into the abyss by that weight. Just as in the fairy tale the father and sister of the boy go in with him to the meal when he has been returned to them, so in the idyllic picture of the Apocalypse a similar promise is held out at the end: "Blessed are they which are called to the marriage-supper of the Lamb" (xix, 9).

XI

THE RIDER ON THE WHITE HORSE
AND THE THOUSAND YEARS

THE NINETEENTH AND TWENTIETH CHAPTERS

THE picture of the Great Whore darkens the heavens like a black cloud. When the cosmic tempest has scattered it, a wonderful symbol of salvation lights up the sky. In the picture of the immaculate Bride the sphere of a Cosmic Marriage is revealed. The whole universe is filled with rejoicing: "Let us be glad and rejoice, and give honour to him; for the marriage of the Lamb is come, and his wife hath made herself ready" (xix, 7). That section of mankind which has escaped the seductions of materialism and the pit, and has submitted wholly to the grace and light of the Spirit, appears as the Bride of the Lamb. In the figure of the Bride, the soul of humanity receives the wedding garment: "And to her was granted that she should be arrayed in fine linen, clean and white, for the fine linen is the righteousness of saints" (xix, 8). Here the mystery of the white robe, that is, of the human being who has to shine from within, irradiating even his bodily nature; attains its supreme fulfilment.

This marriage has world-wide human import. The guests at the wedding feast, also clothed in the wedding garment, press in from every direction and are greeted by the solemn apocalyptic beatitude, "Blessed are they which are called unto the marriage supper of the Lamb" (xix, 9).* The guests are mankind, summoned as a whole to the marriage, which is at the same time the reception of a most holy Communion. The motif of betrothal, the marriage of the Soul with the Spirit, has appeared again and again, both in pre-Christian times and in the history of Christendom, as a poetic picture of the joy of redemption. The Song of Solomon, the "Song of Songs" in the Old Testament with its hymns of love between Bride and Bridegroom, is not completely fulfilled until the last chapter of the Apocalypse. In the Gospel it is Christ Himself Who in a most solemn hour uses the same prophetic picture. While the storm-clouds of catastrophe are already gathering, in His last instruction on

* Seven Beatitudes are woven into the whole of the Apocalypse. This is the fourth.

the Mount of Olives, He gives the intimate circle of His disciples the parable of the Five Wise and Five Foolish Virgins. It is in this way that He opens that concentrated "Apocalypse" of the future, through which His disciples are equipped for thousands of years ahead for their apostolic mission. He speaks of His own Second Coming, and describes it as a Marriage. When this Mystery is one day fulfilled it will be seen which human souls are ready for it and which are not.

At the peak of the Middle Ages a rich anthology of books of poetry and devotion grew up round the mystery of the Marriage of Soul and Spirit. The Flemish mystic, Jan van Ruysbroeck (1293–1381), who belonged to the group of the "Friends of God" and to the council of the "Brothers of Communal Life", wrote the wonderful little book, *The Adornment of the Spiritual Wedding*. Like all books of this type, it is a kind of breviary, a book of meditation in which the soul is led forward step by step through the stages by which it will attain to inward penetration by the divine, and will become the Bride of Christ. *The Chymical Wedding* of Christian Rosenkreuz is both a conclusion and a climax to the meditative poetry of the Middle Ages. This little book was written at the beginning of the seventeenth century by Johannes Valentinus Andreae, who later, as Ecclesiastical Commissioner in Swabia, became a good churchman and wished to have nothing more to do with the precious thing which, as a young man, he had been inspired to create. The significance of this book lies in the fact that its store of pictures presents a means by which medieval mysticism may be developed into a way of discipline for the soul, suited to the approaching age of Natural Science. "Chymical Wedding" means literally *chemical wedding*. But it is not a chemistry of material substances, but a union between the human soul and the divine Spirit which resembles the chemical union of two substances, and extends the effect of the process of spiritual permeation into the realm of the body. For a long time pictures of the Spiritual Wedding were kept alive in fairy tales. Why is there so often a wedding at the end of the fairy tales? This is because they depict what happens within the soul. So they also describe how the soul finds the spirit, or the spirit finds the soul. When the young man who is regarded as a simpleton in the fairy tale eventually passes all the tests, and so frees the king's daughter from the spell and wins her as his bride, we see how the soul, imprisoned in the tower of the body, can eventually be released through the courage of the Higher Ego. But there are also fairy stories which, like the parable of the Ten Virgins, show the soul on the path of suffering and trial, until the king's son comes to wake her from her spellbound sleep, and make her his bride. To these belong, among others, *Snow White* and the *Sleeping Beauty*. In a variety of poetic forms, apocalyptic visions of Christ shine through the fairy tales.

What does the Apocalypse mean when it speaks of the "marriage of the Lamb"? Are we to understand simply *Christ* by the Lamb? Among the Beings of the higher worlds, there is none in whom cosmic love and the capacity for sacrifice have been so completely embodied as in Christ. Nevertheless, through the picture of the Lamb we are directed to an all-embracing world-principle. We perceive in it Love as the essence of God, as it is when it can be fully revealed through the openness of men's hearts. The world in which it is possible that love can turn into wrath has sunk into the abyss. Humanity is the loving bride. To the "love from below" "love from above" can answer, undiminished and undimmed. The mystery is fulfilled of which Goethe speaks at the end of *Faust*:

> "Whoe'er aspires unweariedly
> Is not beyond redeeming,
> And if he feels the grace of Love
> That from on high is given,
> The blessed Hosts that wait above,
> Shall welcome him to heaven."

A special secret concerning Christ is expressed, however, when in the picture of the Great Marriage the Lamb appears too. It has been mentioned that the Lamb is met with twice in the structure of the Apocalypse. Both in the far past and in the future a sacrificial deed of Christ brings decisive benefit to humanity, as did the one which formed the central turning-point of history. It was the primal sacrifice of the Lamb that set Creation in motion. The future sacrifice of divine Love begins to be revealed when, with the new manifestation of Christ, the new Creation springs up. The parable of the Ten Virgins in the Gospel and the second picture of the Lamb in the Apocalypse indicate that the path to the Betrothal and the Wedding Feast lies open when the sphere of Christ is revealed to mankind in a new way.

It is by no means the case that the call to the Wedding Feast brings nothing but bliss and security. Even that section of humanity which escapes the Babylonian plunge into the abyss finds that the step from the Whore to the Bride requires continuous and intensive spiritual activity. Without co-operation from Man's inmost being, a new Babylon is for ever rising of itself. So a battle must be fought. Between the two cities which the writer of the Apocalypse saw in a great double vision at the end of the path, there comes a warlike host galloping on white horses. Once before we have witnessed an apocalyptic conflict. The battle between Michael and the Dragon was fought out between two armies, the troops of Michael and those of the Adversary. Now there is a metamorphosis of that conflict. Instead of the joy of the royal Marriage Feast, as might have been expected, Heaven opens and the Rider on the White Horse appears in splendour. His army follows him, also riding on white horses. The robes of pure shining linen in which the wedding guests were clad are now seen as the robes of the army. Could the hosts of the White Rider be the same as those we saw before? Has a sudden battle-cry called them away from the Wedding Feast?

In religious circles where the pictures of the Apocalypse are placed at the service of Utopian fantasy, the motifs of Chapters 19 and 20 play a particularly important part. Some people like to imagine that a political constellation may soon appear on the physical plane which will bring about the dawn of the Millennium. Thus time and again they watch for the great Horseman to come riding on his charger as the instrument of the expected miracle. But this is a complete misunderstanding of the Revelation of St. John; we must seek in the realm of Spirit for the events described to us here. Only when we can perceive them there do we begin to realize how profoundly their influence can extend into earthly events. Indeed, the battle fought by the army of the White Rider is closely connected with the destinies and conduct of men on Earth. The war of the hosts of Michael with the forces of the Dragon took place in Heaven. The result of the Archangel's victory was that the powers of the Adversary were "cast out into the Earth"; and there for the first time they give full vent to their rage. They make their assault upon Man in the thousand different temptations of the Two Beasts, involving him in tensions and perplexities of soul and spirit which must work themselves out in ever greater historic crises and catastrophes. Thus men must finish the work begun by the Angels' victory in Heaven. The task of Michael has passed over to men, and is set anew in every epoch of historical evolution. The inspiring picture of the battle waged by the White Rider is a prevision of the final phase of this struggle.

Whenever the Apocalypse depicts a battle a female figure appears before it. Before Michael's war in Heaven we saw the Woman clothed with the Sun—the higher human soul. She stands under the sign of birth and life; the future is hers. Before the battle of the White Rider the Whore Babylon appears—the lower, earthbound soul of humanity. Because she is the Great Whore she has no son; she is barren. Only a semblance of life proceeds from her, and she has no future. With all the glittering ornaments that hang about her, she is only a mask of death and destruction.

Since the figures shown by the Seer are, as it were, characters appearing in a drama which proceeds from act to act, we may ask what becomes of the male child born of the Woman in Heaven, who was menaced by the Dragon. He is caught up to the Throne of God, for protection; but one day he will grow up and become a man, and the Apocalypse itself lets us recognize him in the White Rider. In Chapter 12 we read, "She brought forth a man-child, who was to rule all nations with a rod of iron" (xii, 5). And of the White Rider we are told, "He shall rule them with a rod of iron" (xix, 15). Michael's war in heaven breaks out in defence of a new force which is to be born in mankind. The ego is quickening in the womb of humanity as well as in the souls of individual men and women. The Adversary who wishes to hinder the birth of the ego is overcome and cast down. Now for long ages ahead humanity on earth must resist the assaults of hostile powers. Men must comfort themselves with the thought that the battle which they have to fight to a finish has already been decided in Heaven in their favour. They may also feel that a higher force has been born and preserved through this heavenly victory though it cannot be embodied at once. At first the new force hovers over men incarnated on Earth, so that it may mature long enough to be able one day to enter into full possession as the true Self of Man. When that happens, the war that Man must carry on in continuance of Michael's war will enter a decisive phase. In the White Rider and his troops that section of mankind which has escaped the enchantment of the Dragon and the Great Whore will receive the knighthood of the Spirit, which makes them ultimately victorious.

The new-born son of the Woman in Heaven who was caught away to the Throne of God returns from Heaven as the White Rider when the time is fulfilled. He is the Son of Man, the higher spiritual human being. Thus these two pictures in chapters 12 and 19 where the name "Son of Man" is mentioned weave together into one whole. The exalted figure who appears in the first chapter, and before whose feet John on Patmos fell as dead, is the picture of the Spirit-Man, the ideal Man as God at the Creation had intended him to be. This picture of the Son of Man, however, was still so completely divine, so entirely filled with the substance of the Christ-Being, Who was the first to embody it fully on earth, that we hardly dared to stand before it as before a mirror of our own true being. In this figure God and Man balance each other. Then, as the sound of the Seven Trumpets died away, the Apocalypse showed us for the second time, with special emphasis, the picture of the Son of Man on the clouds of Heaven with the sickle in his hand ready to gather in the harvest of the world. Here the Son of Man appears entirely divine. We must recognize him as a revelation of the Second Coming of Christ. When Christ approaches Man anew from the spiritual world, He comes in the true image of Man according to which everything must be decided. But when the Son of Man has developed into the Rider on the White Horse it is now the human side which is emphasized. Here is the Human Being himself who has stood the great test. Man cannot of his own strength restore in himself the archetype of his true higher being, and so become the Son of Man. He can only do it by allowing the Christ Ego to dwell within his own ego, thus making himself a vessel for the Son of God. We are clearly shown, however, that this is not possible through a merely passive attitude, but only through intensive inner activity. This is the meaning of the transformation of the wedding guests into the troops of the White Rider.

The call to the wedding has sounded. Close as he now is to Christ, John's soul is still only full of humility and devotion. "And I fell at his feet to worship him" (xix, 10). But he receives an answer which exhorts him to assume quite a different spiritual attitude. "See thou do it not. I am thy fellow servant, and of thy brethren." It seems surprising at first that Christ should reject the worship of Man. But at this stage of evolution He wishes to be the Friend and Brother, rather than the Lord of Man. Does not this remind us of a most sacred scene in the Gospel? On Maundy Thursday Christ has washed the disciples' feet, and celebrated the Holy Meal with them. After the meal, in St. John's Gospel Christ gives the disciples the instruction which is commonly called the Farewell Discourses. One of the central points is the words, "Henceforth I call you not servants . . . I have called you friends" (xv, 15). Where the Mystery of Communion is fulfilled there is the dawn of freedom. Humility must be united in the soul with courage, for Christ wills not only to be Brother and Friend to Man. He also expects that Man should summon up courage to become a friend of God and a brother of Christ. St. Paul's words, "Not I, but Christ in me," will have no reality unless Man ventures to bridge the gulf which separates God and Man. *Faith*, as humility and courage of soul, alone makes possible the indwelling of the Christ Ego in the human ego.

Immediately after the Seer John experiences the octave of that hour in which he lay on Jesus' breast and heard His exhortation to friendship with God, the heavens open and the picture of the White Rider appears to him. Through the grace of Communion, Man must grow mature enough to look into this picture as into a mirror, thereby awakening in himself the inner strength to become a fellow warrior with Christ.

If a man were able to let his human nature be permeated through and through by the Being of Christ, he might say: "I recognize myself in the Rider on the White Horse." The different names by which the Rider is called can be signposts on the road to such identification. The first name is translated in the Authorized Version of the Bible as "faithful and true" (xix, 11). The inadequacy of this rendering will only be fully realized in times to come. The words translated "faithful and true" should be understood as "He is the bearer of Faith and Truth." Two world principles, Faith and Knowledge, are combined in a living synthesis by the Rider on the White Horse. He lives in a spiritual realm where Faith and Knowledge are reconciled. Here the Bible itself refutes the doctrine which, since the Middle Ages, has separated faith in revelation and knowledge acquired by reason. This division has robbed religious life of its spiritual intensity and impetus, making Christian piety assume an inwardly passive character. The flame of spiritual activity can be kindled again by the Revelation of St. John so that a higher knowledge can come from faith, and faith can bring warmth and inspiration to knowledge. Head and heart will work together when we are no longer content with a religious life which is divorced from thought. The picture of the White Horse has already appeared once in the Apocalypse. It came on the scene when the first of the Seven Seals was opened. Now after we have been through all the cycles of Seals, Trumpets and Vials of Wrath it is seen again, carrying the White Rider. We have seen that the first Seals show the stages which the divine gift of Intelligence has passed through in the course of evolution. The White Horse showed that human Intelligence first consisted in the share which Man still had in the thoughts of God Himself. The pictures of the Red, White and Pale Horse represent the loss which Man would have to endure if he drew down the divine forces of thought deeper into his own nature and correspondingly into earthly darkness. The original revelation of God must be lost. But if after passing through the dangerous valley of egohood, humanity desires to find the power to rise again, this cannot be done without thought. We must resist the temptation, through growing weary of our abstract, shadowy thinking, of throwing overboard the heritage of past millennia of thought, in order to live out of natural instinctive forces of the soul. In our age this danger has become acute. Even though our thinking has fallen into mere intellectualism, we must not lose faith in thinking as such. We must determine to redeem our thinking. From the fact that our present ways of thought no longer furnish help for the most intimate concerns of life, one conclusion alone can be drawn—that in future thinking must be purer, and more inspired by the heart. Especially in the name of Christianity, the resurrection of thinking must become a foremost aim. Christian theology and practice in the last thousand years have been equally to blame for allowing knowledge based on thought to fall out of the sphere of religion.

In the renewed picture of the White Horse whose Rider is "bearer of Faith and Truth", the Apocalypse shows the power of Thinking redeemed by Christ. The Rider on the White Horse has eyes like flames of fire and many golden crowns on his head. The man of the future will develop a life of thought that will be filled both with the fire of inspiration and the quiet light of wisdom. Academic abstraction will give way to living knowledge of the spirit, and a deep interest in it. Sense-perception gains new life when it is extended to the sphere of the supersensible which lives and weaves behind the whole sense-world. The fire of the Spirit in the human eye opens it to perceive the Spirit in all things. The golden crowns on the head of the Rider show that he is once more endowed with the wisdom of true divine thoughts, which he does not "think out" for himself, but which come to him as Heaven's gracious response to his own spiritual activity.

The second name of the Rider on the White Horse is not actually spoken. "He had a name written that no man knew but he himself" (xix, 12). There is one name which can always only be spoken by the one who bears it. This is the secret of the little word "I". Everyone can say "I" only of himself; no one can apply this name to anyone else. But this name of the Rider on the White Horse contains yet another secret. Besides the fact that no one except the bearer of it can utter it, no one except himself can even *understand* it. If we simply say "I" to ourselves, we indicate thereby our human personality so far as we are conscious of it. We cannot stop short at this *I* without becoming closed in and spiritually sterile. We must strive to provide a home in our *I* for a higher Being. The words "Not I, but Christ in me", teach us to be "I" in such a way that Another says the word through us. This is the secret hidden in the second name of the White Rider. It indicates the ego which is filled by God and so bears the divine *I* in the human *I*. Thus the second name becomes the seed or bud of the third. This name is written on the robe which the Rider wears. It is white, but sprinkled with blood. The harmony of white and red so often painted in the Apocalypse appears again on a new and higher level. The colours of spirit and soul are united, but here it is no longer the human soul's own inner warmth which meets the light of the spirit: the blood of Man unites with the blood of Christ. Here is the Mystery of the Grail. The soul purified by the indwelling Christ grows into union with the Spirit.

This robe bears the Name, "The Logos of God". How does this human being come to be called "the Word of God"? Through the indwelling of Christ Man receives a force which does not only operate inwardly, but radiates outward from him. The speech of Man becomes one with the speech of Christ, Who is the "Logos of God" Himself. But even when Man is not speaking, he is a living Word of God through the indwelling of Christ. No matter whether it is directly noticeable or not, he can be a very real revelation to those around him. In him the Creation of the world continues, of which it is written in the Prologue of St. John's Gospel: out of the Logos all things were made. We feel something of the magic weapon which is at the disposal of the White Rider and his hosts. The two-edged sword which comes out of his mouth in fact corresponds to the Name that is on the blood-sprinkled vesture, transmuted into both inner and outer activity. Man himself, Christ-filled, attains to a share in the magical power of creation especially in the speaking of the Word. In his hand the Rider carries the rod of iron whose authority to "rule all nations" has already been mentioned prophetically when the Woman in Heaven gave birth to the child. The picture of the rod of iron appeared for the first time in the fourth Message. Those in the Church of Thyatira who had stood the test were promised the rod of iron whereby they would become shepherds of the nations, but would also have authority to "break them in pieces like the potter's vessels on Earth" (ii, 27). This is the rod of egohood. When anyone first becomes an "ego-man", all kinds of old bonds and natural connections will be broken. But when the rod of iron is wielded in the hand of the Rider on the White Horse, the ego will have developed so that now a force proceeds from him which can form community. The loss of the old blood ties will be compensated by the new spiritual community of those who have attained to their Higher Ego through the indwelling of Christ. At first the principle of personality opposes that of community, but when the individual ego-man learns to develop beyond himself and to become receptive for higher things, the promised power of creation will show itself in the social sphere as the quality of brotherliness. Communities are no longer formed as gifts of Nature, but as the work of Man inspired by God. Then the iron rod becomes the shepherd's crook. A universal human priesthood is evolved whereby the wounds of separation, hatred and social chaos may be healed.

When *I* is spoken in the sense of the iron rod, a *we* sounds with it. The *I* no longer speaks out of arrogance and a craving for power, but out of priestly selflessness, in the name of the many. An instructive example of this is in the Act of Consecration of Man.* Whereas in the first part, especially during the Offertory, the wording is in the *we* form, it finally passes over in the Communion to the *I* form. But the *I* spoken here by the celebrating priest signifies *we*. In its progress through the Gospel, the Offering and the Transubstantiation, the spiritual community is formed through an actual coming together in harmony of every Higher Ego. From here onwards, the Ego of the congregation speaks, with which every fellow-worshipper can identify himself. And when the celebrant at the altar takes bread and wine with the words, "I take the bread," "I take the wine," then it is all the more a classic example of the personal super-personal element, into which we can grow through the secret of the rod of iron. With the *I* of the community, all the individuals present speak these words through the mouth of the priest and make their Communion with him, before the individuals later go up to the altar for their personal receiving of Communion.

The fourth name of the White Rider is written on his thigh: "King of kings and Lord of lords." In the Old Testament, Jacob was left with a limp after wrestling by night with the Archangel Michael, and so lost his balance. He was the first who had to adapt himself to the growing

* The Communion Service of The Christian Community.

171

preponderance of outward over inward influences. In the sign of the Son of Man, however, men must develop a new equilibrium between the divine and the human; so in the very part of the body where the loss first occurred, the name is inscribed which it would be the greatest arrogance for a man to attribute to himself. This name signifies that only the Man of the future who has become One with Christ will know the full secret of freedom and spiritual sovereignty. The prospect revealed here definitely puts a stop to the old way of thinking which only emphasizes the distance between sinful Man and God. Man is sinful; but he may, and must, go the way which the pictures of the Apocalypse point out to him.

With the appearance of the Rider on the White Horse light is thrown on a significant word in the twelfth chapter of the Apocalypse, a word which directly precedes the beginning of the War in Heaven. When the Child of the Woman clothed with the Sun is born, it is said, "She brought forth a son, a man-child" (xii, 5). Might not the emphasis on the male sex of the Child seem superfluous? Spiritually, however, it indicates a new beginning of supreme importance.

The figure of the Woman in Heaven represents the soul of mankind as it has so far developed. The spiritual ego, the masculine principle, has not yet entered humanity on Earth. It still rests in the heart of God. But when the Woman in Heaven brings forth her son, the male principle begins to enter earthly evolution, and for the first time it becomes possible to speak of a spirituality that really belongs to the planet Earth and to the human race upon it. It is just this beginning of the male principle which is threatened by the Dragon, for here the Adversary recognizes the power which will become its rival for the lordship of the Earth. So the tender new-born Child would have been exposed to hostile attack if the Archangel Michael, as representative of the new spiritual male principle, had not intervened with his troops against the forces of the Dragon. When the man-child grows up, he will have the Archangel as teacher and example. The ideal of spiritual virility will meet him in this form and go before him again and again, teaching him, as Rider on the White Horse, to continue the battle on the human plane. When the spiritual ego has entered fully into humanity, and the son of the Woman has grown to manhood as a warrior of God, then the decisive battle can be fought. Fulfilment comes at the same time to both soul and spirit, the feminine and masculine principles in Man: the Soul becomes the Bride, the Spirit a Knight of God.

Through the intervention of the White Rider a further act in the threefold drama opens. The first catastrophe, the fall of Babylon, has already taken place. Civilization which has succumbed to materialism collapses of its own accord: no outside force is required to overthrow it, for materialism itself leads *ad absurdum*. It overbalances and plunges into the abyss. Everything now valued as impressive and successful will prove illusory unless Man learns to bring supersensible realities and spiritual values into his thoughts and plans.

The second great catastrophe, the fall of the Beast and the False Prophet, was brought about by the Rider on the White Horse and his followers. At first the Beast carried the Whore on his back, but then turned against her and effected her complete destruction. Now he is himself cast down, together with his spokesmen—those who practise "black" magic. Now it is not only human beings who fall into the abyss. Superhuman demonic powers are overthrown by the sword of the Rider. This can come about without visible weapons, for the time will come when men and women working with God will quietly and unobtrusively bring about results far beyond what is now the human range. But the very fact that there are people, and communities, who strive to make themselves true bearers of Christ, will effect changes even in the outward course of history. This need no longer be unintelligible today, since we have been obliged to observe that even weather conditions on the Earth become different as a result of what we think, feel and do. But the White Magic of future Christendom will not develop if those who want to be Christian persist through wrong ideas of divine mercy in observing a merely passive piety. Faith must be strengthened in the heart to become a force of the Ego by no longer keeping aloof from knowledge, but by making close alliance with it. This fiery power of Christ-filled thinking, speaking and doing brings about the fall of the Beast and of the black magicians whom it has attracted. The Beast tries to keep men at the stage of the soul only (that is, at the animal stage), and to hinder them from developing the spiritual part of their nature which is their true being. But when in spite of this the flame of the spiritual Ego lights up, it overcomes the demonic power which sets up the image of the Beast and stamps its sign on the forehead and hand of Man.

The Beast and his accomplices fall into the "Lake of Fire"—a drastic apocalyptic picture. When it is said of a morally unreliable man that he is sunk in a *slough* of corruption, the suggestion is that he is caught more and more by the force of suction from the depths, so that eventually he can no longer escape from it. The humorous story of Baron von Münchhausen, who pulled himself out of the bog by his own pigtail, may seem nonsense if taken literally; yet it is a striking parable of the task which constantly faces Man in the moral sphere. The slough into which the Beast and the false Prophet are plunged by the White Rider has not come into being through a mixture of earth and water. The Apocalypse conjures up the picture of a volcanic crater bubbling with boiling lava. Here the depths of the pit and the flames of cosmic conflagration are combined. When the fires die down, the slough with all that it has engulfed petrifies into a hard volcanic stone—the slag which will be cast off when the Earth rises to its new Aeon.

The third cataclysm is the fall of Satan. After the great city of Babylon, and Leviathan the many-headed, many-horned Beast—the Luciferic tempter—have been overthrown, Behemoth, the cold Ahrimanic demon of death, still remains to be overcome. When Michael had cast his enemy into the depths, this power appeared on Earth as the two-horned Beast. Its dangerous nature is hidden behind the apparently insignificant form of a lamb. It is really the opposite of the Lamb—the anti-lamb. It is the very embodiment of coldheartedness and incapacity for sacrifice, of cosmic lack of Love. Thus it is also the opposite of the Being of Christ. As Christ is the Genius of the Sun, so this Beast is the Sun-demon, the actual Antichrist. It is impossible even for the White Rider to overthrow this Adversary. Superhuman and superearthly powers must intervene. "I saw an Angel come down from Heaven, having the key of the bottomless pit and a great chain in his hand. He laid hold on Satan and bound him a thousand years, and cast him into the bottomless pit" (xx, 1–2). Even the powers of Heaven are unable finally to overthrow the power of Satan. It is only possible to chain it for a thousand years. After that it is freed again for a time, and with it the whole of Hell is let loose: "and when the thousand years are expired, Satan shall be loosed out of his prison, and shall go out to deceive the nations" (xx, 7–8). No picture of the Apocalypse has been so hopelessly misunderstood and misused as the "reign of a thousand years", the "millennium". Not only materialistic sects of the West, but also politicians and dictators have stimulated fanatical expectations that the dawn of the Thousand Years is imminent or has already come. A primitive belief in miracles based on religious pride and egoism gives rise to Utopian dreams of an earthly paradise. Such illusions have contributed greatly to the present chaos. They have thrown dust into men's eyes, preventing insight into

174

the real situation. Actually, the opposite of such fantasies is the truth.

The reign of a Thousand Years is a rhythmical pause, recurring as a help to Man against the powers of the pit. For the evolution of mankind proceeds in waves. Ages in which the gates of Hell are closed, but in which the good spiritual powers also keep in the background so that Man may develop his own strength, are followed by apocalyptic, concentrated times in which humanity is put to severe tests. In periods of peaceful evolution men become absorbed in earthly concerns, and may so far forget the existence of a supersensible world that they develop philosophical ideas to prove the non-existence of that world. Then in some overwhelming catastrophe the supersensible sphere suddenly penetrates right into everyday life—particularly the powers of the pit, which do not need to be evoked by the spiritual activity of Man. They are all the more successful because through the blindness of men they can do their work in disguise. Evil itself makes its appearance as a community-forming influence. This is shown by the Apocalypse in the hordes of Gog and Magog. Eventually, through the chaos and suffering inflicted on them by the unleashed power of Satan, men begin once more to reckon with the fact of supersensible spheres and forces. Then perhaps they will begin to see that opposite the open gates of Hell, Heaven too stands open again, and that they may take their place on the side of the good powers in the battle for the Spirit.

At the present time a peaceful period of a thousand years has run its course. The Thousand Years does not need to be taken as a literal number; it signifies a whole epoch. After the intense activity of the first Christian centuries with its times of persecution had died down, mankind was left alone for a while both by Heaven and Hell. The significance of the present lies in the spiritual battle which humanity must fight to preserve the forces gathered by all its past experience.

The vision of the Seer penetrates beyond the rhythm of the Thousand Years and the subsequent ages of conflict to the time of fulfilment when, after the fiercest epoch of its emancipation, the power of Satan is finally overthrown. Then Death itself also sinks into the Pit (xx, 14).

Illusions about the Thousand Years have arisen mainly from a misunderstanding of what the Apocalypse says about their content. It has been overlooked that the writer of the Apocalypse is also describing changes taking place in the realm of the dead, i.e. in the supersensible world. In the sphere of human souls which have passed through death there occur in the course of world-destiny cycles of a thousand years in which calm follows storm. Then among the dead there appears a distinct grouping into camps, which should be regarded as a preparation for the division of spirits. In each group a fundamental apocalyptic mystery is revealed. Those souls which have passed over into existence after death without having kindled the light of union with Christ on Earth, have no life: they lie under the spell of the *second death*. But those souls which have brought out of their life on Earth, as a seed of true immortality, a union of their human nature with the Christ-being, are able to rise into the Sun sphere of Christ. Here is the mystery of the *first resurrection*.

For those who have died with Christ, the reign of a Thousand Years is the sphere of blessedness (which the materialistic interpretation misunderstands as an earthly condition). A new element is introduced when the indwelling of Christ in souls on Earth begins to blossom and bear fruit in souls after death. The Apocalypse describes how these souls not only have true life-forces at their disposal, but have also a share in the creative power of Christ. "They lived and reigned with Christ a thousand years" (xx, 4). The essence of the power of Christ is the victory over death by Resurrection, the power to permeate and transform into spirit all existence, even the substance of the earthly body. The dead in Christ have a share in this through the first Resurrection, which becomes full reality among them long before it can be anything more than a seed on Earth. It is not only a grace bestowed on them, but a creative, cosmic task in which they may actively participate as fellow-workers with God and Christ. It is a materialistic way of thinking that pictures the Resurrection of the dead as if they would rise from their graves clothed with their restored physical bodies. The power of the first Resurrection streams from Heaven to Earth, making it possible for souls to help the destinies of men and women on Earth. And so the apocalyptic beatitude: "Blessed and holy is he that hath part in the first resurrection, on such the second death hath no power" (xx, 6) applies to the dead who are united with Christ and at the same time to those on Earth who, in active collaboration with the sphere of the dead, can carry this power into their earthly life.

On the other side appear those of the dead who have brought no spark of Christ's light with them from the Earth, but only the darkness and weight of temporal existence. While on Earth they have already evoked the spectre of the Second Death by directing their attention only to material interests. Thus they have prepared the way for the death of their soul together with their body. Abstract thinking, if it never goes beyond the world of the senses, easily imagines the immortality which it attributes to the soul as holding good for every human being in the same way. Certainly no human soul ceases to exist after death. But there are differences in immortality. The point is whether the soul possesses the light of consciousness whereby it really continues to *live*, or whether this is extinguished by the Second Death. It is only when, after the Thousand Years, times of "unchaining" again occur, and everything is in movement in Heaven and on Earth, that the ban on the dead is relaxed (xx, 5). Even for souls "asleep" the field of destiny is lit up by the raging of a cosmic storm.

In the midst of the spiritual battle, the possibilities of light and darkness become universally visible. As the end of the Earth's history approaches, decisions will become more and more definite. In the end the fall of Satan will drag down the realm of the dead also into the abyss. "And death and the realm of shades [Greek, *Hades*] were cast into the lake of fire. This is the second death" (xx, 14).*

In the spiritual sphere the "Millennium" is to be found at any time, even when the power of Satan is released on Earth. "The Reign of a Thousand Years is always among us," says Novalis. Through the mystery of the indwelling Christ Man can stand in a different relationship to death and to life. The Second Death loses its power over him, and the rising sun of the Resurrection sends its beams into his life. The number of the Adversary—666—is, as we have seen, the sign of the ever-increasing *tempo* of life, which brings restlessness and discord into human souls. On the other hand, the number One Thousand is the sign of "Eternity in Time"; it betokens the peace which is a spiritual art learnt through devotion. Whoever lives in the "inner millennium" can collaborate in the downfall of Antichrist and the building of the Heavenly Jerusalem. If the earthly, historical city of Jerusalem bears the name "city of peace", how much more does the divine city which comes down from Heaven!

---

* Here a short reference may be permitted to the thought of repeated lives on Earth without which every reflection on eternal destiny must end in a blind alley, the more deeply it penetrates into apocalyptic ideas. The Revelation of St. John does not expressly mention this conception, but takes it for granted at least in the way it regards as inconclusive the moral and spiritual decision which death brings at the end of one life on Earth. It reckons with possibilities of further development and new decisions. Since, however, Christ has united Himself to the Earth, the necessity by which true progress of the soul depends on finding and permeating itself with Him eventually leads to the thought of repeated lives on Earth.

XII

THE HEAVENLY JERUSALEM

THE TWENTY-FIRST AND TWENTY-SECOND CHAPTERS

AFTER the dramatic pictures of the cycles of Seven, the victorious intervention of the White Rider, and the dividing of the spirits between Whore and Bride, the path of the Apocalypse of St. John seems to lead at last into realms of pure bliss. We are surrounded by the golden glory of the Eternal City.

Traditional Christianity has more easily assimilated the mood of the Heavenly Jerusalem than anything else in the Apocalypse. The glorious vision of the consummation of human existence, stripped of all its limitations and hardships, answered to the deepest hopes of human souls, and has inspired very moving religious poetry. One of the best known English examples of this kind is probably the hymn beginning:

> "Jerusalem the golden
> With milk and honey blest,
> Beneath thy contemplation
> Sink heart and voice oppressed."

But even here, where religious feeling in its poetic expression rises nearer to a super-personal level than anywhere else, the egoistic desire for the "next" world is not altogether laid aside—the egoistic mood which is so closely bound up with traditional piety, and which has so largely prevented organized Christianity from grasping the super-personal objective content of the Apocalypse. "Could I but dwell for ever beside this shining throne!" as another hymn puts it. This other-worldly, egoistic desire for Heaven, from which the healthy feeling of modern people turns away, is quite unjustifiably deduced from the picture of the Heavenly Jerusalem. Indeed, to claim support for egoistic piety from the last chapter of the Apocalypse is fundamentally to falsify it. We are fatally mistaken, and will meet a tragic disappointment, if we fancy that after having shed the burden of life on earth the soul will simply enter into the golden streets of the Heavenly City. The New Jerusalem does not lie in another world. We need only notice how the writer of the Apocalypse describes the position in which the Eternal City showed itself to him. In this picture Heaven is moving towards the Earth. This descent is in itself a refutation of an escapist point of view.

In the usual interpretation of the last book of the Bible a strange paradox has come about. By far the largest part of the Apocalypse has been misunderstood in that it has been taken to refer to this material world; the pictures of the Seer were applied to earthly people and events. The vision of the Heavenly Jerusalem, on the other hand, has been taken as belonging to the world beyond. The reverse is true. In the Heavenly City a spiritual sphere is described which is ready to penetrate our earthly world. It is the characteristic direction of Christ Himself, for He descended from the heights of Heaven to become Man on Earth. He has brought Heaven to Earth so that the heavenly spirit may permeate the earthly. The Christianity of the future will be a Christianity which comes from above; it will supersede the Christianity from below which strives, out of egoistic religious longing for salvation, for the "next" world. The Heavenly Jerusalem is the beginning, not only of the new Heaven, but also of the new Earth. It is in the sphere of the Earth, which is renewed by being interpenetrated by Heaven, that the secrets of the Heavenly Jerusalem are to be found.

Thus the two Cities stand opposed to each other at the end of the Apocalypse. The Great Whore who falls into the abyss represents the darkening and tarnishing of the spiritual by the earthly—the materializing of spiritual things. The Heavenly Jerusalem, the Bride, brings down spiritual formative forces into the Earth—and spiritualizes matter.

With this vision Christianity reveals its character as the final stage and consummation of the religious history of mankind.

The farther we go back into pre-Christian times, the simpler is the character of all religious life. The divine forces in the Kingdoms of Nature were the primary objects of worship. People of ancient times revered the spiritual element in tree and cloud, in river and mountain, in the march of the seasons, for their souls were still able to perceive the reality in dreams and visions. And while the pre-Christian religions were directed to the cosmic sphere, they had at the same time a retrospective character; they turned back to the divine Beings out of whom and through whose creative working our world has come into being. All ideas about the Gods and all mythologies of pre-Christian eras are based on ancient human memory, on a clairvoyant looking back into the ages of the world's creation. And the same Gods who created the world were seen continuing the work of creation in the kingdoms of Nature.

Towards the middle of the history of mankind, a movement set in which ceased to turn its attention to the divine in Nature. Its classical representative was the religion of the Old Testament, especially of the later times when the more comprehensive Israelitish element was replaced by the one-sided Jewish influence. Judaism came into being as the strenuous opponent of heathendom; a consciously non-cosmic religion developed among a race for which contact with the cosmic Nature-religions of their neighbours became almost revolting. Judaism concentrated its religious life entirely within man's own being, so that eventually only the educational and moral side of religion—the Law— was left. It was regarded as a serious crime to look up to the Stars, the Sun or the Moon, and to see and worship in them the activity of divine Beings. This transition through a stage of inner concentration was necessary, in spite of the loss of warmth and colour, because only by this method could the principle of the free Ego enter humanity.

Eventually, through the loving sacrament of the Incarnation, Death and Resurrection of Christ, Christianity came into the world. Up to this very day it has again and again misunderstood its own true nature. It has regarded itself as a continuation of Old Testament religion and so has placed itself in opposition to all cosmic religious thought, as being "heathen". But in fact Christianity ushers in the third stage on the path of human evolution. Once more, on a new level, it leads to an experience of the divine in Nature. But it does not return to the old Gods, the primal creative Beings of the world. Christianity is the religion which is devoted to that divine Power Who progressively permeates all earthly existence, and at the end of the Earth-aeon will have made it altogether into His own flesh and blood. This is the meaning of the Resurrection of Christ. The Communion in Bread and Wine is the sign that the Christ penetrates and trans- forms earthly matter with His Being. By this means He forms and develops the very seed of a new Earth. The old cosmic religions, in their retrospective character, are orientated towards the myths of Creation. They have their centre of gravity in Genesis, which stands at the *beginning* of the Bible. Christianity looks into the future, and the more its outlook is orientated by the Apocalypse, the *last* book of the Bible, the more it will find its true character. There the door opens on to the New Creation, which through the power emanating from the

Death and Resurrection of Christ, will be permeated anew by the divine. This New Creation appears in the vision of the Heavenly Jerusalem. So we may say that while pre-Christian religions worshipped the God of Creation, Christianity worships the God of Consummation. It follows the Being who leads to, nay *is*, the highest, holiest goal of future evolution.

True Christianity is more comprehensive than any other religion could be, at any time. Christ, Who once walked the Earth as Man in order to implant Himself in earthly Nature as the seed of spiritual transformation, is the fulfilment of all "heathen" prophecies as well as of the Old Testament. He Who by passing through His Incarnation, Death and Resurrection became the God of the consummation of earthly creation, is none other than the Logos "by whom all things were made and without whom was not any thing made that was made". In Him lives the "fullness of the Godhead", the Highest Ego, and the substance of the Divine powers which were worshipped also by pre-Christian "heathen" humanity. Christ Himself says this in the Revelation of St. John, "I am the alpha and the omega, the beginning and the ending . . . which was, and is, and which is to come." A Christianity which labours under the restrictive spirit of the Old Testament can have no living future. Only a Christianity conscious of being the third great stage on the spiritual path of mankind can develop the full cosmic greatness inherent in it, and will be able to offer men the knowledge and the forces that they need in the dramatic progress of human destiny.

In order to establish and safeguard the cosmic dimensions of the Apocalypse we must endeavour to read in its calendar of cycles not only the sequence of civilizations, but also that of the planetary cycles of evolution of the earthly globe itself. If we refer the stages of the Apocalypse to the very largest evolutionary cycles, then the seventh Trumpet reveals how the whole Earth-aeon of humanity comes to an end. As we have seen, it is not altogether untrue that the "last Trump" heralds the end of our world, the doomsday of our Aeon. But this "end of the world" is not an absolute annihilation, just as indeed the death of a man does not mean that he becomes non-existent. Evolution continues in supersensible forms of existence in the spiritual regions which lie beyond the Threshold. What follows on the cycle of the Seven Trumpets, i.e. the outpouring of the Vials of Wrath and the double picture of Babylon and Jerusalem, refers (if we apply the most comprehensive standard of time) to the cosmic trials of the whole earthly globe; to the processes of elimination, purification and rejection to which the planetary existence of mankind is subject when the earthly cycle of time has run its course. Our planet "Earth" passed through great stages of cosmic transformation before it assumed its present form. Geologists and astronomers have come to the conclusion that at one time the Earth must have been united with the Moon, and still further back with the Sun also, in one cosmic body. Not until the separation from Sun and Moon was the Earth brought into the material, physical condition which we know, and which a materialistic Science constantly tends to project back into all the ages of the distant past. Correspondingly, the future evolutionary stages of our planet, concerning which Science offers only such barren conceptions as that of entropy, universal death by heat, will consist in processes of reabsorption into greater cosmic units. The solemn Marriage motifs in the last chapters of the Apocalypse refer to such unions: "The marriage of the Lamb is come, and his wife hath made herself ready" (xix, 7). "And I, John, saw the Holy City, New Jerusalem, coming down . . . as a bride adorned for her husband" (xxi, 2).

The part of Earth and of humanity which appears in the picture of the Heavenly City as rescued from the destruction of the world, is the bride who prepares herself for the marriage with Christ, and thereby lays the foundation for the new Earth and the new Heaven. *The "Marriage of the Lamb" is also a cosmological truth.* Some day the Earth will again be united with the Sun. Neither Earth nor Sun, however, will then be in the material, physical condition in which they exist at present, or which is attributed to them at present. Then it will be revealed that "Nature" does not follow mechanical laws apart from the spiritual and moral sphere, as has been supposed during the few short centuries since the dawn of Natural Science. Then it will come to light that the destiny of the planet is determined by the reality of spiritual and moral forces. The dividing of spirits causes great cosmic changes. The reuniting of the planet Earth with the Being of the Sun necessarily involves also a cosmic split. A kind of "Moon" will drop out of the universal conflagration as slag. What is and will remain no more than material will be seized by a cosmic *rigor mortis* and plunge into the depths like the lava of a volcanic eruption. Together with the Sun, the Earth which will have become itself a Sun, will pass over into a state which is no longer material. This future incarnation of the Earth is called by Spiritual Science the "Jupiter" existence. It is the complete realization of the Heavenly Jerusalem. And the slag which falls out and hardens to a moon-like cosmic body is the final condition of the Babylonian part of mankind which plunges to its doom in the bottomless pit.

The discovery of these vast planetary perspectives in the Revelation of St. John takes nothing away from its permanent topical character. On the contrary, the spiritual laws inherent in the progress of the great cycles make those secrets of destiny comprehensible for the first time, to which humanity is subject also within the shorter epochs experienced as periods of history. There are crossroads in history, in which Past, Present and Future merge into one another, and in which the Apocalypse as a whole and in detail has a topical significance that increases from day to day. At such moments, remnants of the past will appear under judgement, and prophecies and presentiments of an inevitable future will be felt. *We are living in such an age today.*

In the ordinary calendar our own age is only a single point of time. What lies behind it is irrevocably past; the turn of the future has not yet come. In contrast, the Apocalypse is a spiritual calendar which like a seed contains in the present the fruit of the past, and the germ of all future growth. And in times when a Threshold is to be crossed, as in our own age where a new consciousness is awakening, those parts of the Apocalypse which follow on the last Trumpet are especially topical. From beyond the Threshold, the Vials of Wrath and the Dividing of Spirits are events reflected into our world. Our time is lit up by rays from the wide expanse of the future and from eternity. Surrounded by the storms which the Trumpets have raised, we can now draw up a balance sheet of the results of human evolution hitherto by means of the Seven Messages and the Seven Seals. Then by facing the challenge of the Vials of Wrath and the gulf between the Whore Babylon and the Bride Jerusalem, we can find the moral and spiritual purposes of the future. Thus periods of great disruption can be at the same time periods of preparation, of sowing and of growth. The beginnings of the fall of Babylon are already around us. On the dark background of contemporary catastrophes, however, the mellow rays of the Holy City also begin to appear, the objective hope of a new civilization, indeed of a new Nature.

The whole extent of the Bible lies between the two visions of Paradise and of the Heavenly Jerusalem. The old Creation, still permeated by the Divine Being, appears in the picture of the *Garden*. The new Creation, filled afresh by God, appears in the picture of a *City*. There may still be remnants of the Garden today, remnants of a Nature still imbued with the Spirit. But it is part of the experience of modern man that he yearns ever more hopelessly for a Nature that is still unspoilt, and which still preserves something of the magic of Paradise. We cannot turn back the wheel of evolution; we must adapt ourselves under Providence to the descent whereby the history of mankind hitherto has been a progressive expulsion from Paradise. Man must learn what could not be learnt in Paradise, what can only be acquired on the stony ground outside. For in the long run Nature can no longer give Man anything. A prospect of hope opens only through the realization that through the Mystery of Golgotha the possibility of a fresh ascent has been offered to Nature too. The New Creation does not, however, appear again as a Garden but in the picture of a City. This means that the future cannot come into existence without the collaboration of Man. The great concluding picture of the New Testament shows that Providence counts on finding men who understand how to build out of the Spirit.

The striking duality between Babylon and Jerusalem at the end of the Apocalypse teaches an impressive lesson about right and wrong ways of building. The uncleanness which makes Babylon the City of the Whore is due to the fact that all building in it is done in the manner of the Tower of Babel, i.e. only from below, whereby the all-too-earthly element is carried up into the Spirit and defiles it. Man can work and build as much as he likes; but if he only builds from below and does not learn to allow the grace of Heaven to enter freely into all his actions, he is only laying the foundation for collapse and destruction. Is not the Tower of Babel crashing everywhere around us today? The causes of the collapse are much more fundamental than is generally supposed. They lie much more in a wrong *method* of thinking than in a wrong *content* of thinking, in wrong opinions. Mankind today thinks wrongly, even in the Science of which it is so proud. Our civilization is Babylonian because we think exclusively "from below". The Heavenly City which derives its thinking and building from above is not merely a concern of the future and of the other world. It can and must be fashioned here and now. To be a Christian means fundamentally to think and build from above, so that into human planning and achievement the co-operative forces of a higher Power can flow. True Christian spirituality includes patience and receptivity, whereby Man allows all earthly thinking and acting to be influenced by the forces he can find on those levels where he may know the Risen Christ, and also his own Higher Self, his true Being.

When the three intimate disciples, Peter, James and John, were on the holy mountain with their Lord, they saw through the earthly figure of Jesus the radiant Spirit-Sun of the Christ, transfiguring the earthly body. Peter was so rapt by the sight of the earthly substance irradiated from above that he said, "It is good for us to be here. Let us make three tabernacles." The phrase "to make tabernacles" can be a striking motto today when homelessness meets mankind like a symbol in so many different ways.

Here a passage from Rudolf Steiner's *How to attain Knowledge of the Higher Worlds* may be helpful. When the disciple on his Path to the Spiritual World approaches the Threshold, he must detach himself from all support he had relied on hitherto; in a sense he must become homeless in order to find a new home in the spirit. Rudolf Steiner describes as follows the step which must be taken at this point: "Just as objects and places in physical space are defined from a fixed point of departure, this too must be the case in the higher world. The student must seek out some place, thoroughly investigate it, and take it spiritually in possession. In this place he must establish his spiritual home, and relate everything else to it. . . . We are born into the physical home without our co-operation, and instinctively absorb, during our childhood, a number of ideas by which everything henceforth is involuntarily coloured. A man, however, himself founds his own spiritual home in full consciousness. His judgement, therefore, based on this spiritual home, is formed in full unhampered freedom. This founding of a spiritual home is called, in the language of occult science, the making of a tabernacle (literally, the 'building of a hut')."

Even he who is not directly blessed, like the three disciples, with the vision of the transfigured Christ, even he who at first only seeks with longing, or surmises the nearness of the Risen Lord, can be admitted into the secret of building a tabernacle. This is the essence of the renewed sacramental life. Every true worshipper comes to the altar at which the Holy Act is celebrated as a disciple who has found the secret of building a tabernacle. To give the Risen Christ a dwelling-place among men, to build a tabernacle for the heavenly in the earthly, for the spiritual in the material, will increasingly become the centre of Christian life, and ultimately of human existence as a whole. This secret may be so expressed: Man must take care that, wherever he himself is, room must be left for the spiritual element. Then a spiritual building from above will be joined to the earthly building below. Something entirely new can come in, restoring youth to the age-worn world, because men learn to bring down from Heaven what can come from there alone. The shining gold of the Heavenly Jerusalem sinks into the soil of the Earth, even though the latter be covered only with ruins and the relics of destruction.

The vision of the Heavenly Jerusalem shows Earth becoming Sun. The golden crystals of the spiritual Sun-sphere pervade our planet. This is also the mystery of transubstantiation, the conversion of Bread and Wine. And this in turn is linked together by mysterious bonds with the Resurrection, whereby Christ wrested from the corruptible earthly body the transubstantiated spirit-body in which He revealed Himself to the disciples. The vision of the Heavenly Jerusalem shows the fulfilment of what was begun on the Hill of Golgotha. Novalis expresses this with poetic exactitude:

" . . . How He by Love alone was driven
    To lie for us beneath the sod.
His Body as the stone was given
    To found the City of our God."*

By making the mystery of Bread and Wine in the renewed Sacrament once more the centre of religious practice, The Christian Community seeks to serve the evolution of the new Creation which is already active within the dying world.

With the Vision of the Heavenly Jerusalem, Seven, the number of Time, gives way to Twelve, the number of Space. When the number Twelve makes its appearance, we enter a spiritual temple which is a variation of the dome of stars, encircled by the twelve signs of the Zodiac. Anyone reading through the whole book of the Apocalypse with a feeling for numbers will share in the experience of Parsifal when he was in the precincts of the Grail: "Time here becomes Space." Out of the ever-moving stream of Time we come to a cosmic Castle of the Grail. The dominion of the number Seven, governing everything that is in constant movement within the human being, is left behind. The number Twelve reveals its mysteries, because the concentrated inwardness here becomes an outer world again. Building is taking place, and a World is being founded. *Man becomes World*. After the Seer has described the dimensions of the Heavenly Jerusalem —the wall with the twelve gates, guarded by twelve Angels, and on the gates the names of the twelve tribes of the Old Testament; on the

* From *Sacred Songs of Novalis* translated by Eileen Hutchins. Selma Publications, Aberdeen.

foundations the names of the twelve Apostles of the New Testament, embellished with the twelve precious stones and the twelve pearls— the Angel with the golden reed takes the measurement and proclaims: *"It is the measure of Man."* The spiritualizing of the New Creation is at the same time a humanizing of it.

As preparation for entry into the Heavenly Jerusalem, wherein Man becomes World, humanity had to be ranged on the holy mountain as the host of 144,000. At that moment the number Twelve already revealed its inherent law. Now the measure of the great Twelve, twelve times twelve, recurs. The wall which the Angel has measured is 144 furlongs in length. The number of the universal entirety of individual possibilities surmounts all individuality and community.

Now the architecture of the Apocalypse as a whole, itself a spiritual building, lies clearly before us. The vision of the Son of Man is the beginning of the path along which the writer of the Apocalypse leads us. The vision of the City is its goal. The revelation of the inmost cosmic secrets begins with Man and shows in the end how Man becomes World. But before he can become World he must become Humanity. When through the power of the Higher Ego Man becomes Humanity, the great Twelve shines forth in the host of those who are gathered round the Lamb on the Holy Mountain. The Twelve becomes the governing law of existence when, under the sign of the Heavenly Jerusalem, Man who through Christ has regained the image of God intended for him, becomes the focus and raw material of a new cosmic Creation, the new Heaven and the new Earth.

The Heavenly City is described as being of the same length, breadth and height. This description alone should be sufficient to refute the sentimental, easy-going ideas of Heaven held by those who picture it in terms of what gave them pleasure on Earth. A great crystal cube emerges as the figure of the Heavenly City. On earth, rock salt, the most common form of salt, crystallizes in cubic form. Is the Heavenly Jerusalem also the fulfilment of the charge which Jesus gave to the disciples in the Sermon on the Mount, "Ye are the salt of the Earth"? In the same context the Heavenly Jerusalem is referred to as from a distance: "A city that is set on a hill cannot be hid." The disciples who according to Christ's charge are to be the salt of the Earth are, in their spirituality, the building material of the Heavenly Jerusalem. In them, Man truly becomes World.

Every further indication of the raw material of the Heavenly City confirms this. The foundations with the names of the Twelve Apostles are adorned with twelve precious stones. The precious stone mentioned in the first place is Jasper, whose brilliance adorns the City in many forms. The City shone in "the glory of God; her light was like unto a stone most precious, even like a jasper stone, clear as crystal." "And the building of the wall of it was of jasper."

In our world, when the Sun rises, the light of the stars is extinguished by the brighter light of the day-star. In alternating day and night we see *either* the stars *or* the Sun. In the Eternal City, Stars and Sun shine at the same time—from within outwards. The glitter of the twelve precious stones is not extinguished by the sunshine of the gold crystals; it is concentrated and deepened: "The City itself was pure gold, like a transparent crystal." "The streets of the City were pure gold, as it were transparent crystal." The ground, the plane upon which everything moves, is gold crystal, through which one can see deep into the world below.

The crystalline gold of which especially the ground of the City is formed, is the further development of the "sea of glass", in which the newly purified creation began to crystallize out from the ocean of evolution. The admixture of red which distinguished the new crystal sea from that of the first creation, because human warmth of soul and the power of love have flowed into the substance of the new world, has now been refined to pure gold which shines like a Sun. "The City has no need of the Sun, neither of the Moon, to shine in it, for the glory of God Himself lightens it, and the Lamb is the light thereof." In the Heavenly City day and night no longer alternate. The "Marriage of the Lamb" is celebrated. Earth and Sun have again become one. The "New Earth" is itself Sun. The principle of the Lamb, the sacrificial love of Christ, has become the point of crystallization of the new world.

Behind the sunlight that brightens our day, the love of the Gods of Creation is hidden. So the love of the God of Consummation, Who as Son of Man is also the centre of all true humanity, will be the source of light for the new Age. The gold crystals are the sunshine of Christ-filled human hearts become World.

If the golden crystals show that the Sun is once more in the Christ-filled Earth, so the precious stones show that once more the differentiated wealth of the Stars is contained in it. Through the love of Man's heart, Earth becomes Sun; through the spiritual purity of his thinking, the Earth becomes star-like, radiant, a concentration of the whole starry firmament. The predominance of jasper as the first and noblest of the precious stones links the pictures of the beginning with those of the end. In the fourth chapter, between the Messages and the Seals, He who sits on the Throne, Father of the worlds, is pictured as a jasper stone. He does not appear in human form, but as a centre of rays, flashing and shining like a precious stone. The power of pure thinking passes over from the Beings of God to Man. (There is a hint of this also in the story of the Holy Grail, for it is said that the Chalice of the Grail was cut out of jasper.) As Man becomes World he causes Creation itself to assume the starry countenance of God. In the Eternal City, the enthroned One becomes the World, the Creator becomes Creation.

And what is the secret of the pearls, of which the twelve gates consist? The oyster forms the pearl by transforming a painful foreign body which has penetrated into its shell. This process of Nature can, and must, become one of the guiding principles of human spiritual life. The gates of the City of God can only be passed through under the sign of the pearl. Only pain and suffering conquered and transformed can enable men to share in the new Creation. Just as the gold shows the Sun in the new Earth and the precious stones cause the stars to shine forth in it, so the pearls are the transformed Moon incorporated in the Earth. When the will of Man has attained to pure endurance through all the trials of destiny, then the New World will have its gates, through which he can enter who has reached maturity.

We have seen that the Whore Babylon also has, in her own way, gold, precious stones and pearls at her disposal. The great lamentation over the fall of Babylon rings out: "Alas, alas, that great City that was clothed in fine linen and purple and scarlet, and decked with gold and precious stones and pearls! For in one hour so great riches is come to nought." Here is appended outward magnificence which, in the Heavenly Jerusalem, is an integral part of a new Creation. The pearls with which the great Whore decks herself do not represent suffering fruitfully endured. The materialistic outlook is characterized by its inability to understand the value and purpose of pain, sickness and death. The Whore Babylon decks herself with the pearls springing from the suffering and tribulation of others. Her principle is power. But the outward assumption of riches only increases the dead weight which ultimately brings about the plunge into the abyss.

In Chapter 12, the Woman in Heaven clothed with the Sun, Moon and Stars appeared as a picture of the Soul of the World and of Man. The picture of the Bride Jerusalem, with gold, pearls and precious stones, is a progressive metamorphosis of this. Now the human soul is no longer clothed with Sun, Moon and Stars alone; she has become

World and carries Sun, Moon and Stars as constituent parts of her own being. Now she has absorbed the Cosmos into herself, she herself has become Cosmos. The inner World becomes the outer World. The City of God is built through the incarnation of the inward Sun, the inward Moon and the inward Stars.

INDEX

193